Newly-Qua
Social Workers

Newly-Qualified Social Workers

A Practice Guide to the Assessed and Supported Year in Employment

STEVEN KEEN, JONATHAN PARKER,
KEITH BROWN and DI GALPIN

**3rd
Edition**

§SAGE | LearningMatters

Learning Matters
An imprint of SAGE Publications Ltd
1 Oliver's Yard
55 City Road
London EC1Y 1SP

SAGE Publications Inc.
2455 Teller Road
Thousand Oaks, California 91320

SAGE Publications India Pvt Ltd
B 1/I 1 Mohan Cooperative Industrial Area
Mathura Road
New Delhi 110 044

SAGE Publications Asia-Pacific Pte Ltd
3 Church Street
#10-04 Samsung Hub
Singapore 049483

Editor: Kate Wharton
Development editor: Lauren Simpson
Production controller: Chris Marke
Project management: Swales & Willis Ltd, Exeter, Devon
Marketing manager: Camille Richmond
Cover design: Wendy Scott
Typeset by: C&M Digitals (P) Ltd, Chennai, India
Printed by CPI Group (UK) Ltd, Croydon, CR0 4YY

Library of Congress Control Number: 2016940554

British Library Cataloguing in Publication Data

A catalogue record for this book is available from the British Library

ISBN: 978-1-4739-7797-6 (pbk)
ISBN: 978-1-4739-7796-9 (hbk)

Contents

V

8 **Contributing to service quality
and development** 127

About the editors

Dr Steven Keen, Senior Lecturer, Bournemouth University
Steven brings together years of wide-ranging management, research, education, consultancy, lecturing, thesis supervision and sports coaching experience in his current role as a Senior Lecturer in Research within the National Centre for Post-Qualifying Social Work and Professional Practice at Bournemouth University.

Dr Jonathan Parker, Professor of Society and Social Welfare, Bournemouth University, and Visiting Professor at Universiti Kebangsaan Malaysia, Universiti Sains Malaysia and Universiti Malaysia Sarawak
Jonathan was one of the founders and director of the Family Assessment and Support Unit, a placement agency attached to the University of Hull, and Head of the Department of Social Work. He was Chair of the Association of Teachers in Social Work Education until 2005, Vice Chair of the UK higher education representative body, the Joint University Council for Social Work Education from 2005–2010 and is a Fellow of the Academy of Social Sciences and Fellow of the Royal Anthropological Institute. He has published widely on disadvantage, marginalisation and violence, Southeast Asia, religion, social work and welfare education internationally.

Professor Keith Brown, Director of the National Centre for Post-Qualifying Social Work and Professional Practice, Bournemouth University
Keith holds academic and professional qualifications in social work, nursing, teaching and management. He has worked in the education and training field for over 25 years, in universities and local authorities and is currently Director of the National Centre for Post-Qualifying Social Work and Professional Practice at Bournemouth University.

Di Galpin, Academic Lead for Social Work, Plymouth University
Di is a qualified social worker and Academic Lead for Social Work at Plymouth University, specialising in the areas of social policy, safeguarding adults and professional judgement in risk and decision-making in practice. She is active in developing and delivering education and CPD to qualifying and qualified health and social care professionals. Di has co-written *Social Work Practice with Adults* (2009, Sage/Learning Matters) as well as acting as an editor/contributor to this text. Di has published on safeguarding adults in the *Journal of Adult Protection*, *Social Policy and Social Work in Transition* and the *Journal of Social Welfare and Family Law*. Di is a keen blogger and tweeter on issues related to practice in health and social care (digalpin.wordpress.com).

Book contributors

Angela, service user
Angela has personal experience of mental health services and worked as a service user representative for 12 years. She has delivered training both locally and nationally and was an 'activist' for Rethink. She is now the co-ordinator of the Bournemouth University Carer and Service User Partnership and feels that her lived experience of mental illness and training experience can offer a unique perspective to newly qualified social workers.

Shelley Baker, social worker, Tregonwell Academy
Shelley qualified as a social worker in 2008. She completed her degree at Bournemouth University. Since qualifying she has worked as an education social worker in a local authority in the south of England and is now school based. Shelley's primary role is to work with children, young people, their families, schools and other professionals to improve school attendance and address presenting welfare issues.

Pru Caldwell-McGee, newly qualified social worker, Dorset County Council
Pru graduated from Bournemouth University in 2015 with a BA (Hons) Social Work degree and is currently working through her ASYE in a front-line childcare team for the Weymouth and Portland area of Dorset. As a mature student, Pru spent many years in the marketing industry and took the life-changing decision to study in order to work in child protection.

Emma Crawford, newly qualified social worker
Emma recently completed her MA in Social Work and currently practises as a newly qualified social worker in a busy childcare team in the north of England.

Jill Davey, Senior Lecturer, Bournemouth University
Jill is a qualified social worker, with over 25 years' experience of working with children and families at both a practitioner and managerial level. Jill holds academic and professional qualifications in both social work and teaching. She teaches on the BA/MA Social Work programmes and has recently and successfully defended her doctorate.

Marion Davis CBE, Independent Consultant

Marion was Strategic Director of Children's Services for Warwickshire, with the job title of Strategic Director of Children, Young People and Families. During that time she was President of the Association of Directors of Children's Services between 2010 and 2011, and a member of the Munro Review Reference Group. She is a qualified social worker with over 30 years' experience as a social worker, manager and Head of Service in both children's and adult services. She has previously worked for Dorset County Council, Devon County Council and Plymouth City Council. She now works independently leading safeguarding peer reviews and is an advisor to the Education Select Committee, as well as having more time to pursue other interests such as travel, photography and yoga.

Dr Lee-Ann Fenge, Deputy Director of the National Centre for Post-Qualifying Social Work and Professional Practice, Bournemouth University

Prior to joining Bournemouth University as a lecturer, Lee-Ann worked as a social worker in a number of adult social services settings in London and Dorset. Her particular research interests include older people, seldom heard groups and integrated care. She has undertaken a number of participatory action research projects, and has published academic papers on participatory action research methodology, co-production in research, diversity and ageing, the impact of the recession on older people, safeguarding and financial abuse and using arts-based research methods with young people with disabilities.

Melanie Forsyth Smith, Bournemouth University

Melanie qualified in social work nearly 30 years ago and held posts in field-work and residential care, before moving into the training and education field, working as a trainer, assessor and practice teacher in statutory, voluntary and education settings. She joined Bournemouth University when post-qualifying training was in its infancy, and is currently leading graduate and Master's level units specifically designed as the first step onto an academically accredited professional development pathway. She has supported thousands of students through post-qualifying development programmes over the last 15 years at Bournemouth University.

Greg Hind, Child Health and Disability Team Manager

For more than 31 years, 19 years in a managerial capacity, Greg has been involved in planning, developing and delivering social work practice in a wide variety of different settings, governmental, local authority and voluntary, in the UK and overseas. He is a qualified social worker and has been an Associate Lecturer with the Open University. His most recent post is as the Child Health and Disability Team Manager for a local authority in the south of England.

Kate Howe, Senior Lecturer in Social Work, Bournemouth University

Kate has worked in social work/social care education for 20 years, having previously worked as a social worker in statutory and third sector agencies. At Bournemouth

University she works in the social work post-qualifying and qualifying teams. She leads the programmes for newly qualified social workers and specialises in supervision and developing emotionally intelligent leadership.

Mark Hutton, Principal Social Worker, Leicestershire County Council
Mark qualified as a social worker in 1991. He currently provides leadership and management to support social work practice for adults in Leicestershire. He has previously been a social work manager in a range of settings, from a daytime referral, crisis intervention and assessment social work service for adults in the community, to social work teams in acute hospitals and intermediate care. In November 2007, he was awarded a BA Hons in Leadership and Management in Health and Social Care and a full Post-Qualifying Social Work Award.

Karen, carer
Karen is the carer of a young man with Down syndrome, who was her foster child from the age of two weeks. Life experiences and work with around 20 social workers over nearly 30 years has given her things to share which she hopes are of value to newly qualified social workers.

Mary Keating, ASYE Project Manager, Skills for Care
Mary is a member of the team responsible for developing and implementing the revised ASYE for adult social work, and leads on supporting employers in child and family social work to meet the requirements for assessment of the ASYE against the Knowledge and Skills Statement (child and family) (2014). Working with the Office of the Chief Social Worker (adult) she was a member of the group who finalised the development of the Knowledge and Skills Statement (adults) (2015) in response to the consultation. Previously within the team Mary led on the development of the standards for ASYE contained in the Professional Capabilities Framework and had been responsible with The College of Social Work for describing and supporting the move to holistic assessment. Mary's social work career includes working in social work education, adult and children's statutory settings, and in therapeutic settings with children and young people.

Marion Macdonald, Workforce Strategy Staff Development and Training Manager
Marion is a Social Care Workforce and Training Manager. She has over 20 years' experience in statutory social care training teams, both as a trainer and a training manager. Marion worked directly with people with learning difficulties for 9 years before and after qualifying as a social worker in 1992.

Lucy Morrison, Good Design Works
Lucy initially worked at the National Centre for Post-Qualifying Social Work and Professional Practice as a research administrator. It was during her time at the university that she became interested and involved in the marketing and design of publications and conference materials. She later played a central role in the

creation of the first National Centre website. In 2013, she set up Good Design Works, a web and graphic design company and still continues to work with Bournemouth University.

Anne Quinney, Senior Lecturer, Bournemouth University

Anne is a Senior Lecturer in Social Work at Bournemouth University. She is the author of *Collaborative Social Work Practice* (Learning Matters), co-author of *Interprofessional Social Work: Effective Collaborative Approaches* (Sage),co-author of *The Social Work Assignments Handbook* (Routledge) and co-author of the *Interprofessional and Interagency Working* e-learning resources for the Social Care Institute of Excellence. Anne was previously the Editor of the peer reviewed journal *Practice: Social Work in Action,* a journal of the British Association of Social Workers (BASW) and is a member of the Editorial Boards of *Practice: Social Work in Action* and the *British Journal of Social Work* and has written widely on technology-enhanced learning. She is a qualified social worker and has worked as a teacher in Sudan and as a social worker and youth worker in Dorset and Scotland.

Angela Parker, practised as Principal Officer, Social Care, Ofsted

Angela worked in social care for over 20 years within adult services, child pro-tection, children with disabilities services, safeguarding and with community projects. In her role as Principal Officer, Social Care for Ofsted she had responsi-bility for managing the social care thematic inspection and survey programme. Thematic inspection and survey reports have been published looking into delays in adoption, protecting disabled children and supporting social workers. Her areas of interest included improving practitioners' awareness of safeguarding issues, espe-cially in relation to children with disabilities, improving outcomes for all vulnerable children and encouraging joined-up working between different organisations.

Emma Perry, Senior Lecturer in Social Work, University of Gloucestershire

Emma completed her Master's degree and Diploma in Social Work at Keele University in 2004. She spent nine years working within adult services, in a variety of roles including Senior Practitioner and Practice Educator. Since 2013 she has been a Senior Lecturer at the University of Gloucestershire and teaches on a variety of mod-ules. She has a particular interest in older people and relationships in later life.

Dr Lynne Rutter, Senior Lecturer, Bournemouth University

Lynne holds academic and professional qualifications in education and has sev-eral years' experience of developing and delivering Bournemouth University health and social care post-qualifying programmes. Her doctoral research focused on the development of professional judgement and knowledge, and she is a co-author of the Learning Matters texts *Critical Thinking and Professional Judgement for Social Work, The Practice Educator's Handbook* and *Promoting Individual and Organisational Learning in Social Work.* Currently she is designing and delivering continuing professional development units for health and social work leadership and service improvement programmes.

Clare Seymour

Clare has worked as a social worker, university lecturer, external examiner, practice educator and independent trainer. She is the co-author of *Courtroom and Report Writing Skills for Social Workers* (2nd edition, Learning Matters, 2011) and *Practical Child Law for Social Workers* (Sage, 2013), and has written the court skills section for Community Care Inform. Her e-mail address is cvseymour@hotmail.co.uk.

Martha Sharp, social worker

Martha began her training at the age of 20, completing a three-year degree in social work at Bournemouth University; here she accomplished two 100-day placements, both in adult and children's services. Shortly after graduating from her training, she found employment in a local authority childcare assessment team, where she started her career as a social worker.

Liz Slinn, social worker

Liz worked as a newly qualified social worker for a county council in the south of England, in a locality team working with children and families, including Children in Need, Child Protection and Looked After Children. She completed her social work degree at the University of Reading following the employment route training.

Chris Willetts, Senior Lecturer in Sociology, Bournemouth University

Chris began working with people with learning difficulties in the early 1980s after leaving university. He has a professional and academic interest in all excluded and marginalised groups. He now works as a Senior Lecturer in the Centre for Social Work and Social Policy at Bournemouth University.

Richard Williams, Senior Lecturer, Bournemouth University

Richard is a registered social worker with 40 years' experience of working with children and families at both practitioner and managerial level. He is currently Programme Leader for the BA (Hons) and MA Social Work programmes.

Anna Woodruff, social worker

Anna qualified as a social worker over 10 years ago. She was part of the first intake for the new social work degree, studying at Trowbridge College, and has been in practice since then, more recently working for a community interest group called Sirona Care.

Foreword

Dame Moira Gibb, Chair, Skills for Care

 Skills for Care is the employer-led body which leads on developing the values, knowledge and skills of the workforce for the adult social care sector. We know how important it is that every one of the 1.5 million people who work in the sector gets good quality support, supervision and development throughout their careers.

However, this is especially true for newly qualified social workers (NQSWs). As employers and social workers tell us, the first year of practice is absolutely vital as NQSWs consolidate the learning from their basic training and develop new knowledge and skills in their first employment setting.

The Assessed and Supported Year in Employment (ASYE) is designed to help all NQSWs, whatever route they have qualified from, develop their skills, knowledge and capability, and strengthen their professional confidence. The ASYE framework provides access to regular and focused support during the first year of employment. There are common expectations for all social workers in all settings. Many of the features of the ASYE build on the strengths of the former NQSW programmes.

The ASYE for social workers in adult and child and family settings is assessed against the new Knowledge and Skills Statements, underpinned by the Professional Capabilities Framework. This assessment of practice will in turn help ensure that the public can have confidence in the capability of the social work profession.

This publication gives a fuller introduction to the ASYE, brings together some of the best current thinking about how we can support NQSWs, but also offers practical support to new graduates coming into the social work profession, setting them on a course of continuing professional development that we trust will become an integral aspect of their career progression.

I hope the wide-ranging contributions in this book will help social workers make a success of the transition from student to professional and on behalf of Skills for Care I would like to wish you a rewarding career in which you can make a difference to the lives of those you serve.

Acknowledgements

This continues to be an unusual book to write, update and indeed edit. On the back of wanting to make more of a difference with our newly qualified social worker research in the South West region, Dr Ivan Gray first had the idea of producing this practice guide; his contributions to these editions are still appreciated and recognised. Six years on we (as editors) also remain very grateful to over 25 contributors – a wonderful mix of people who use services, carers, service and strategic managers, experienced and newly qualified social workers alike, employers, ASYE project managers and academics – continued heartfelt thanks to you all. Thank you also to all the anonymous peer reviewers from the above-mentioned groups. And finally, thank you to Kate Wharton and Lauren Simpson for keeping us all, very cheerfully, on track . . . again!

Chapter 1

Please mind the gap

Steven Keen and Jonathan Parker

Welcome to this practice guide for aspiring or newly qualified social workers. If you have just successfully completed your social work qualifying programme, very well done and many congratulations; we know this is hard work! If you are at the beginning or in the middle of a qualifying programme, keep on reading – this book is also for you. We hope it will inspire you to aim for excellence in your practice, even though the world of social work, in England especially, appears complex and its future uncertain, if the recent closure of The College of Social Work is anything to go by. Aside from death and taxes, one thing is certain . . . 'change' is here to stay – so, you might as well get used to it. The change from qualifying to qualified social worker is an important one. That is why we have written this book. Employers should not expect you to be fully formed social workers on qualifying, instead recognising that you are on a journey of development, one that needs to 'mind the gap'.

How many times have you heard these familiar words? In the late 1960s it became impractical for London Underground staff continually to warn passengers about the gap between train and platform. The equivalent phrase in France, Hong Kong, Singapore, Australia and the United States highlights the same problem – trains do not quite fit their stations. Likewise, newly qualified social workers often find they do not fit comfortably into their new organisations. Whether you have qualified as a social worker in England (Bates *et al.*, 2010; Novell, 2014), Ireland (National Social Work Qualifications Board (NSWQB, 2004)) or Australia (McDonald, 2007) appears to make no difference – the breach between qualification and first post is likely to be significant. Newly qualified social workers (NQSWs) often describe their first year in practice using very graphic terms (see also Skills for Care, 2011).

- *The ASYE is an excellent idea, but unfortunately it has become an onerous task in itself on top of a complex caseload. I worked well into the early hours to get pieces finished, not due to poor time management but the realities of surviving the job* (Schraer, 2016).

- *Frankly, peer support from other NQSWs has been the life saver* (Carpenter et al., 2011, p37).

- *It was a baptism of fire* (Bates et al., 2010, p21).

- *I constantly felt I was just keeping my head above water* (Revans, 2008, p15).

- *I have been repeatedly told I have a protected caseload, but no one is clear what an average caseload is, so it's impossible to work out what 80% of that should be* (Schraer, 2016).

- *There's plenty of nights when I'm lying in bed and I'm worrying and I've got that knot in my stomach* (Jack and Donnellan, 2010, p310).

Whether you are a newly qualified social worker or someone who is about to qualify, this book will help you to 'mind that gap' and make the transition towards your Assessed and Supported Year in Employment (ASYE).

Most social work textbooks focus on social work practice, social work skills or on how to study for your social work degree (see Parker and Bradley, 2014; Trevithick, 2012; Walker, 2011). Few texts directly address the gap or crucial transition period between finishing off the social work degree and managing the first years of practice. As such, this book offers down to earth, practical guidance on applying for your first post and managing your first few years. It includes useful sections on topics such as ASYE, induction, supervision, dealing with conflict, court skills, report writing and team working – and is written by a group of over 25 authors with extensive qualifying and post-qualifying social work education, and social work practice experience – be they people who use services, carers, managers, academics or newly qualified social workers.

Our interest in this transition period was fired initially by a research project tracking the learning and development needs of 22 newly qualified social workers in the South West (UK) region (Bates *et al.*, 2010). It is to this research project that we turn briefly.

The first social workers to graduate with the new degree did so in the summer of 2006. Later that year, Skills for Care commissioned Bournemouth University to track newly qualified social workers in the South West region through their first year of employment. They asked us to do three things:

- to evaluate their perceptions of the effectiveness of the new social work degree;
- to evaluate their perceptions of the effectiveness of their induction and/or probation periods;
- to track their progress towards post-qualifying social work education.

We also sought the perspective of people who use services, carers and line managers on the learning and development needs of these newly qualified social workers. What we found out through the use of multiple questionnaires, interviews and focus groups surprised us.

Blewitt and Tunstall (2008) raise the question whether generic qualifying programmes enable social workers to work equally well in children's *and* adult services. Some research suggests the answer is 'no'; just one-third of newly qualified children's workers believe their degree course prepared them for their jobs (Sellick, 2008). Incidentally, this 'readiness to enter practice' debate still rages (see Narey, 2014 and Croisdale-Appleby, 2014, e.g. p69). However, in our sample (all from local authority children's or adult services) about three-quarters of newly qualified social workers and their line managers agreed that the social work degree provided workers with the right knowledge, understanding and skills for their current post – a finding that remained almost constant over the nine months of the evaluation (Bates *et al.*, 2010). The evaluation of England's social work degree reports a similarly positive experience of teaching and learning (Evaluation of Social Work Degree Qualifications in England Team (ESWDQET), 2008; Orme *et al.*, 2009; also see Grant *et al.*, 2014). Yet, this study and Bates *et al.* (2010) also report negative findings. About a quarter of our sample did not feel prepared by their qualifying programme in areas such as report writing and dealing with conflict; the issue that stood out though was the development of court skills (Brown *et al.*, 2007; Bates *et al.*, 2010).

About three-quarters of our sample underwent a workplace-based induction. Yet, during interviews it became clear that few had been given a structured induction – that is, one that helped them move into their new role in a clear, planned and organised fashion (also see Moriarty *et al.*, 2011 and Grant and Kinman, 2014). Finally, three newly qualified social workers claimed to know nothing about continuing professional development opportunities – this, of course, was *not* confirmed by their line managers.

You will notice from the contents page that this practice guide is a result of and a response to these research findings, and we have used your colleagues' experiences to structure it. These findings even fuelled debates in the House of Lords (Hansard, 2007). Subsequent to these debates, the government asked the then Children's Workforce Development Council (CWDC) to develop a three-year pilot programme for newly qualified social workers working in children's services to help them strengthen their knowledge, skills and confidence (DfES/DH, 2006; CWDC, 2008, 2008a). This programme started in 2008 alongside Skills for Care's programme for social workers working in adult services. In 2012 these programmes were replaced by an Assessed and Supported Year in Employment, or ASYE for all newly qualified social workers in England. Importantly ASYE was and is open to the statutory, voluntary and private sectors and involved assessment against ASYE capabilities as part of the Professional Capabilities Framework (PCF) (BASW, 2015). The PCF provides social workers and employers alike with an understanding of the appropriate capabilities to be developed as part of continuing professional development. For social workers in Northern Ireland, Wales and Scotland, these are still underpinned by the National Occupational Standards for Social Work (e.g. see **www.ccwales.org.uk/national-occupational-standards/** and **www.niscc. info/files/AYE/201405_AYEGuidanceForRegistrantsAndEmployers_Publication_ MAY2014V1_JH.pdf**).

Since 1 April 2015 a revised ASYE framework has been introduced following the introductions of the recent Knowledge and Skills Statements for Social Workers (DfE, 2014; DH, 2015). So, the third edition of this practice guide is also a response to the revised ASYE framework and these Statements in that all of them are covered to a lesser or greater extent throughout.

These welcome interventions come at a time of continued change in the world of social work practice resulting from radical reform of the public sector (Jordan and Jordan, 2006; Jordan and Drakeford, 2012). Since the New Labour government was first elected in 1997, the social and health care sector was subject to a 'modernising' agenda heralded by the Department of Health (DH) White Paper *Modernising Social Services* (DH, 1998). This agenda focused on public service improvement through increased regulation, inspection and monitoring (Parker, 2007; Parker and Doel, 2013). The fiscal crisis which started in 2007 caused shockwaves throughout the world of social welfare and social work and, since the coalition government came to power in 2010, services have been rationalised, some prioritised, and some integrated with others. Children and families' services have, in many authorities, been separated from adult social care. There is a continuing emphasis on working collaboratively with other disciplines and agencies to improve services rather than being constrained by their professional roles (Barr *et al.*, 2008; Quinney, 2012). The involvement of carers and people who use services in designing and leading services continues to be promoted. The Health and Social Care Act 2012, Children and Families Act 2014, Care Act 2014 and the transfer of social work's regulatory functions from the General Social Care Council to the Health and Care Professions Council (**www.hcpc.org.uk**) require commitment and adherence. Employing agencies will require social workers to contribute to performance assessment frameworks and service inspections to promote improvement and development (Sinclair, 2008). Treading a path through such a complex world requires models of social work practice that maintain the value base, yet can also facilitate the development of services and their management and promote personal and professional growth.

This practice guide should help you tread such a path. The flow of the chapters that follow has slightly changed again from the second edition in that there is more of an emphasis on the ASYE at the beginning of the book. Importantly, each chapter starts with a statement about how the text will help you to demonstrate certain ASYE-level professional capabilities and Knowledge and Skills Statements. Chapter 2 starts with the concepts of continuing professional development and critical reflection leading into a discussion of the ASYE whilst Chapter 3 provides welcome ASYE guidance and insight from Skills for Care and the Department for Education. Chapter 4 highlights the transition period between finishing off the social work degree and starting a new job; this chapter will help you to think through issues not only around choosing your first social work post, but also tips on how to apply for it. Chapter 5 will help you to clarify your expectations regarding induction, probation and supervision – and sketches out your role and responsibilities within these processes.

Chapter 6 addresses specific personal issues such as emotions, stress and the management of conflict whilst the final two chapters focus on the workplace. Chapter 7 reiterates the team, partnership and multidisciplinary nature of social work practice working, while Chapter 8 will help you understand your potential contribution to the development of services within the context of business planning, managerialism and learning cultures. The appendices pick up on those findings we mentioned earlier and those ASYE-level capabilities and statements that are not covered in the above chapters – they are designed to be helpful snapshots for newly qualified social workers into issues such as diversity, social justice, safeguarding, court skills, writing skills and child protection, providing signposts along the way. Further reading sections, practical tasks, critical commentaries and case studies within both chapters and appendices, written by managers, people who use services, carers, experienced practitioners, newly qualified social workers and academics bring alive the above topics – and make this book what it is intended to be – a practical, down-to-earth practice guide for newly qualified (or about to qualify) social workers entering their first years of practice.

Please note that many of the names of the newly qualified social workers, carers and people who use services have been changed.

FURTHER READING

ASYE

Skills for Care has given over part of its website to the ASYE.

Adult social work: **www.skillsforcare.org.uk/Learning-development/The-ASYE-adults/The-Assessed-and-Supported-Year-in-Employment-Adults.aspx**

Child and family social work: **www.skillsforcare.org.uk/Learning-development/The-ASYE-child-and-family/The-ASYE-for-child-and-family-services.aspx**

Health and Care Professions Council

The link below provides a series of other links to the Standards of Proficiency for Social Workers in England document as well as the mapping of these standards against the PCF. Please note that in January 2016 Nicky Morgan, then Secretary of State for Education, announced the creation of a new regulatory body for social workers across children's and adults' social care. The most recent report on Social Work Reform is available from the House of Commons education committee here: **http://www. publications.parliament.uk/pa/cm201617/cmselect/cmeduc/201/201.pdf?utm_source=201&utm_ medium=module&utm_campaign=modulereports&wb48617274=A94ABDF8**

www.hpc-uk.org/publications/standards/index.asp?id=569

A revised Standards of Conduct, Performance and Ethics document was published in 2016: **www. hcpc-uk.org/aboutregistration/standards/standardsofconductperformanceandethics/**

Knowledge and Skills Statements

Adult social work: **www.gov.uk/government/consultations/adult-social-work-knowledge-and-skills**

www.gov.uk/government/uploads/system/uploads/attachment_data/file/411957/KSS.pdf

Child and family social work: **www.gov.uk/government/uploads/system/uploads/attachment_data/ file/379033/Consultation_on_knowledge_and_skills_for_child_and_family_social_work_-_ government_response.pdf**

Please note that you will find the statements on page 14 of the above document.

PCF

BASW, the British Association of Social Workers, has taken over ownership of the PCF. Available from: **www.basw.co.uk/resource/?id=1137**

The College of Social Work's recent review of the PCF is available from: **www.basw.co.uk/resource/?id=4083**

There is even a PCF app, downloadable from the App Store for Apple products or Google Play for the Android version.

Research with newly qualified social workers

If you want to go deeper into published research articles that plot the lives of newly qualified workers from a number of different perspectives, consider plundering the following list:

Carpenter, J, Shardlow, S, Patsios, D and Wood, M (2015) Developing the confidence and competence of newly qualified child and family social workers in England: outcomes of a national programme. *British Journal of Social Work*, 45: 153–76.

Hussein, S, Moriarty, J, Stevens, M, Sharpe, E and Manthorpe, J (2014) Organisational factors, job satisfaction and intention to leave among newly qualified social workers in England. *Social Work Education*, 33: 381–96.

Jack, G and Donnellan, H (2010) Recognising the person within the developing professional: tracking the early careers of newly qualified child care social workers in three local authorities in England. *Social Work Education*, 29: 305–18.

Kearns, S and McArdle, K (2012) 'Doing it right?' – accessing the narratives of identity of newly qualified social workers through the lens of resilience: 'I am, I have, I can'. *Child and Family Social Work*, 17: 385–94.

Manthorpe, J, Moriarty, J, Stevens, M, Hussein, S and Sharpe, E (2014) The 'making' of social workers: findings from interviews with managers. *Practice: Social Work in Action*, 26: 97–111.

Manthorpe, J, Moriarty, J, Hussein, S, Stevens, M and Sharpe, E (2015) Content and purpose of supervision in social work practice in England: views of newly qualified social workers, managers and directors. *British Journal of Social Work*, 45: 52–68.

Schraer, R (2016) Patchy implementation of the ASYE leaves newly qualified social workers facing unprotected caseloads. *Community Care* 27 January 2016. Available from: **www.communitycare. co.uk/2016/01/27/patchy-implementation-asye-leaves-newly-qualified-social-workers-facing-unprotected-caseloads**

Chapter 2

CPD, critical reflection and the ASYE

Steven Keen, Lynne Rutter, Keith Brown and Di Galpin with contributions from Angela (NQSW) and Jane (social worker)

PROFESSIONAL CAPABILITIES FRAMEWORK

This chapter will help you to demonstrate the following ASYE-level capabilities:

1. Professionalism: identify and behave as a professional social worker, committed to professional development.

    *   Identify your learning needs; assume responsibility for improving your practice through appropriate professional development.

6. Critical reflection and analysis: apply critical reflection and analysis to inform and provide a rationale for professional decision-making.

    *   Use reflective practice techniques to evaluate and critically analyse information, gained from a variety of sources, to construct and test hypotheses and make explicit evidence-informed decisions.

9. Professional leadership: take responsibility for the professional learning and development of others through supervision, mentoring, assessing, research, teaching, leadership and management.

    *   Take steps to enable the learning and development of others.

KNOWLEDGE AND SKILLS STATEMENTS

This chapter will help you demonstrate the following requirements:

Child and family:
7. Analysis, decision-making, planning and review.
10. Organisational context.

Adult:

8. Supervision, critical reflection and analysis.
9. Organisational context.
10. Professional ethics and leadership.

You are never too old to learn

The phrase 'you are never too old to learn' is exactly what the concept of lifelong learning is all about (Commission for European Communities (CEC), 2007).

> *Learning one set of skills at school, technical college or university is no longer enough to carry people throughout their working life. But there is one basic skill that is becoming increasingly important in today's fast-changing technological universe: being able to learn and adapt to the new skills and training that will be required.*

(OECD, 2007, p1)

The concept of lifelong learning is here to stay and will continue to be a widely held policy object among the Organisation for Economic Co-operation and Development (OECD) countries, not least in the UK, where the number of bodies and agencies working in this learning and skills system remains breathtaking.

The main difference between the generic concept of lifelong learning and continuing professional development (CPD) is the focus on the professional (Higham, 2013). Therefore, CPD emphasises the importance of personal development to the professional practice of social workers in particular, but is not just confined to education and qualifications – it embraces any learning activity. CPD also emphasises that learning is the responsibility of the professional and, like lifelong learning, recognises the importance of the effectiveness of professionals as learners and their commitment to learning as the only constants in an otherwise fast-changing world – one where today's skills and understanding may not meet tomorrow's tasks. CPD has as its ultimate outcome the improvement of services and can start with the question: *What kind of service do we want to deliver?* (Skinner, 2005, p14).

Times of change can result in greater strain and stress, as well as offering good opportunities for development. As we pointed out in the previous chapter, the world of social work and social care is no stranger to change. In recent years, we have witnessed a raft of new policy, legislation and associated organisations in our sector that have changed both the practice and role of social workers in addition to providing the strategic impetus for CPD to become an integrated part of this world, including the introduction of Ofsted, the Care Quality Commission, Health and Care Professions Council (HCPC), Professional Capabilities Framework (PCF) and Knowledge and Skills

Statements (KSS), to name but a few. In part, they highlight the critical importance of your Assessed and Supported Year in Employment (ASYE) as the official beginning and a continuation of your professional learning that actually should never end. We will specifically look at the ASYE later in this chapter as a precursor to Chapter 3, which has been written by an individual who has been part of the development of the ASYE since its inception. Put in its proper context though, the ASYE is part of your wider CPD journey and it is to this we now turn in detail. As we do so, we stress the importance of critical reflection.

Your CPD journey

Recognition of the need for social work practitioners to engage in learning activities has increased in the UK since the early 1990s, as government, employers and employees have identified the need for CPD (Pietroni, 1991; DH, 1998; Higham, 2013). Long-standing evidence in a range of industries shows that accessible career pathways and workforce development opportunities are critical in retaining staff and creating a motivated and stable workforce (Parker *et al.*, 2006; Skinner, 2005). Today, many discussions around CPD focus on these economic and/or political arguments. Put another way, vocational learning helps meet targets designed to ensure the workforce is suitably qualified. Yet, this viewpoint tends to overshadow the personal and socially transformative aspects of participating in CPD. CPD makes complete sense in many ways – it has its own rewards for the individual as well as organisations. **But often the individual is forgotten** (Galpin, 2009). This is why we view CPD as a three-way responsibility between employers, those prescribing and/or providing the learning opportunities, and you, the practitioner. By working together collaboratively, tensions can be managed by allowing reciprocal advice and support to meet one another's needs in the ever-changing world of social work (see Brown *et al.*, 2012, pp23–41, for guidance on how to manage these partnerships). Each has different responsibilities.

The individual's responsibilities are:

- to take a proactive approach in formulating and engaging in learning activities;
- to ensure they meet PCF, Knowledge and Skills Statements and HCPC registration requirements.

The employer's responsibilities are:

- to meet workforce planning requirements to ensure the service is able to fulfil its statutory duties;
- to support individuals in meeting professional registration requirements;
- to support individuals in their pursuit of learning opportunities; this may include financial, study leave and mentoring opportunities.

The provider's responsibilities are:

* to provide opportunities for CPD activity that meet individual needs and the needs of employers;
* to ensure CPD opportunities enable professional learning and development.

But what is CPD?

CPD is defined by Skills for Care (2010, p1) as a:

> *planned learning and development activity that develops, maintains or extends knowledge, skills, understanding or performance. It can include a wide range of activity, designed to equip a worker to provide quality social care and/or support their career development.*

As such, it is any activity that contributes to lifelong learning and is represented diagrammatically in Figure 2.1. CPD usually involves four main stages within an ongoing cycle which is driven by learning needs and objectives, and which in turn allow relevant choices of learning activities/opportunities to be made, plus corresponding evaluation of that learning. CPD can be a managed process supported by organisational policy and procedures, but it is best if you are able to take responsibility for it.

Figure 2.1   The CPD cycle (Brown et al., 2012, p55)

CPD, therefore, applies to all levels of workers and managers and has as its outcome the improvement of services.

In very broad terms, CPD consists of three main types of provision:

- Formal learning – leading to recognised awards and qualifications; may involve further academic study, e.g. post-qualifying modular Master's level courses could be undertaken as stand-alone units, or combined to create a full degree. Higher education programmes will be validated against nationally agreed standards.

- Informal, i.e. non-accredited learning – such as in-house workshops, induction programmes, secondments, mentoring, action learning sets or e-learning modules.

- Experiential learning – such as peer discussion, coaching others, case study reviews, supervising staff or students.

CPD is therefore varied and not just confined to training and/or qualifications. In other words, CPD will not always be provided via a course or programme. Key building blocks are needed to underpin, develop and sustain any type of CPD provision – ranging from effective staff supervision and appraisal systems, succession planning, practice learning, clear leadership and management roles, to an embedded organisational culture of learning (Parker *et al.*, 2006). Enthusiasts are needed at a local level to champion CPD, and flexible learning methods alongside monetary and responsibility-related incentives are also important. Perhaps one of the main underpinning features is the necessity of evaluating CPD, whether it occurs within a formalised programme or not. There should be a change and/or increase in understanding, knowledge or experience as a result of CPD, i.e. some type of learning. We show later how a framework for critical thinking and reflection may aid this 'evidencing' process.

You can see that at whatever level CPD is being undertaken, or however it is being done, it will be about developing practice in some way and measuring this development. In many ways, it is only when you commence work and operate as a qualified social worker that you begin to reflect on your learning and experience to date, and begin to realise what you do not know. So, CPD is vital in order to give you the opportunity to reflect and consolidate your learning to date and to plan your development. To this end, the appendices in this book cover a number of areas that newly qualified social workers highlight they need development in – be they court or writing skills, or safeguarding – please use them as appropriate.

But what does this mean for the newly qualified social worker? As you've seen, this chapter is not focused on employers and the delivery of services – although Chapter 8 is – or even providers of CPD. The focus of this chapter is on *you,* and on where *you* want to be professionally in one to five years' time – ASYE is the beginning of this journey. If you have never considered where you want to be in five years' time, spend some time now thinking about your response and on the next activity. Angela's case study should be helpful as you deliberate on where you want to be professionally in the coming years.

CASE STUDY 2.1

Where do I want to be in a few years' time? Angela's story

I was told I could answer this question honestly so . . . in a few years' time, I would like to be sitting on a tropical beach with my loved ones, remembering fondly the days when I used to be in social work! By then, the numerous excuses as to why I should not do the next post-qualifying module will all have been exhausted and I won't be struggling through the last unit of the course whilst trying to balance working, eating, sleeping and family life. On a serious note, having thought about the concept of lifelong learning, it is helpful to consider where I have come from in order to try and answer the question, where do I want to be in a few years' time?

The path to becoming a social worker began when I started work as an administrator for social services and was then encouraged to do the new social work degree. Prior to this I had studied for three years to obtain a degree in social sciences. It all sounds nicely academic, but apart from the placements I had little experience of actually doing the job, and the thought of doing any more 'official' studying has deterred me at present from pursuing any further formal academic qualifications.

However, since getting my first job as a newly qualified social worker, my knowledge and experience have obviously increased. I have found that I quickly started to engage in an almost constant flow of learning and development coming from various different sources such as classroom-based trainers, people who use services, other colleagues, line managers and so on. This knowledge has helped me on a personal and professional level, which in turn has had a positive effect on my practice.

*I have found the internal training courses provided within my authority especially helpful as they seem to be able to balance knowledge along with practical application. Alongside this, I have had the opportunity to follow a slightly hazy (at present) interest in social work research and have applied to train as a mentor/possible teacher through the Learning and Skills Improvement Service (**www.excellencegateway.org.uk**). These are two specific areas of interest to me and may actually provide part of the answer as to where I want to be in a few years' time.*

There seem to be a number of opportunities now for social workers to pursue a wide variety of interests, and if you are unsure of where you want to be, then my advice would be to not be afraid to experiment, for instance, by shadowing colleagues until you find something that fits with you.

At the end of the day, I want to be the best social work practitioner that I can be. I realise now more than ever that in order to achieve this, it will not be a 'one-off' event. It is much more of a journey that requires a commitment to engage with the process of lifelong learning in whatever form that takes.

ACTIVITY 2.1

Where do you want to be in a few years' time?

Think about what you are good at and what you like to do.

Think about where you want to be, and/or where you want to work, in one to five years' time.

Think about what skills and knowledge you would like to develop during this time. Please feel free to revisit your undergraduate professional development plan or skills analysis.

Thinking about the future will no doubt have caused you to ponder on your current practice. Practice can become routine as you forget why you came into the profession in the first place. This is why it is important to consider why you might engage in CPD. Learning new things can make us more aware of the gaps in our knowledge and skills. Think about driving; would you pass your driving test if you took it tomorrow? Probably not . . . over the years we will have picked up bad habits, but these will not have stopped us from, for example, driving to work. Practice is a bit like this – how many bad habits do we pick up along the way, when we continue to work in the same way, day in, day out?

ACTIVITY 2.2

In his book about England's rise to Rugby World Cup glory, head coach, now Sir Clive Woodward, tells the story of how he prepared his squad for thinking in detail (Woodward and Potanin, 2004, pp165–7). Using an exercise from organisational consultant Humphrey Walters, he asked his players to look at the sentence in capitals below, and tell him how many F's they saw within it – take about 30 seconds and do the same.

> *FINISHED FILES ARE THE RESULT OF MANY YEARS OF SCIENTIFIC STUDY COMBINED WITH THE EXPERIENCE OF MANY YEARS*

When we, the authors, did this exercise for the first time, we all saw three F's. Studies show that 95 per cent of people will only see three F's (Woodward and Potanin, 2004, p166) – the F's in FINISHED, FILES and SCIENTIFIC. In actual fact there are six F's. We so take for granted the word 'OF' that our brains have learned to filter it out of our vision. The point of including this task is this – what do we take for granted in the way we practise? In our everyday work, what do we filter out so that we no longer see it? Sometimes the act of just stopping, thinking about and reflecting on our practice can bring about some interesting results.

Critical thinking and reflection for CPD

Reviewing and reflecting on practice is important for developing capability. Rolfe *et al.* (2001) show that developing practice and learning cannot be separated. The development of practice is a lifelong activity; it generates experiential knowledge and so to practise is also to learn. The use of CPD progress records, personal learning plans or portfolios (Skills for Care, 2006, 2010; Hull *et al.*, 2004; or see **www. hpc-uk.org/apply/uk/forms/**) can be an effective way to achieve and evidence such learning. For many it leads to insights and new understandings. However, reviewing and developing practice can also be threatening and provoke anxiety. It is hard work, involving self-doubt and mental blocks. Professional knowledge comprises theoretical knowledge and experience, as well as the understanding of process – these are complex ideas to deal with. Critical thinking and reflection on practice, therefore, can be invaluable tools to review, consolidate and develop practice because they provide the necessary guidance and instructive frameworks associated with experiential learning or portfolios of evidence; and with producing robust evidence of such learning. Texts such as *Critical Thinking and Professional Judgement for Social Work* (Rutter and Brown, 2015) and *Professional Decision-Making and Risk in Social Work* (Taylor, 2013) aim to support and develop this process, and the following ideas are adapted from these books as a proposed model of how to evidence CPD.

What is critical thinking and reflection?

Critical thinking and reflection are processes that allow you to think back on experience more deeply and 'drill down' to identify relevant underpinning knowledge (experiential and theoretical) and values, as well as the professional reasoning and decision-making that make up your expertise. Not only this, they allow a more questioning and creative approach – highlighting different options, alternatives or implications that could inform and help you develop future practice – thereby ensuring that CPD does what it says on the tin; in other words, it continues in time, adopts a professional approach and is developmental.

Why think and reflect critically?

In our experience, the greatest area of weakness for a newly qualified social worker portfolio is the level of critical reflection and analysis (Rutter and Brown, 2015). Critical thinking and reflection should not produce cynics, but practitioners aware of the reality of practice, who are committed, well-informed, rational and supported by relevant and valid skills and knowledge. These 'critical practitioners' will be the type of staff people using social care services need to meet their needs and who they can trust and respect.

On a day-to-day level, there are dangers associated with the development of expertise in practice. As we tried to demonstrate earlier with the exercise in Activity 2.2, any practice can easily fall into purely intuitive and routine methods because they are safer and less time-consuming. We sometimes develop rules of thumb and standardise our approaches to problems in order to survive our workloads. However, these habitual practices do not demonstrate explicit professional judgement or decision-making. Using critical thinking and reflection to develop professional expertise in the sense of sound professional judgement will take you beyond repeating the same experience or implicitly developing your own implicit rules of thumb. Rather, you can explore and understand your reasoning, judgement, decisions and actions in meaningful ways, and develop new perspectives for future practice. The main outcome will be an evaluation of the learning and development pertaining to future practice: the development of self as a critical practitioner (Adams *et al.,* 2002) undertaking sound professional judgement. The aim is to get you to think beyond the acknowledgement and description of feelings, or the elements of a particular situation, to an evaluation of how you dealt with it – i.e. your thinking processes, and the resulting decisions and actions.

How can this be achieved?

Critical thinking and reflection can be triggered by the recognition of something not 'normal' – possibly an unexpected action or outcome (positive as well as negative) or an intuitive feeling of unease. Supervision can be used to pick up on and explore these situations, and your supervisor or mentor may be able to spot and challenge unhelpful practice. Although we will return to the advantages of supervision later in the following chapter and again in Chapter 5, please understand here that there are real benefits in keeping up to date in a professional area of practice and having the necessary critical skills. Such a practitioner will have more knowledge and awareness to recognise incidents for what they are and have more self-confidence to deal with them explicitly. Initially, frameworks to help critical reflection can be used to guide further thought and exploration. The next activity and Table 2.1 will enable you to link various aspects of practice to certain critical thinking activities, to demonstrate and develop critical practice for CPD.

ACTIVITY 2.3

Thinking and reflecting critically: part 1

Use the left-hand side of Table 2.1 to identify the relevant aspects of practice you want to explore and then move across to the right-hand column to see which particular critical thinking activities are likely to support them. By understanding and discussing practice in these terms, you can more readily articulate your capability, notice where further development is necessary and see where extra training or education is appropriate to support development. For example, you may have relevant knowledge about Deprivation of Liberty legislation (DH, 2005) but realise you now need more information about the specific implications of this legislation and how to apply it. To find such information may require further reading or training.

Table 2.1 Elements and activities of critical 'expert' practice

'Expert' practice areas	Embedded critical thinking
1. Awareness, control and evaluation of thinking processes	Thinking about thinking (meta-thinking). Recognising and questioning arguments, etc.
	Identifying and challenging own and others' assumptions.
2. Developing clusters of knowledge	Keeping up to date; reading the literature. Integrating values and experience.
	Holding views based on valid experiential evidence but seeking and accepting relevant but alternative viewpoints and perspectives.
	Generating and evaluating practice-based knowledge.
3. Assessment of situations in depth – 'naming and framing'	Gaining alternative perspective/s or reframing a situation.
	Understanding when more information and input is required, knowing where and how to get it.
Selection and adaptation of 'schema' or framework that fits	Lateral/creative/flexible thinking; problem forming and solving.
4. Decisions leading to action	Decision-making and planning; use of discretion; responsibility; risk assessment.
	Seeking out and taking proper account of all stakeholders' input.
	Thinking through the means–end relationship as well as the implications of decisions and actions.
	Predicting possible outcomes, allowing for alternatives.
5. Monitoring progress and evaluating outcomes. Adapting and changing where necessary. Ongoing learning	Formulating clear aims/objectives at start, getting feedback and making judgements.
	Using feedback and evaluation from all concerned parties, especially people who use services.
	Making informal leaning more explicit. Embedding formal learning.
	Sharing and developing learning within the organisation.

(Adapted from Rutter and Brown, 2015, p58)

The next practical task offers you a series of progressive steps to think critically about a practice experience (see Table 2.2). As such it demonstrates that there are multiple dimensions to critical reflection.

ACTIVITY 2.4

Thinking and reflecting critically: part 2

Identify a practice experience you wish to think more critically about. Start by thinking about the main descriptive details and use the examples and questions in Table 2.2 to guide you. Then work on this material by identifying, analysing and evaluating the key points and issues, your input and the outcomes, and finally draw out the learning from this evaluation and show how it can affect or impact your practice. So, there is an evaluated conclusion (i.e. something that can be appropriately assessed) in terms of your understanding and learning and development. This is a key purpose of CPD, especially if you are not undertaking a formal course.

Table 2.2   Dimensions of critical reflection

Dimensions	Example
Description Be aware of important and relevant aspects of self and the situation – including your feelings and thoughts concerning complex issues and dilemmas.	For example, if you were reflecting on a home visit, you might consider the details concerning your role, the situation of the person you were visiting and their feelings, how you prepared for the visit and the timing of it. What were you feeling? What do you want to achieve? What did you notice? What do you now see as significant? What seemed unfamiliar?
Critical analysis Identify and explore significant aspects and issues of this situation, e.g. feelings, behaviours, reasoning, decisions, actions, etc. Challenge or question underlying assumptions, knowledge, experience, etc.	Using the same example what were the key issues in the way you communicated? What were your objectives and why? Why did you use particular techniques during the visit? How was this visit different from previous ones? Are the differences significant? What were your assumptions? What could you have failed to notice?
Evaluation Judge your reasoning, decisions as well as the outcomes. Show additional insight into relevant issues; wider contexts; different perspectives.	Again using the same example, perhaps consider how well you met your objectives. Also consider why you thought a particular technique was appropriate. Was this reasoned through explicitly or not? Did you make a conscious decision or a more intuitive one? What are the potential and apparent risks with either of these approaches?
Learning Finally, consider the learning that has come from this reflection and how you might share it.	What does this mean for your practice? A consideration of the above could lead you to ideas for future practice, both in terms of your own learning needs and improvements in service provision. How has this changed your thinking?

(Adapted from Rutter and Brown, 2015, p35)

Both of these frameworks (Tables 2.1 and 2.2) can be used within supervision sessions, self-directed learning activities or in association with a formal course. They can also be used as tools to demonstrate the learning associated with CPD, especially for ASYE but also how you make professional judgements.

Professional judgement

You will be starting to reflect on the way you come to decisions in more detail here (i.e. exploring how you think and reason things through, and make judgements). As indicated in the activity, some decisions are made in a more conscious manner than others. Munro (2011) refers to the analytical and intuitive dimensions of thinking. We may be able to take the time for a deliberate, systematic approach to a decision, or more usually we only have an opportunity to make a fast instinctive response. Although you will not be able to fully 'capture' what is happening, making an effort to uncover, explore and understand some of the elusive aspects of professional judgement increases the possibility of becoming more aware of them in action and developing them more meaningfully for CPD. This can be achieved not just for your learning, but also for reasons of accountability and for you to be able to share such knowledge and understanding with colleagues. Analytical or intuitive approaches to decision-making are not necessarily right or wrong, biased or unbiased – they are just more or less appropriate for a particular situation. Understanding the situation and the requirements on you are therefore key aspects of critical thinking. Kemmis (1985) shows that it is practical reasoning (as opposed to academic or technical reasoning) that is able to consider what is most appropriate for a situation, and how to best act in that situation; it is a moral activity, it considers both means and ends, and allows for complexity. Such practical reasoning (see Table 2.3) is therefore said to be a key part of professional judgement-making (Kondrat, 1992; Beckett and Hager, 2002).

One fundamental feature of practical reasoning is that there is no established process to it because it is happening in an active, complex and evolving or uncertain situation. Practical reasoning, therefore, cannot be viewed or approached as a prescriptive list of rules to be followed, but there are particular features and principles associated with it. It is important that these are understood in order to make practical reasoning as good as it can be, and to allow an objective and critical evaluation of it where possible as you reflect on a decision or judgement you made.

When reflecting on your thinking be aware that thought processes are more complex than simply being analytical or intuitive. Kahneman (2011) talks about the uneasy interaction of 'fast' and 'slow' thinking and argues that even if we think we are using

Table 2.3   Framework of practical reasoning principles

Practical reasoning principles

Situational appreciation, i.e. sensitivity to, and discernment of, the particular characteristics and features of a situation (including ethics, circumstances and needs).

Attention paid to the complexity and uncertainty of a situation, i.e. this is not ignored or overly reduced.

Transparent purpose and intentions, e.g. explicable aims/objectives.

Critical appraisal and interpretation of formal and informal knowledge, skills, attributes and values.

A clear exchange between the particular characteristics and features of the situation (e.g. a person's behaviour) and the wider context (e.g. social/cultural norms) in order to gain a fully informed view; as well as between subjective (personal) and objective (neutral) perspectives.

A moral and reasonable relationship is established between goals/objectives and resulting decisions/actions via a critically reflective, reciprocal dialogue between means (how we do something) and ends (the outcome).

Critical thinking is used within the process to:

> weigh up risks, options, pros and cons, contingencies;
> adjudicate between competing goals and demands;
> generate and deliberate between alternatives, choices;
> create review or monitoring points;
> take into account relevant constraints and limitations.

Outcomes, decisions/actions are prudent, appropriate and useful to the situation's needs, etc.

New understanding and meaning (expertise) is developed.

(Taken from Rutter and Brown, 2015, p20)

slow analytical thinking to make choices and decisions, we are influenced all the time by our fast intuitive thinking. Nevertheless, we can still reflect and aim to understand and improve both these aspects of our thinking using different models.

There are a number of analytical problem-solving and decision-making models that can help direct and improve our analytical thinking, e.g. see Chapter 8 and Adair (2010). They provide a series of steps that make sure we define our aims and objectives, collect relevant information, generate feasible options and evaluate them carefully. They act as prescriptive stages to follow. In contrast, Klein's (2004) work develops a descriptive and naturalistic model of decision-making (Recognition Primed Decision-Making) that can prove useful to help us analyse our more intuitive thinking. It provides an interesting set of ideas that help explain how we 'naturally' decide what to do in a fast-moving situation. The two key components are:

1. Sizing up the situation – this involves recognising relevant 'cues' which let you recognise a certain 'pattern'. This relates to the 'naming and framing' idea seen earlier in Table 2.1. Once we recognise a pattern we gain a 'sense' of that situation – we know what cues are going to be important and need to be monitored. We know what goals we might be able to accomplish. We have an idea of what to expect next.

2. These patterns also include ideas for a response – a course of action to follow. Identifying a course of action that makes sense for that situation, and then evaluating that course of action by imagining it is the second component.

In other words, recognition of the familiar and non-familiar in a situation means being able to identify cues and their significance – this is pattern matching and is the first phase or component. Knowledge of a range of acceptable courses of action and being able to think them through requires mental simulation – this is the second phase. This second phase is also called a singular evaluation approach because each option for action is evaluated in turn and on its own merits in response to the initial pattern matching. This is in contrast to an analytical model that would initially create a range of differing options in order to evaluate them against each other.

Large sets of internalised cues and patterns are required in order to size up situations as well as a store of mental models of action to then imagine and evaluate a responsive course of action effectively. So, this approach is reliant on continuing experiential learning to build and update such expertise so that cues and patterns are not only identified but their significance and relevance to any subsequent decisions are also understood too.

Motivation

By using the practical reasoning principles and the analytical and intuitive thinking models to inform and help focus your reflection, professional judgement can be explored in more depth, and areas of development can be identified for CPD purposes. Of course, issues regarding confidence and experience play an important part here – as a newly qualified practitioner you will naturally rely on others and their judgements more than an experienced practitioner would. However, you can start to reflect on how far that reliance should extend, as well as on how you are developing and relying on your own professional judgement. For more information on this topic and as you progress in your career, refer to Rutter's (2012) *Continuing Professional Development in Social Work.*

Regardless of the quality of CPD provision and support structures, only you can provide the motivation to learn. Admittedly, that motivation may be based on external factors such as monetary reward, but more often than not it may be based on a desire to make a difference in the lives of people in vulnerable situations and/or at risk. Thinking about what motivates you to learn is important and should help develop your own practitioner-centred approach to CPD, as Jane notes in her case study.

CASE STUDY **2.2**

Jane's CPD story

I have thoroughly enjoyed my Master's degree in Adult Social Work and feel that I have gained a great deal from it. I started the course three years after completing my Master's level social work qualification. I enrolled as I wished to continue my professional development and return to formal learning.

Colleagues have commented that my confidence has grown and I feel that my practice has improved. The course has provided a valuable opportunity to step back, analyse, reflect and consider my work and why we do what we do, which so easily becomes lost in a busy workplace. I now take a much more critical approach to government policies and agendas and have greater understanding of their likely impact upon local authorities, front-line workers and ultimately my role.

Some of the material covered on the course may be familiar to those who have recently qualified. However, the usefulness of revisiting this should not be overlooked. The views and beliefs that I held when I qualified have shifted and evolved as a result of spending several years actually 'doing' social work. Theories and material is looked at from a different and more critical stance that experience brings.

One of the most enjoyable aspects of the course was the chance to join with other practitioners away from the pressures of the work environment and share thoughts, feelings and frustrations of the job. This is a rare opportunity and I feel that I learnt a great deal through discussions with others.

I am currently completing the Enabling Work Based Learning module and am now supervising a final year student. Although the thought of being responsible for someone else's learning was initially a little daunting I am really enjoying the experience. Having a student is sharpening up my practice and knowledge and keeping me on my toes!

Anyone considering a formal CPD award needs to look beyond just the academic qualification. There is the potential to gain so much more from CPD provision; you will grow as a practitioner, professional and possibly as an individual too. My skills base has expanded significantly which is not just going to benefit me but also my employer, be it current or prospective. Rather than just considering a particular award in terms of its end result, see it as a journey where there is much to learn along the way.

The first activity in this chapter encouraged you to think about where you want to be and what skills you would like to develop in the next few years. The following activity will cause you to think more about the key subject areas we have covered so far in this chapter and your own approach to CPD before we move on to introduce the ASYE.

ACTIVITY 2.5

Continuing professional development

How might you develop a personalised and meaningful approach to CPD? Here are some topic areas and related questions to reflect on.

The context of CPD: *are you clear why you are participating in CPD? Is it all about registration, job chances, improving job satisfaction or service outcomes for people who use services? Is it about improving your work environment or supporting others in the workplace?*

Partnership: *who is involved in your likely CPD partnerships? What are these partnerships like and how can they be improved? What CPD opportunities is your employer offering?*

Reflection: *are you able to stop and reflect on practice? What barriers stop this process? How might you remove or lessen these barriers?*

Motivation: *what is your motivation to learn? What factors might improve your motivation to learn in the future?*

At this point it might be useful for you to draw up an action plan. Within the plan, include a timeline, a list of key partnerships you might like to develop and how, and other activities you could engage in.

Assessed and Supported Year in Employment

As we highlighted at the end of the first chapter, there is a growing body of evidence highlighting the importance of the transition that you are just about to make or have just made, that is, from qualifying programme to the workplace (for examples, see Moriarty *et al.*, 2011). In 2009, the Social Work Task Force recognised that the problem with qualifying education was that it was not reliably preparing individuals for the demands of practice. This led to the recommendation for an Assessed and Supported Year in Employment or ASYE (SWTF, 2009) replacing previous programmes for newly qualified social workers in September 2012, and subsequently updated in April 2015 (Skills for Care, 2015) following the introduction of the KSS for social workers in adult and child services (DfE, 2014; DH, 2015). The following chapter will guide you through the implications of these changes in further detail and point you to the helpful Skills for Care online resources (see **www.skillsforcare. org.uk/Topics/Social-work/Social-work.aspx**). For now though, understand that ASYE aims to ensure that newly qualified social workers receive nationally consistent support throughout their first year and therefore involves assessment to meet KSS as well as PCF requirements. ASYE dovetails with other developments in the sector including the updated Standards for Employers of Social Workers in England (LGA, 2014). There is to be no direct link between ASYE, registration and regulation; once you have finished your social work degree you will be able to register with the Health and Care Professions Council if you work in England (see **www.hcpc-uk.org**). Though please note that in January 2016 Nicky Morgan, then Secretary of State for Education, announced the creation of a new regulatory body for social workers across all children's and adults' social care, so this situation may change in the future.

ACTIVITY 2.6

Familiarity

Re-familiarise yourself with the Standards of Proficiency (SoP), Knowledge and Skills Statements and PCF (ASYE capabilities) by accessing the following links:

SoP: **www.hcpc-uk.org/publications/standards/index.asp?id=569**

www.hpc-uk.org/publications/index.asp?id=1141#publicationSearchResults

Knowledge and Skills Statement (child and family): **www.gov.uk/government/uploads/ system/uploads/attachment_data/file/379033/Consultation_on_knowledge_and_ skills_for_child_and_family_social_work_-_government_response.pdf**

Knowledge and Skills Statement (adult): **www.gov.uk/government/uploads/system/ uploads/attachment_data/file/411957/KSS.pdf**

PCF: **www.basw.co.uk/resource/?id=1137**

In order to understand what is or will be required of you as a social worker, a key question to consider is what are the main similarities and differences between these requirements?

To figure this out, it may be helpful to initially consider what is the overall aim of each document, e.g. the aim of the Standards of Proficiency document is to detail expectations of a social worker's knowledge and abilities so they can register with the HCPC and start practising. How does this differ with the aims of the KSS and PCF? There are a number of 'mapping' documents that should help you. Access these at:

Mapping of HCPC standards against the PCF: **www.hpc-uk.org/publications/standards/ index.asp?id=569**

Mapping PCF to KSS: **www.skillsforcare.org.uk/Learning-development/The-ASYE-child- and-family/Practice-examples-and-templates.aspx**

ASYE is an employer-led process that has two main aspects – that you, as the newly qualified social worker, are assessed and supported. Therefore, there are three main stakeholders – the newly qualified worker, employer and assessor. The main role of the newly qualified social worker is to meet the above standards. The main role of the assessor is to ensure effective support and assessment arrangements are in place. In practice, this means that he or she will make a professional recommendation (more on this in the next chapter) that will be moderated 'internally' by your employer or a group of employers and possibly externally (e.g. see **www.skillsforcare.org.uk/ Learning-development/The-ASYE-adults/Internal-assessment-confirmation-and-moderation.aspx**). It will be important for you to make the most of this relationship with your assessor/mentor. Some employers provide guidance on how you might do this (e.g. **bournemouthcs.proceduresonline.com/pdfs/asye_handbook.pdf**) but as a general rule of thumb take responsibility to develop this relationship by building mutual respect and trust; be as open and honest as you can; and remember that it is a reciprocal, i.e. two-way relationship. What this means is that no one individual alone will take responsibility for your final ASYE assessment. Finding out from your employer or prospective employer about their ASYE programme is critical.

ACTIVITY 2.7

ASYE programmes

How would you describe the key elements of your employer's or prospective employer's ASYE programme?

Partnership? Flexible? Professional confidence? Competence? Capability? Support? Assessment?

How will you be supported throughout the year?

Proformas? Induction period? Probation period? Reviews? Observations? Link to academic qualifications? Reduced workloads? Frequency of reflective supervision? Link to pay and progression? Moderation? Final assessment/outcome?

What are the arrangements for probation, induction, appraisal, resolving appeals and complaints?

Pass/fail predictions? Extensions? Action plans? Probation?

Whichever way your employer has chosen to complete the ASYE, clarity over assessment procedures is critical. In other words, employers are ultimately responsible and accountable for their assessment decisions and determining any appeal or complaint procedures. Yet, these processes do not take away from you the responsibility for your own development. That's why it is important to look out for employers who will support you through the ASYE process and beyond into your future career as an experienced, advanced and ultimately strategic practitioner. A good employer will have a well-established CPD career framework for its staff. Often linked in partnership with a university, this framework will provide a clear focus and structure for your professional development and is perhaps equally or possibly more important than 'rates of pay', as it's all part of their investment in your career. Our advice is to look for employers that offer clear ASYE and CPD opportunities linked with universities, as these will offer you nationally recognised awards that will be valued as such. In completing these awards and ASYE requirements you will be required to manage effective study alongside managing a caseload. The final part of this ASYE sub-section provides our hints and tips to achieve a good balance in managing the completion of ASYE expectations.

- Start 'thinking' early – think about how you can combine your 'day job' with the completion of ASYE documentation outcomes. Think about how you study best, as knowing how you function most effectively will enable choices around how, when and where you ASYE documentation. Think about how you can use any spare time, e.g. it may be as simple as watching less television or using your commute to work more effectively. Do check out the time management matrix in Figure 6.2.

- Take a project management approach – there is more on this in Chapter 8 but for now, you may find it helpful to plot your major milestones on a timeline. Then you can break these milestones down into smaller tasks, working out what needs to come first and by when. You may find that as your see yourself completing these smaller tasks this helps motivate you to keep on track. In short, our advice is to be organised.

- How about an ASYE buddy? Some may find pairing up with a fellow newly qualified social worker a helpful way of maintaining motivation and commitment to completing ASYE-related documentation and outcomes.

- Take a day off every week – if you can take a whole 24-hour period to relax every week. We think you'll be surprised at how refreshing it is.

The chapter that follows will provide further detail on the ASYE.

Summary of key points

- The ability to continually and professionally learn, develop and adapt are key skills that newly qualified social workers need to embrace.

- Although CPD is viewed as a three-way responsibility between employers, providers and practitioners it is best if you are able to take responsibility for, and develop your own practitioner-centred approach to, it.

- Reviewing and reflecting on your practice is critically important for developing your capability and enhancing learning associated with CPD, especially for ASYE.

- ASYE is the official beginning and a continuation of your professional learning that should never end and aims to ensure that newly qualified social workers receive nationally consistent support throughout their first year in practice. It is important that you check how you will be supported by your employer or any prospective employer throughout this process and how you might maintain a good balance between achieving ASYE-related outcomes whilst working.

FURTHER READING

Klein, G (2004) *The power of intuition.* New York: Currency Books.

This book explores intuition as a tangible skill that allows us to recognise patterns and cues as a natural learning process from experience over time.

Rutter, L (2012) *Continuing professional development in social work*. London: Sage/Learning Matters.

Rutter, L and Brown, K (2015) *Critical thinking and professional judgement in social work*, 4th edn. London: Sage/Learning Matters.

Both the above highly recommended books contain practical, down-to-earth guidance in easily digestible formats.

Williams, S and Rutter, L (2015) *The practice educator's handbook*. London: Sage/Learning Matters.

This book, although primarily written for busy social workers involved in supporting, enabling and assessing learners in the workplace, will provide newly qualified social workers with invaluable guidance and indeed a 'heads-up' on their own development.

Chapter 3
The social work Assessed and Supported Year in Employment (ASYE)

Mary Keating

Please note that whilst the ASYE covers all capabilities and statements in a holistic manner, this chapter focuses, in particular, on those listed below.

PROFESSIONAL CAPABILITIES FRAMEWORK

This chapter will help you to demonstrate the following ASYE-level capabilities:

1. Professionalism: identify and behave as a professional social worker, committed to professional development.

   - Make proactive use of supervision to reflect critically on practice, explore different approaches to your work, support your development across the nine capabilities and understand the boundaries of professional accountability.

6. Critical reflection and analysis: apply critical reflection and analysis to inform and provide a rational for professional decision-making.

   - Show creativity in tackling and solving problems, by considering a range of options to solve dilemmas.

   - Use reflective practice techniques to evaluate and critically analyse information, gained from a variety of sources, to construct and test hypotheses and make explicit evidence-informed decisions.

KNOWLEDGE AND SKILLS STATEMENTS

This chapter will help you demonstrate the following requirements:

Child and family:

   7. Analysis, decision-making, planning and review.
   9. The role of supervision.
   10. Organisational context.

Adult:

3. Person-centred practice.
8. Supervision, critical reflection and analysis.
9. Organisational context.
10. Professional ethics and leadership.

This chapter is predominantly for newly qualified social workers (NQSWs) undertaking the Assessed and Supported Year in Employment (ASYE) but it should also be useful for their assessors. It examines the current arrangements for the support and assessment of the ASYE as required by the two Knowledge and Skills Statements (KSS) published by the Department for Education (2014) and the Department of Health (2015). The publication of these statements has introduced some differences in the arrangements for the assessment of NQSWs in adult and child and family settings. The final picture of how the Approved Child and Family Practitioner (ACFP) assessment and accreditation will link with the ASYE in child and family social work settings is still in development; however, it's likely that the ASYE will continue as an induction year.

This chapter will give you a basic understanding of the ASYE. It will consider the similarities and the differences between the assessment frameworks in child and family and adult social work, highlight how you can build on your qualifying education experience to enhance your experience of the ASYE and give you some tips on how you can prepare for your first year in employment. It also contains many case studies of NQSW experience like the one below.

Skills for Care was involved in developing the original framework and guidance introduced in 2012. We were also responsible for developing the ASYE capability statements in the PCF.

More recently we were part of the group, working closely with the office of the Chief Social Worker (adults) to finalise the development of the KSS for social workers in adult services (DH, 2015) in response to the consultation.

Skills for Care (2015) worked with employers on the revision and design of new ASYE materials to meet the requirements of the KSS (adults) (DH, 2015) and is responsible, through a contract with the Department for Education, for the provision of support to employers in child and family services as they implement the new requirements for ASYE, including assessment against the KSS (child and family) (DfE, 2014).

CASE STUDY **3.1**

NQSW experience: newly qualified child and family social worker

'The ASYE allowed me to find my social work style and learn in a supportive environment which I believe has now led me to be a confident social worker – if I had personally gone straight in without the ASYE I would have struggled . . . the difference from being a social work student to a social worker is enormous and ASYE bridges that gap.'

How we got here

Helping new social workers to make the transition from qualifying education to the world of professional work is not new. In 2008, the Children's Workforce Development Council (CWDC) introduced a framework for the assessment of NQSWs in child and family services followed in 2009 by the introduction of Skills for Care's NQSW framework for social workers in adult services. The introduction of special arrangements for the first year in practice brought social work in line with other regulated professions, who were already running induction schemes. Since this date, the management of and process for this first year in practice has undergone several changes.

As the previous chapter notes, the ASYE was introduced in September 2012, building on the previous NQSW frameworks. The major change was that the ASYE, rather than having separate frameworks, was now a generic framework. The ASYE was designed as an employer-led and managed scheme but the social work education reviews of 2014 (e.g. Croisdale-Appleby, 2014) noted the potential for discrepancies in the way employers might be delivering and assessing the ASYE, thereby creating a potential lack of consistency in assessment across the country. The Chief Social Workers, in part, responded to these concerns by publishing the KSS:

- Knowledge and Skills Statement for social workers in adult services: **https://www.goo. gl/OaEFSD**.

- Knowledge and Skills Statement for child and family social work: **https://www.goo. gl/RwCWVX**.

These statements describe what social workers should be able to do at the end of their first year in practice and are looked at in more detail later in this chapter.

At the same time as the publication of the KSS (child and family social work) (DH, 2014), the Secretary of State for Education announced the government's intention to develop a new assessment and accreditation system for three levels of professional practice for children's social workers in England.

- Nicky Morgan announces children's social work reforms: **https://www.gov.uk/ government/speeches/nicky-morgan-announces-childrens-social-work- reforms** and **https://www.gov.uk/government/news/nicky-morgan-unveils- plans-to-transform-childrens-social-work**.

- Consultation on knowledge and skills for child and family social work. Government response: **https://www.goo.gl/R4iDhd**.

The first level of these, the Approved Child and Family Practitioner status (ACFP) (p11 of the consultation on knowledge and skills for child and family social work, Government response), is intended for those social workers who are working with our most at risk children – children in need (Children Act 1989), that is, children in need of protection and children in public care. An assessment and accreditation process is currently being developed for the ACFP and during this 'proof of concept' phase, decisions have not yet been made on which social workers employed in child and family settings will be required to sit the assessment. Testing of the ACFP assessment and accreditation commenced in November 2015. Despite the introduction of the ACFP, it is expected that core aspects of the ASYE will continue to be delivered, because of the proven benefits for people who need care and support, NQSWs and organisations (see Case Study 3.2). Therefore, social workers in child and family settings should find this chapter useful to understand the core support and development requirements for the ASYE.

CASE STUDY **3.2**

NQSW experience: newly qualified child and family social worker

'I think most newly qualified workers have some anxieties about starting their first post in social work – the ASYE programme . . . has been invaluable for me during this time. Being a front-line children's social worker has been a challenging and rewarding experience; I have been impressed at the high level of training and development opportunities the ASYE has provided, helping to develop my skills, knowledge and confidence which are required to meet the needs of the children and provide families with the best possible service.'

For those of you who are taking up your first social work post in adult services, the KSS for social workers in adult services (DH, 2015) provides a clear statement of the ASYE requirements. The intention of the Chief Social Worker (Adults) has been to ensure that a nationally consistent assessment framework is in place in which both NQSWs and employers could have full confidence. In practice, this means that the evidence requirements are standardised, and that internal and external moderation processes, including a national moderation process, are in place to measure the standards across the country. From your point of view there is clarity about what is expected of you, and you can be reassured that the support and the standard of the assessment is being scrutinised through an internal and external moderation process. Details of the assessment and moderation requirements can be found on the Skills for Care website: **www.skillsforcare.org.uk/internalmoderation**.

Central to the previous ASYE framework, introduced in 2012 in England, were a number of products developed by the Social Work Reform Board (SWRB, 2010). These products influenced the design and the delivery of the ASYE, for example, the Standards for Employers and Supervision Framework (SWRB, 2012) laid down expectations of the support and supervision arrangements that would apply to the first year. This meant that for the first time there was transparency for NQSWs and employers about the expectations of support for this protected year, and these same arrangements will continue to apply to you (via the revised Current Standards for Employers document (LGA, 2014)) as you progress through the current ASYE framework. At the same time the assessment standard for the ASYE moved from the National Occupational Standards to the standards contained in the Professional Capabilities Framework (PCF) for Social Workers in England (BASW, 2015). The PCF signalled a move away from a mechanistic competency approach to assessment and replaced it with progressive, holistic assessment. A holistic assessment remains a requirement of ASYE assessment following the incorporation of the KSSs.

Why support the first year in practice?

The NQSW experiences in these case studies are just some of many examples expressing this appreciation and enthusiasm for the support and guidance that they have received in their first year of practice. A number of large- and small-scale evaluations of the NQSW framework and the subsequent ASYE in child and family and adult services have reiterated and reinforced key messages about the value of the protected year (see Case Study 3.3).

Key messages about the ASYE:

- Two-thirds of NQSWs agreed that supervision had improved the quality of their practice (Skills for Care, 2011). Regular structured supervision was rated as the most beneficial component of the programme (Carpenter *et al.*, 2011).

- More NQSWs are completing personal development plans and embarking on post-qualifying education. Three-quarters of NQSWs agreed with the statement, 'My employer takes my professional development seriously' (Skills for Care, 2011).

- Two-thirds of NQSWs agreed that the overall quality of their practice had 'improved a great deal' and so had their 'own professional abilities'.

- The vast majority of NQSWs stated their supervision was supporting their reflective practice either very or quite well (Skills for Care, 2013).

- NQSWs and supervisors/assessors identified a range of benefits for the NQSW in taking part in the ASYE, the main one of which was the 'development of professional confidence' (Skills for Care, 2013).

- For NQSWs, the main messages to sell the ASYE to another NQSW included time for reflection, receiving structured support and guidance and the importance of peer support (Skills for Care, 2013).

- A quarter of social workers who responded a year after completing the ASYE, felt that the ASYE had prepared them 'very well' for the transition from student to social worker and almost three-fifths felt it had prepared them 'fairly well' (Skills for Care, 2015).

CASE STUDY 3.3

NQSW experience: newly qualified adult social worker

'I have found my ASYE year to be a good opportunity for learning and development . . . I feel that the programme has been a useful tool that has enabled me to integrate well into an Adult Social Care Team during my first year as a qualified social worker. I look forward to my next step in my career as a social worker.'

There is a danger that an NQSW could approach the ASYE thinking that it is more of the same, i.e. another, albeit very long, practice placement. It is important that you don't fall into that way of thinking. We'd like you to think of it instead as the year where you consolidate the learning from your qualifying training and develop new learning pertinent to the setting in which you are employed.

As an NQSW, you are now working as a registered social worker and everything relates back to your practice, so developing good habits in this first year will stand you in good stead for the rest of your career. Do grasp this golden opportunity with both hands. This is not just about assessment; it is about your right to a supported and protected year in which you can find your feet in the social work setting with all its complexities and challenges. You will still be expected to hit the ground running . . . but jogging, not sprinting.

CASE STUDY **3.4**

NQSW experience: newly qualified adult social worker

'The ASYE year is a good bridge of the gap between finishing university and going into a full-time career. The sessions have promoted critical reflection in a comfortable, relaxed and friendly environment. I feel that [names removed] have been really supportive and encouraging throughout the ASYE and I believe these qualities have developed me as a practitioner and as a person. I feel the ASYE year has put me in good stead for a career in social work.'

The KSS and the PCF: how they support your learning and assessment

If you are not already familiar with the two KSSs, now is the time to refer to the statement that is most applicable to your intended or actual first employment setting. The KSSs describe what social workers should know and be able to do at the end of their first year in practice. They will help you get started in your first post, providing a useful tool to help you think about the specific skills and knowledge that you will require for the context in which you are employed.

Both statements support the use of the PCF as the generic standard for all social workers. The KSSs do not reiterate all of the PCF capabilities because they were designed to contextualise not replicate the PCF. You will be familiar with the content and the expectations of the PCF from your qualifying education but now is the time to understand the requirements of the next level for the ASYE. The knowledge and skills set out in the published statements are specific to either child and family social work or adult social work. The PCF is the overarching standards framework intended to be applicable to all social workers in whatever role or setting. A review of the PCF has recently been undertaken by The College of Social Work (TCSW, 2015) and includes a recommendation about how relationships and connections between new standards and the PCF can be managed. Following the closure of TCSW, the responsibility for taking forward the recommendations has been passed to the British Association of Social Workers (BASW).

The KSS for social workers in adult services (2015) reflects the changing context of social work in adult services. Working within the parameters of new and recent legislation, including the Care Act (2014) and the Mental Capacity Act (DH, 2005), it places an emphasis on statutory health and well-being outcomes. Together with the Care Act, this statement provides the opening for social workers in adult services to grasp an opportunity to take a leadership role and be recognised as central to the development of a robust and caring adult social care sector.

The ASYE assessment in adult services requires that social workers demonstrate legal literacy through the application of these and other pieces of legislation. The statement places an emphasis on the skills and values of working in partnership with people in need of care and support and on supporting independence and well-being.

ASYE assessment requires demonstration of understanding, application and management of all aspects of risk and safeguarding including positive risk-taking. There are clear expectations of the knowledge requirements, including human development, personalisation, the social model of disability and the impact of trauma and loss etc. There is an increased emphasis on the social worker as professionally confident, demonstrating a professional social work identity and taking a leadership role in all settings including interprofessional working. Such professional confidence requires the ability to continually update knowledge using evidence-based interventions and reflecting on practice. How you can be supported in this process will be discussed later in this chapter but the ASYE will assist you in becoming that highly professional confident leader.

If you are starting a career in a child and family setting, the KSS for child and family social work will help you to understand the specific knowledge, skills and responsibilities that are required of every social worker working in a child and family setting. In the introduction to the statement, Isabelle Trowler, Chief Social Worker (child and family) says: *The statement affirms just how skilled and wise we expect our social workers to be to meet these challenges*. The statement will provide you with the detail of the combined aspects of skills and wisdom.

The statement places an emphasis on the development and demonstration of interpersonal, relationship building and empathic skills, but in the context of the social worker as the authoritative professional capable of using knowledge and evidence-based practice.

Through the reflective process the child and family social worker, over the course of the year, is expected to develop a combination of evidence-based practice that draws on knowledge, including legal literacy, and practice experience to understand, assess and work with children and families. Central to this is the recognition of potential harm and risk, and the importance of developing skills in this area. There is an expectation that the social worker will demonstrate the ability to lead investigations on allegations of significant harm, albeit in consultation with others.

Throughout your qualifying programme you will have developed your knowledge base but you may not have covered everything in detail. The statement provides a list of core knowledge requirements, including an understanding of child development, and the impact of mental health, substance misuse and domestic abuse on children and families. The list is not exhaustive and you will need to identify the knowledge requirements that are specific to your employment setting. As in the KSS for adults the statement emphasises the ability to reflect, analyse and demonstrate reasoned, defensible decision-making. Your development as a professional will be through a combination of all of these capabilities (see Case Studies 3.5 and 3.6).

CASE STUDY 3.5

NQSW experience: newly qualified adult social worker

'The ASYE programme has been very positive for me in being able to put into practice the skills and knowledge I gained from my degree. Taking full advantage of the training and supervision included has increased my confidence and belief in my practice.'

CASE STUDY 3.6

NQSW experience: newly qualified child social worker

'During the year I believe I have gained experience and confidence within my work as a direct result of knowing support is there if needed. Consequently, I have been able to improve and grow in areas of work in which I was already relatively confident, whilst also being supported to gain confidence in areas of work I have not previously experienced. This has been particularly relevant within legal and court processes, as until they are experienced what to expect is not known – by shadowing a supportive consultant the process becomes a little less scary.'

The relationship of the KSS to the PCF

Having analysed the key elements of the KSS, you may well be wondering about the role of the PCF in identifying learning needs and in the assessment process. It is important to remember that the PCF is the generic framework and provides the standards for social workers throughout their careers, not just at qualifying and ASYE levels. As such it is the bedrock when identifying the learning that you will need to prioritise as you progress through your ASYE year.

As we pointed out in the previous chapter, understanding the relationship between the two should be instructive, i.e. the KSSs set out what a social worker working with adults or children and families should know and be able to do by the end of the ASYE and these are designed to strengthen and enhance the PCF. The PCF is the overarching standard for all social workers and in providing detail of the capabilities at each level it pinpoints the profession's expectations. The PCF can also be used as a diagnostic tool and will assist you in identifying your learning needs.

Example

When you commence your ASYE you will be expected to undertake an audit of your knowledge and skills against the relevant KSS. You might identify that you need to develop your ability to use *practice evidence and research to inform complex judgements and decisions* (DH 2015, statement 8). You can analyse the detail of what and how this can be achieved by referring to the PCF. If you want further detail about how the KSS and the PCF overlap, there are mapping documents on the Skills for Care website that you will find useful: **www.skillsforcare.org.uk/asyegoodpractice**.

Assessment of the ASYE: similarities and differences

The PCF was a product of the SWRB (2012) and seen as central to the successful introduction of the final social work reforms and products. The importance of the PCF for you as an NQSW is several-fold. We have already seen how it can be used as a diagnostic tool and to inform professional development activity, but perhaps even more importantly than this, the PCF was designed to support the development of the profession and the capability and confidence of every individual social worker.

Because social work practice is a complex activity, it requires the interplay of knowledge, skills and values, which is exemplified by the PCF. Although there are nine separate PCF domains, these need to be seen as interdependent as they interact in professional practice. There are overlaps between the capabilities and many practice issues will be relevant to more than one domain. Moreover, understanding what a social worker does can only be complete by taking into account all nine domains working in interaction with each other. In order to assess this complexity a holistic assessment is required.

Additionally, the KSSs require an understanding and demonstration of the complex activity that makes up the social work task, making the holistic assessment of the ASYE a necessity.

The revisions to the ASYE have created an opportunity to improve the guidance and information on holistic assessment to ensure that progressive development is supported and evidenced. Your ASYE is not a snapshot assessment, but requires demonstration of your progression over the year.

In adult ASYE the revisions to the framework have strengthened the centrality of critical reflection in all aspects of professional development to ensure that the voice and feedback from people using the service is at the heart of the reflection.

Support for and demonstration of progressive development over the year is linked to a cycle of critically reflective logs and reviews. The ASYE (adults) guidance is separated into the record of support and progressive assessment (RSPA) and the critical reflection log (CRL). The RSPA should be completed by the assessor and the CRL should be completed by the NQSW. In practice, the two documents are interwoven so if your first post is in adult services you need to familiarise yourself with both documents. These can be found on the Skills for Care website: **www.skillsforcare.org.uk/asye**.

In child and family social work, the ASYE assessment framework and requirements are not prescribed in the same way. In practice, many employers will be either doing something similar to the new adult framework or will continue to follow the guidance issued for the introduction of the ASYE (2012). In both cases there will be an initial audit against the KSS to inform learning needs and your professional development plan. Guidance on both of these frameworks and examples of what evidence requirements employers in child and family social work are using can be found on the Skills for Care website: **www.skillsforcare.org.uk/asyecf**.

Although the introduction of the two separate KSSs and the introduction of the ACFP appear to signal a departure from the generic ASYE assessment framework that was introduced in September 2012, you can be reassured that in the immediate future the assessment requirements will remain similar. As adult social work tests how it can develop a nationally consistent assessment of ASYE, child and family social work is also testing an assessment and accreditation framework. It is possible that what appears to be two divergent tracks may converge again in the future as each learns the lessons from the other's experience. As you can see from Table 3.1, there are more similarities than there are differences.

Critical reflection and the development of professional practice and judgement

Central to social work practice and to the development of professional judgement and expertise is the ability of every social worker to critically reflect on their work. Table 3.1 shows that the ability to critically reflect on practice and to demonstrate this is central to the assessment of the ASYE in both child and family and adult settings.

Table 3.1   Similarities and differences between child and family and adult ASYE assessment requirements

ASYE assessment requirements	Adult	Child and family
Audit against the KSS	Yes	Yes
Learning agreement and PDP	Yes	Yes
Direct observations	Minimum of three	Yes, but number not prescribed
Feedback from other professionals	Minimum of three	Highly recommended but number not prescribed
Feedback from people in need of care and support, children and their carers	Minimum of three	Highly recommended but number not prescribed
Critical reflection	Critical reflection log or equivalent	Required but no prescribed format
Assessment of record and report writing	Yes	Highly recommended
Holistic assessment	Yes against the KSS and the PCF	Yes against the KSS and the PCF
Moderation	Required	Recommended

Through this reflective process, the insight and learning will ensure that your practice is continually improved. The practice of critical reflection is something that you will have already commenced in your qualifying education and you should revisit any programme guidance you have been given.

The reflective process is not confined to your qualifying training and the ASYE because the purpose of this emphasis on critically reflective practice at these stages is to ensure that the process is embedded and develops with you as you progress throughout your career. This is the point we made in the previous chapter.

One source that provides important detail of what is meant by reflective practice is the PCF domain – critical reflection and analysis. Both of the KSSs place significant emphasis on the development and use of reflective practice, framed within an understanding of theory, legislation and research in order to be able to develop and articulate your reasoned, evidence-based decision-making. The Skills for Care website provides further information on critical reflection and gives pointers for how you can conduct critically reflective dialogues: **www.skillsforcare.org.uk/asye**.

To support the progressive development of reflective practice the critical reflection log, originally created for use in ASYE (adults), has also been adapted for use in child and family settings and can be used to guide you through the process.

Feedback from people in need of care and support, children, young people, their families and carers

Central to any reflection on practice is the ability to continually take account of and respond to feedback from people in need of care and support. This feedback will be implicit as well as explicit whether collected formally or on an ongoing basis and all these aspects need to be considered in understanding the implications for your practice. At every stage of their work, social workers are expected to consider, obtain evidence from, and respond appropriately to, the views of the people they are supporting about the social work intervention and the professional relationship the social worker has with them.

There is no single correct way by which a social worker should seek feedback, and indeed best practice would dictate that the process and tools will differ according to the situation and those being supported. The Skills for Care website provides more information on how to develop feedback from people in need of care and support: **www.skillsforcare.org.uk/gatheringfeedback**. At the beginning of the critical reflection log you will be asked to consider and plan for how you will collect this feedback.

Professional supervision

As an NQSW, you will receive professional supervision regularly from your line manager, or from another experienced social worker if your line manager isn't a registered social worker or for other operational reasons. Supervision is not just about reporting on your day-to-day social work practice with your line manager, clarifying policies and procedures and agreeing the next steps, although these are all important. Supervision is crucial as it should give you the opportunity to critically reflect on your practice and enable you to grow and develop in confidence and capability as a social worker.

Your supervisor should help you to review all aspects of your practice, including, for example, your direct work with the people you support and as a member of a team or working with other partners or external organisations. Most importantly, reflective supervision sessions should help you to develop skills in critical analysis and reflective practice by providing a forum for you to explore your practice. The aim is for you to become highly skilled in this area and you should use supervision to share and gain feedback on your insights and ideas. You should take a proactive approach and prepare for supervision sessions and suggest items for the agenda. Chapter 5 will explore these ideas further.

Support: what can you expect?

We have spent a lot of time describing and considering the implications for the assessment of the ASYE, however, the other side of the coin is the agreement between employer and NQSW around the level of support that you can expect. The latest Standards for Employers document (LGA, 2014) lists the support expectations for the ASYE. By doing so it 'mainstreamed' the level of support for those undertaking the ASYE within an overall expectation of support that applies to all employers, managers and social workers.

The Department for Education and the Department of Health expect that you will be given the required level of support as you progress through the ASYE as your employer receives funding to enable them to put this support in place.

Having a completed record of support and progressive assessment of the learning agreement at the start of programme is an important part of the ASYE, as it sets out how support and assessment will be undertaken between the employer and the NQSW. It also helps to clarify the roles and responsibilities of all those involved and includes:

* details of the frequency of reflective supervision;

* a statement on a reduced workload during the first year of employment;

* a professional development plan;

* a time allocation for professional development.

This support and assessment/learning agreement should be reviewed regularly – at least at three and six months. This review will be an opportunity for all involved to come together to consider how well your assessment is progressing and to, put in place action plans if necessary. This is also the time for all parties to consider and, importantly, record whether all aspects of the agreement are being adhered to, and that includes contributions and comments from the NQSW on the level of support received. Support can also come in the form of a peer-led NQSW forum as Case Study 3.7 points out.

CASE STUDY 3.7

NQSW experience: newly qualified children and families social worker

'Having a forum to meet with other newly qualified social workers gave me the basis to be able to discuss any issues of being a "newbie" and gave me the confidence to be able develop professionally whilst feeling supported and understood' (social worker, children with disabilities).

Are you eligible for the ASYE?

The ASYE is an induction year supporting NQSWs to establish themselves on the first step of their professional career. The expectation is that the learning gained in qualifying education is consolidated and that new knowledge and skills are developed in practice relevant to the employment setting. The learning gained during your qualification programme needs to remain current and should not become a distant memory with no practice experience or continuing professional development (CPD) between leaving university and the ASYE. To be eligible for the ASYE there must be no more than two years between graduation and commencing your first role.

There has been some concern expressed that this may disqualify some qualified and registered social workers who have been unable to find social work posts immediately. There is, however, a caveat to the two-year time boundary in that it is possible beyond this timescale for the employer to assure themselves of the currency of the social worker's knowledge and skills. In addition, re-registration with the Health and Care Professions Council (HCPC) is required every two years and in order to re-register, NQSWs will need to be able to evidence they have kept knowledge and skills updated through CPD activity; see **www.hpc-uk.org** for more information.

Registered social workers who are employed in private, voluntary, health and education are eligible for the ASYE. Those employed in other roles that may not be described as 'social work' are also eligible to undertake the ASYE as long as their employment includes work of a sufficient level and kind to meet the expectations of the relevant KSS and the PCF. Case Study 3.8 provides a good example of this.

This is because we are living in a constantly changing world for the delivery of social work services. Social workers are, and will increasingly be, found employed outside of local authorities in smaller agencies, social enterprises, community interest groups, social work practices and in multidisciplinary teams. The intention has been to provide an ASYE framework that can be flexibly implemented across a diverse range of employment settings and roles.

The ASYE is available to all social workers working with adults in adult services who contribute to delivering statutory health and well-being outcomes for people and their carers, regardless of the sector in which they are employed. The Care Act (2014) creates a legal obligation on all providers of care to ensure individual well-being – physical, mental and emotional – is at the centre of service provision. Furthermore, it places a universal obligation on local authorities and their partners to provide for the well-being needs of all local people, not just those in receipt of state-funded care and support. This means that all services that help prevent, delay and reduce the need for care and support are covered by the definition of statutory well-being outcomes.

CASE STUDY 3.8

NQSW experience: newly qualified child and families social worker

'As I am not employed directly as a social worker I have found the ASYE very helpful in allowing me to keep in touch with my social work values and ethics. The ASYE has also supported me and enabled me to continue learning and professional development.'

Similarly, the ASYE in child and families services is also available for social workers in a diversity of settings as long as they can meet the requirements of the KSS. Large numbers of social workers in such diverse settings as private fostering and adoption agencies, schools and hospices have already undertaken the ASYE.

Increasing numbers of employers and NQSWs outside of statutory provision are being registered to receive funding for the ASYE. Employers report that the ASYE is beneficial in terms of staff recruitment and retention, service efficiency and improved quality of service provision. Further information and comment from employers and NQSWs can be seen in the video clips on the Skills for Care website: **www.skillsfor care.org.uk/independentsectorasye**.

If you are an NQSW employed in social care or other related field and you feel that your job includes work of a sufficient level and kind to meet the expectations of the KSS and the PCF, then talk to your employer about registering for the ASYE.

Social workers are increasingly employed on short-term contracts in local authority, health and social care settings. Your employer is not prevented from registering you for the ASYE if the contract is for less than a year. You can start with one employer and finish with another if your new employer is willing to support you in this process. It will be the new employer who will decide on the sufficiency of evidence that you present for assessment, and this can include any statements from previous employers about your progression, the standard achieved and any evidence to illustrate your development. This allows some flexibility but also puts an onus on the NQSW to ensure that the evidence and statements are available to be transferred to the next employer and that this new employer is willing to continue to provide the relevant support and assessment.

In a similar way, this will also apply to agency workers; however, in this scenario the recruitment agency and the commissioning agency will need to decide who will register and receive funding for the NQSW. This decision will need to be based on who, in this situation, will provide the support and the assessment. Both parties and the employee would need to agree on the responsibilities for supervision, assessment and the funding to support this. The supervision arrangement would need to be laid out clearly in the learning agreement. In many instances the feasibility of these arrangements for those on short-term contracts and agency workers may well depend on the length of contract.

The ASYE has intentionally been designed as a year-long programme of support and assessment. This means that there is no fast track to achieving the ASYE and the converse is also true that under normal circumstances it will not take longer than a year to complete. As an NQSW it is in your interest to ensure that you receive support over a whole year as you embed your practice. The year will be automatically extended if you work part time, go on maternity leave or are off sick for a period of time or for whatever reason the support arrangements are not available to you. In all of these cases, you should ensure that the length of the extension and the reason are clearly documented. It is important to note that the year will not be extended if the reason is to do with your capability; in this case the expectation is that under normal circumstances all NQSWs should be able to reach the standard within one year.

ACTIVITY **3.1**

In advance of taking up your post, or even in advance of an interview, here are some useful tips to help you prepare. Engaging in this self-assessment will not only help you to identify your learning needs, but will also help you identify, from your experience to date, the knowledge and strengths that you have and can bring to the role.

Familiarise yourself with the relevant KSS

Practise auditing your current knowledge and skills against the expectations detailed in the KSS. This will help you when you are completing this for real at the start of the ASYE. Examples of audit tools can be found on the Skills for Care website: **www.skillsforcare. org.uk/asyegoodpractice**

Familiarise yourself with the ASYE level of the PCF

Go back to your final placement report and review the future learning needs identified by the assessor. Think about these in the context of the role that you are undertaking and the KSS requirements. Use the PCF at the ASYE level to help you to clarify your learning needs. The first section of the critical reflection log will give you guidance and help you to organise your thoughts.

Identify your model of reflective practice

Think about what you have discovered on your qualifying course about your learning style and the model of reflective practice that suits you. If you want more information about this area check out the Skills for Care website: **www.skillsforcare.org.uk/ asyecriticalreflection**.

(Continued)

ACTIVITY **3.1** *continued*

Develop your analytical skills

Both of the KSSs stress the importance of critical reflection in the development of analytical skills for decision-making. Employers are looking for a reflective analytical approach in new social workers and how this develops over the year. How might you develop your analytical skills in the next year?

Collect feedback from people in need of care and support

Start to think about and plan for how you will collect feedback from people in need of care and support. How you do this will depend on your service group and setting. The Skills for Care website provides more information: **www.skillsforcare.org.uk/ gatheringfeedback**.

Final thoughts

Social workers will enter the ASYE year with different levels of experience and knowledge. The audit that you will undertake against the KSS and the analysis of the level and detail expected of you in the PCF will provide you with an accurate measure of all that you need to learn and achieve over the year. It's important to remember that the ASYE expects you to show progression regardless of your starting point so it's important for those more experienced social workers to ensure that they continually improve and progress as this is central to the assessment and must be demonstrated over the year.

You will be supported throughout the year by ensuring that you have a reduced caseload and protected time for the professional development activity that you have identified at the start and at regular review points throughout the year. Over the year the level of complexity of your caseload will increase and you will be expected to become more autonomous in your practice and decision-making.

The KSS, the PCF and indications from the developing ACFP assessment place greater emphasis on your ability to reflect in and on your practice. The reflective supervision process and, where available, other support in the form of workshops, action learning sets and group supervision will provide you with the settings to explore your practice and develop these skills. If you are in a setting where other levels of support outside of individual reflective supervision are not available, there is nothing to stop you setting up peer support and supervision arrangements. The section on critical reflection and holistic assessment and the completed example of the critical reflection log will support you in this process: **www.skillsforcare.org.uk/asyecriticalreflection**.

The ASYE is an employer owned and administered programme and the final assessment decision therefore sits with the employer. The Knowledge and Skills Statement for social workers in adult services has resulted in more standardisation and a requirement for assessment decisions to be moderated.

KSS for child and family social work requires the assessment decision to be defensible by being accurate, valid, robust and sufficient although there are no requirements for employers to follow standardised arrangements for the process.

CASE STUDY 3.9

NQSW experience: newly qualified adult social worker

'I am pleased to read in the report that I have asked for guidance appropriately and when necessary. I have noticed that as my knowledge and experience has grown over the year, the level of support has changed. I continue to seek advice from others and managers; however, I do feel that I have developed my ability to use my own initiative more and to use relevant previous experience to inform particular areas of current work. I am pleased to see that this development has been referred to in my report also.'

Summary of key points

- This chapter has shown that despite the apparent differences in the arrangements of ASYE for adult and child and family social work, we see that in practice there are many more similarities than differences. The arrangements for assessment and moderation prescribed for social workers in adult services are in many cases being adopted for child and family social work settings. Many local social work partnerships are already moderating the ASYE assessment process and assessment decisions across a number of employers including both adult and child and family settings. In time this should ensure that the assessment decisions made in Durham will be the same as those made in Devon, meaning you can be assured that there will be a transparency in the decision-making and that you have reached a national standard whether you work in statutory, voluntary, private, child and family or adult settings.

- The value to you of being able to undertake the ASYE is enormous; you will have noted the positive comments from NQSWs throughout this chapter (e.g. see Case Study 3.9) who have completed the programme so talk to other NQSWs if you can.

- A certificate of successful completion of the programme will be issued by Daisy Bogg Consultancy on behalf of the Department of Health for social workers in adult services. The Department for Education will be sharing more information on child and family ASYE certification shortly.

- The responsibility for the success of the ASYE scheme is a joint one. The employer provides you with the appropriate support and you take responsibility for your learning in practice. This is the beginning of your career as a professional social worker, so make the most of the support and take the initiative for your learning, which will pay dividends in terms of your professional confidence, resilience and joy in being part of this young but vital international profession.

FURTHER READING

British Association of Social Workers (BASW) (2015) *BASW England Response to the Review of the Professional Capabilities Framework*. **https://www.basw.co.uk/resource/?id=4085**

Local Government Association (LGA) (2014) *Standards for Employers of Social Workers in England*. **http://www.goo.gl/Cm9tY3**

Skills for Care (2013) *ASYE Longitudinal Report One: Social Worker and Supervisor Surveys*. Leeds: Skills for Care.

Chapter 4
Managing transitions

Lee-Ann Fenge with contributions from Mark Hutton (manager), Tom (NQSW) and Tom's university tutors

Introduction

In this chapter we will consider the impact that acquiring a new role as a qualified social worker has on you, and ways of planning for such a change of status. This will include your transition to becoming a newly qualified practitioner and your Assessed and Supported Year in Employment (ASYE), the focus of the previous chapter. This process will involve developing self-awareness and adaptability in the face of change. There should be resonance here with the knowledge and experience you will have gained as a social work student in terms of working with individuals who face change and transitions within their life course. The knowledge and experience you will have gained as part of your social work degree therefore has application to the transitions and changes you will encounter in the early stages of your practice as a social worker. This chapter is structured to help you to prepare for the transition from student to qualified social work practitioner so that your transition is successful with the minimum of stress and disruption.

You will have been working towards this point throughout your qualifying education. Indeed, your journey to a career within social work may have been much longer, including achieving relevant work experience and qualifications to gain entry onto a social work degree. This can be viewed as a voluntary transition, where you have had time to consider the various options open to you (Fouad and Bynner, 2008).

You may have been clear at the start of your degree about the area in which you ultimately want to practise, or this may have gradually emerged during the course of your studies and experience on placement. You may be surprised that the area you are now considering for a career, or are engaged in as a qualified practitioner, is not something you would have considered at the start of your degree. You may still be unclear as to what type of setting and user group you eventually want to work with, and may still be considering several options. This is a time of opportunity and change, and it is important that you reflect deeply on where you want your career to develop and what opportunities might be open to you. Chapter 2 should have been further help to you here as it addressed your continuing professional development.

As a newly qualified practitioner, the first few weeks and months of your life in the professional community *can set the stage for a successful and gratifying career – or lead to stagnation, disillusionment and attrition* (Pare and Le Maistre, 2006, p363). This transition will now take place as part of your ASYE. Linked to the Professional Capabilities Framework and Knowledge and Skills Statements, the ASYE is designed to support you as you become a newly qualified social worker. The Croisdale-Appelby report (2014, p70) into social work education recognised the value of the ASYE programme as a mechanism to bridge the gap between qualification and qualified practice, particularly as *it offers some degree of protection to newly qualified social workers in terms of workload relief, support and supervision.*

It is expected that, once qualified, you complete the ASYE in 12 months. To support this process of transition during your ASYE period, you and your employer will complete, for example, a record of support. It is therefore important that you anticipate and prepare well for this transition from student to qualified social work practitioner and the ASYE period. No doubt you will also face continued transitions throughout your professional life as you choose to specialise in particular areas of practice, and move towards advanced-level practice and/or management.

Transition research

So, what does research tell us about the transition from student to practitioner? Research into trends of social work employment suggests graduates enter employment quickly, with over half in 1996 and 2001 working in social work within one month of graduating (Lyons and Manion, 2004). This period is a time of change as you make the transition from identifying as a student social worker to becoming a qualified practitioner. The context of your practice will therefore change from one which is undertaken within a university structured process of knowledge and practice education, to one which is structured by your employing organisation and practice context. As a social work student your experience of practice has occurred within condensed timeframes and assessment processes (O'Connor and Leonard, 2014). As a qualified practitioner, increasingly your practice will be influenced by organisational systems, resources and constraints, and your own developing autonomy and reflexivity about practice.

Research suggests most newly qualified social workers struggle with the duality of their roles and need support in establishing coping mechanisms and work–life balance (Revans, 2008). In a recent survey of newly qualified social workers most graduates described their increased confidence in practice but identified that they expected to receive considerable support and guidance in their workplaces as they transition into qualified practice (Tham and Lynch, 2014). The ASYE process should facilitate this transition enabling you to cope better with the changing demands of qualified practice, and this is supported by research that highlights the positive impact that a programme of supervision and support can have on self-efficacy during the ASYE process (Carpenter *et al.*, 2015). The package of support offered by employers during the newly qualified phase is also linked to job satisfaction, and this includes feelings of being well-prepared and able to put social work values into practice (Hussein *et al.*, 2014).

So what might your ongoing post-qualification support needs be? Bates *et al.* (2010) undertook research with newly qualified practitioners which suggests a range of ongoing post-qualification development needs, including developing assessment, report writing, record keeping, time and case management skills. Alongside these ongoing development needs it is suggested that newly qualified practitioners need to feel that their employers appreciate the difficult job they are doing, and that employers show a commitment to providing the resources and support necessary to enable them to do it well (Jack and Donnellan, 2010). This is important in terms of employer engagement with ASYE and the support provided to newly qualified practitioners during this time of transition.

ACTIVITY **4.1**

Thinking back . . . and forward

Thinking back to your final practice portfolio assessment as a student social worker, what future learning needs did you and your practice educator identify? How might these be addressed during the ASYE process?

As you move into your ASYE period, you will need to develop a personal development plan, which will support you to look at areas of transition as well as areas you wish to develop further during your first period of employment as a qualified social worker. It may be helpful to consider key goals within your first year as a qualified practitioner and how these will be achieved during the ASYE period. Identify the resources and learning opportunities needed to achieve these goals.

Research from the nursing and the allied health professions can help us understand the impact of transition from student to qualified practitioner. Research suggests that the experience of being a newly qualified nurse can lead to feelings of uncertainty and chaos (Wangensteen *et al.*, 2008). Similarly trainee doctors have been found to experience distress, burnout and depression during both training and in the early years of medical practice (Dyrbye *et al.*, 2014). Graduate paramedics have reported initially feeling out of their depth without sufficient knowledge and this can be exacerbated by unsupportive workplace cultures which have a negative impact on the new graduate (Kennedy *et al.*, 2015). However, support mechanisms within employer organisations have been found to reduce stress during this transitional phase (Edwards *et al.*, 2015), and acceptance into the workplace culture allows access to valuable inside knowledge (Kennedy *et al.*, 2015).

What can we conclude from this research? Simply this – the transition from student to newly qualified practitioner, across a range of disciplines, can be stressful and unsettling. It involves a process of moving from the culture of an educational establishment to the organisational culture of the workplace (Schrader, 2008); a process of seeing oneself as a graduate practitioner; a process of developing an awareness of your own expectations and what they mean; and a process of understanding the expectations of your new employer and colleagues as well.

Therefore, the context of the work environment, including both formal and informal support mechanisms, and how readily new staff members are welcomed and supported in the workplace culture is important. Although you will have gained practice experience through social work placements, the status of a student social worker in placement is different from that of a newly qualified social worker. The expectations you have of your own practice, the expectations of your employer and the expectations of people who use services and carers may be different, and part of your transition will be to cope with any mismatch that exists. This process involves you moving on from being immersed in your higher education 'community of practice' to your social work practitioner 'community of practice' (Wenger, 1998). Therefore, you are, or will be, engaged in a process of sense-making (Weick, 1995), one in which you are making sense of your changing identity from that of a student to a newly qualified practitioner.

Sense-making

Weick (1995, p17) identifies six characteristics of sense-making. Sense-making is:

- **grounded in identity production** – your emerging identity as a social work practitioner;

- **retrospective** – we rely on what we know to make sense of our present situation;

- **enactive of sensible environments** – the organisational environment plays a key role in the way you make sense of yourself as a practitioner; we therefore rely on what others are doing to frame our understanding of events;

- **social** – we do not make sense of ourselves in a vacuum and our understanding is often contingent on the conduct of others;

- **ongoing** – sense-making never stops as it is an ongoing process;

- **focused on and by extracted cues** – we rely on cues that we extract from our working environment, and which we use to make it seem plausible; therefore sense-making processes are driven by what is plausible rather than by what is accurate.

Weick (1995, p20) suggests that how you make sense of your situation is grounded in the identity you develop of yourself in relation to others. So, in developing your professional identity it is important that you look back to the experiences that have been influential in the past, as well as being aware of the factors that will influence you in your new post. It is also important to remind yourself of your successes and positive experiences to ensure that you carry them with you into your new job.

ACTIVITY 4.2

Preparing for transition: part 1

Assess your own growth and achievement as a student social worker.

A number of elements are involved in a successful transition from student to newly qualified social worker, which include recognising the knowledge and transferable skills you have acquired throughout the social work degree. Often it is easy to underestimate or forget all the strengths that you already have. This task requires that you review and list specific areas of growth and achievement as a student social worker. For example, this may include the experience of group work gained in placement, or a specific area you studied on your course.

What changes have taken place for you over the past three years, e.g. emotional, psychological, relational, geographical? Have there been pivotal learning experiences? What were the most important and/or pivotal learning experiences? What were the biggest challenges? What will you build on or try to replicate in your new post?

At the end of the exercise, review the list. Is it longer than you expected? Are there any surprises included on it?

This exercise will not only enable you to review your own growth and development, but may help you identify areas that you need to develop further in the future. For example, you may feel your understanding and practice experience has provided you with grounding in general mental health policy and practice, but that you really want to develop a more specific understanding of the Mental Capacity Act 2005 (DH, 2005).

Transitions and role change

As we experience transitions in our lives we have to make a series of adjustments and changes as we enter the transition process. A transition has been described as a discontinuity in a person's life space (Adams *et al.*, 1976, p5). However, as discussed earlier in the chapter, the transition you currently face as a soon-to-be, or newly qualified, social worker is something that you have control over and you can plan for.

Research suggests that if we can anticipate change or choose to make a change, we are able to adjust more readily to the transition (Blair, 2000). To adapt successfully from student to qualified worker, it is important to prepare and plan for this transition – which might mean not applying for (and accepting) the first job you come across. This preparation involves taking time to plan what options are open to you, and what might be your most suitable first post to assist you in your longer-term career goals. Research exploring factors influencing career choice highlights the importance of professional socialisation (Rubin *et al.*, 1986). Your academic study and placement experiences will have influenced your choice of career focus – together with other factors such as your individual characteristics, friends and family.

Even though the transition from student to qualified practitioner is planned in some way, each individual will perceive the change differently, and will cope with the transition in a different way (Parkes, 1971). Personal choice and decision-making are important for both perceptions and outcomes of transitions (Ronka *et al.*, 2003). So, how will you as an individual take control of and adjust to the change from student to qualified practitioner? Blair (2000) offers a helpful four stage model of work role transition, consisting of cycles of preparation, encounters, adjustment and stabilisation. We explore each one in turn in the activities below before considering how you might find a job.

ACTIVITY **4.3**

Preparing for transition: part 2

Think about the changes you will face in your transition from student to qualified social worker. These might be positive such as changes in your financial status from student to paid qualified worker, or negative in terms of losing the support of your student peer group. The following list offers suggestions but is not exhaustive.

- *Identity* – *at the crux of any transition from student to qualified worker is a change in identity. This not only means that other people will see you differently, but you will also think about yourself differently, once qualified. You may feel relieved that your years of study are over for the time being, but you may also sense fear and a little trepidation. Koerin et al. (1990) suggest that as the transition from student to qualified social worker involves endings, students may react in many different ways. This may mean that some students become overwhelmed by the thought of being in the real world (Koerin et al., 1990, p202) and as a result try to avoid these thoughts by*

(Continued)

ACTIVITY 4.3 *continued*

delaying looking for a social work job. Others may become overly anxious and invest inordinate time and energy in the job search process.

How does being qualified make you feel?

Think about how you can manage these feelings by taking control of, and making decisions about, your future.

- **Relationships** – how will the end of your life as a student social worker impact on your relationships? For the past three years you have been part of a student cohort, and may have experienced both positive and negative experiences with your peer group. Inevitably, the end of your studies will mean moving on from your current peer group and the support you may have derived from them. Try to anticipate any feelings of loss that may be associated with this process, and explore ways of coping with this change.

- **Living arrangements** – where will you live after the end of your studies? Does the end of your student life also mean a change in your living arrangements? For example, have you been sharing a house with fellow students and will this now change?

- **Location** – will you remain in the same location as your university, return to your family home and/or relocate to find work? What impact might any of these decisions have on your existing support networks?

ACTIVITY 4.4

Encounter

Once you have been appointed to your first newly qualified role, it will be useful to explore what your expectations of this role are. The reality of the workplace could be very different from your expectations (Marsh and Triseliotis, 1996).

Try writing down any expectations you have – about the induction period, the type of work you will be undertaking, quality of supervision, support of colleagues and the nature of the workplace you are about to enter.

It may be useful to review this list two or three months into your new working life when you have encountered the realities of practice as a newly qualified practitioner.

At that time, ask yourself if there is a mismatch between your expectations and the reality of practice? If there is, it might be worth asking yourself the question, what can I do about this? What can you live with and what can you change or adjust to? Chapter 6 will be of further help to you in this area.

ACTIVITY 4.5

Adjustment and stabilisation

Adjusting successfully to a newly qualified practitioner role is essential for future confidence as a practitioner, and is a critical factor if a worker is to continue to practise in that field (Moscrip and Brown, 2002). Adjusting successfully to the transition from student to qualified practitioner involves personal change, role development and relationship building. Essential to this process is the gaining of support from your supervisor and the wider team, and managing your induction. These themes, in particular, are discussed in more detail in the next chapter and Chapter 7 (joining and contributing to a team), but for now, begin to think about how you might enable and gain this support.

Successful adjustment will lead to stabilisation in your new role. This will involve increased trust, commitment and effectiveness involving both the tasks you undertake and the people you work with. A key part of achieving a feeling of stability in your work role is increasing your capability as a practitioner. Support from colleagues and managers is also vital in building confidence during this time (Brumfitt et al., 2005).

The following section considers how you might find a job in order to make these stable and well-adjusted transitions.

Finding a job

The vacancy situation can vary across the country, thereby affecting the availability of posts. It may not be possible to get an ideal fit between the type of post you want, in the exact setting and location you desire. You may need to be flexible in your expectations, and take a view that your first role is a stepping stone to open up new experiences and broaden future horizons. Activity 4.4 should have helped you reflect upon your expectations of your first post.

Social workers can do many different types of jobs in a wide variety of settings, including the statutory, voluntary and private sectors, although most newly qualified social workers appear to choose the statutory sector for their first post (Bates *et al.*, 2010). Making a decision about where you want to work in your first post is crucial and will set you on your path to future career development. A key element of the rite of passage from student to qualified practitioner is your registration with the Health and Care Professions Council (see **www.hcpc-uk.org**). However, if a qualified role is not readily available, you may need to consider employment in an unqualified position as an interim measure.

Career choice and targeting your career search

There are many different ways to begin your search for a social work job. You may be considering posts within the statutory, voluntary and/or private sectors so it is important to cast your net widely when looking for adverts. Think about using the following five ideas:

- **Social networks:** use them to identify employment opportunities: through your placement experiences you may have already established some social networks to alert you to jobs that are coming up. It is therefore a good idea to keep in contact with former colleagues that you have worked alongside during your placements.

- **Social media:** the internet makes it easy to search websites such as **www.community care.co.uk/jobs** and **www.baswjobs.com** for social work vacancies. Many local authorities and recruitment agencies also have their own websites, so that a search for suitable jobs can be at your fingertips. Social media sites such as LinkedIn can support you to develop a network of professional contacts in your chosen field, and may help you identify future opportunities as well as share information about your own developing experience and interests.

- **Newspapers:** newspapers such as *The Guardian* often advertise social work posts on a weekly basis, together with the local press.

- **Open days or job fairs:** some employers will hold open days or job fairs.

- **Recruitment agencies:** if appropriate, think about using national and/or local social work/care recruitment agencies.

Applying for a new social work role

Here are some suggestions which may increase your chances of being called for interview.

- Presenting yourself effectively to a prospective employer is very important and should not be underestimated, as this is the first stage in the selection process. Many agencies have a 'safe recruitment' process which means that your application may be rejected if you do not provide a full employment history with all dates accounted for. Other applications may be eliminated straight away if they are poorly presented or generally appear vague.

- A well-prepared job application is essential, as it represents all a prospective employer will know about you until the interview stage. You may be required to complete a specific application form, and/or provide an up-to-date curriculum vitae (CV). The CV should provide enough information in a clear and concise manner, avoiding unnecessary frills. It should be written in a clear format, using not less than a 12-point font. A well-structured format will include sub-headings to help the reader identify key issues. Include your skills, qualifications and experience, and highlight your unique selling points and strengths. You will need to persuade the prospective employer that you are the right person for the job. A muddled, complicated or overly long CV will be less attractive.

- Make sure that you follow the instructions sent to you in the information pack. If you are requested to complete a handwritten application form, make sure that your presentation is neat. As applications are often photocopied, it is important to use a good quality black pen. Also, look for key words within the job description and/or person specification, and make sure that you refer to those that apply to you. Use the job description and/or person specification to structure your application and/or your CV to show those short-listing that you have the characteristics they are looking for. Use **their** wording to help signpost your application.

- Make sure that your spelling and grammar are correct, and that the application reads coherently. Ask someone else to double-check or proof-read your application before you send it off.

- Keep a copy of your application form. If you get an interview make sure you study it prior to attendance. Keeping a copy will also help you to complete other applications in the future.

- You will normally be asked to provide two referees. At least one should be able to comment on your educational background, and this may be your personal tutor or another person nominated by your university. If you have a choice, select someone who can comment on both your academic ability and practice experience. It is courteous to inform referees each time you apply for a different post, so that they do not unexpectedly receive requests.

What follows is a series of three case studies. The first is a newly qualified social worker's account on applying for his first job; the second is the university perspective on Tom's account; and the final case study is an employer's perspective (unrelated to Tom).

CASE STUDY **4.1**

Tom: applying for my first job

I made the decision in year two of the social work degree that the area of practice that I wanted to pursue as a qualified worker was education social work. Tutors were encouraging us to start applying for jobs prior to finishing the course which at the time felt like an added pressure, but I now appreciate this encouragement. It was a struggle to contemplate completing application forms and preparing for interviews whilst struggling to meet the demands of assignment deadlines. However, when I saw an advertisement for education social workers, I knew that I should take this opportunity since these jobs were fairly rare. I would advise you to start applying early if there are jobs which you are interested in.

I was advised to contact the team manager to have an informal chat prior to applying. I was really pleased I did this because it reassured me that being a newly qualified worker wouldn't disadvantage me. It also gave me an indication of what I should be researching in preparation for the interview and enabled a degree of familiarity when I was interviewed – both put me at ease.

(Continued)

CASE STUDY 4.1 *continued*

On receipt of the application form I experienced feelings of self-doubt when I saw the essential and desirable criteria. This was when I contacted my tutor for support. She reinforced to me that skills are transferable and enabled me to see that I actually had much of the experience that they were looking for, just in a different area of practice. Don't be put off applying for a job when you see the criteria; just draw on the skills, knowledge and expertise that you do have. My tutor also highlighted the importance of being concise, since employers don't want to read an essay about you.

In preparation for the interview, I arranged to see the tutor who specialised in this area of practice. He was able to give me guidance on what the current issues are and the key documents, legislation and so on that I should familiarise myself with. This was really beneficial since it saved me time from ploughing through the wealth of information that I had found on the internet.

The interview consisted of a written assessment followed by a verbal interview with three panel members. Time management was essential for the written assessment since it would have been easy to spend the whole time on the first question! In terms of the interview I was pleased that I'd read through my application form numerous times, as much of what they asked me was based on that. When asking people for interview tips, something that kept coming up was to make sure that I had some questions ready. Knowing that I had these under my belt gave me confidence and turned the tables, since I was effectively interviewing the job to see if it was suitable for me. I was offered one of the posts and started later in the year.

As you can see from the case study, identifying your chosen area and seizing opportunities when they arise are key to securing your first social work position. This includes remaining vigilant to job opportunities and adverts whilst still in your final year, and drawing on the expertise of university tutors through the application process. Preparing for your interview includes finding out as much as you can about the setting and context of practice, including relevant policies and legislation. These points are reinforced by Tom's university tutors in Case Study 4.2.

CASE STUDY 4.2

Asking for help: the university perspective

How do you go from being a supported student, surrounded by people who care about your learning and development who have often vast amounts of knowledge and contacts in the social care field, to being a newly qualified social worker in full-time social work practice?

(Continued)

When Tom obtained an interview to work as an education social worker he spoke to his tutor to ask for advice about the interview. His tutor passed Tom along to me as I had up-to-date experience of working in the educational field and a feel for the issues that the manager who was leading the service would be facing. This manager would most likely be assessing the interviewee as someone who could contribute to these current issues. Tom and I sat down for two hours, with an open e-mail to be used to attach files that we were talking about, for example, current Department for Education guidance, up-to-date evaluations of Children's Trusts and what works to improve school attendance, including documentation surrounding persistent absences.

I knew that Tom was a hard worker, so I knew he would do his research. Tom was happy to do the reading and had the interpersonal skills to communicate effectively at interview. I knew the Head of Service, who was likely to be leading the interview, would be keenly focused on the need to respond to schools identified as having persistent absence. So, when Tom went into the interview he was up to date with current issues, demonstrated he had done some research, linked current issues with evidence of what has a positive impact and had the interpersonal skills to communicate this effectively. Tom was appointed and, naturally, was delighted. He got the job in preference to other candidates who had more experience and were potentially better qualified. The feedback that Tom received was that he impressed by being well prepared; he had researched the role effectively and was clearly enthusiastic. It's really important that you talk to people who know the field.

As the tutors indicate, while they can provide guidance this is no substitute for being well prepared in order to impress a prospective employer. This is why an employer's or manager's perspective is so helpful at this point in the chapter.

Mark Hutton: the employer perspective

Applying for your first social work post will be a new experience for you – you are likely to be overwhelmed with the application process and all it entails. Think about how you can demonstrate a sense of your commitment, interest and experience in the post you are applying for, highlighting your strengths, what attributes you can bring to the post and what your learning needs are likely to be. I am more likely to be interested in your application if you give a concise account of yourself and what you feel would be your contribution to the job you are applying for, as well as being able to clearly identify your likely development and learning needs.

(Continued)

Remember that your application is likely to be one of the many that I receive, so it is important that you convey a real sense of yourself (your skills, knowledge and experience) within it, as this will bring it to life, making it more interesting for the short-listing panel to read. But remember, 'be concise' and keep your information relevant!

If you are unsure as to whether to apply for a post in the first instance, and if informal enquiries are welcomed as part of the application process, consider the questions you want to ask, and make contact with the employer. They are likely to be very willing to answer any questions you may have, and this process should give you a better sense of the job, which you will then be able to transfer into your application and use later in preparation for interview.

When completing the application form, look at the essential and desirable criteria outlined in the job description and person specification and ensure you demonstrate your skills, knowledge and experience by making reference to them using personal, work and placement experiences. If there is an area of the essential criteria where you have limited skills, do not let this put you off continuing with the application. Instead, identify what you believe you would need to do to 'fill the gap', then set to gathering the evidence through research, making reference to your findings in the application form, and how you would expect to develop your experience if you were the success-ful candidate. Most employers, when taking on a newly qualified social worker, will be just as keen to understand the motivation, interest and enthusiasm of the person applying for the job, alongside their skills and experience of the tasks required to ful-fil the job requirements. You may also wish to consider what you identified were your strengths and weaknesses at the end of your social work training, making reference to them in your application. This shows the employer that you are dedicated to pro-gressing and developing and it will stand you in good stead when the time comes for you to commence an ASYE programme.

If you are short-listed for interview you will have already conveyed a good account of yourself. The interview is your opportunity to meet us, the employer, and is as much for you to decide if you like what you see as it is for the employer to find out about you. Interviews can be in differing formats, but the questions covered will certainly relate to the job purpose, essential and desirable criteria, the person specification and current practice – including legislation and policy – so be prepared! If you don't under-stand the question, ask for it to be clarified, and take your time giving a response. Make reference to the statements you made in the application form where they are relevant to the question being answered, expanding on them where you feel confident to do so. Finally, where the employer asks you if you have any specific questions to ask them, a well-prepared candidate will ask questions about access to support, supervi-sion and guidance from employers and tailored development opportunities, including the ASYE. I wish you all the very best with making a successful transition into your first social work post.

The transition from student to qualified practitioner will continue into ASYE and beyond. Just as getting your first post is the start of a longer transition, this chapter has opened up a number of issues that we will pick up in later chapters. The first of these, Chapter 5, relates to how high-quality induction, probation and supervision processes can help support you in your professional role.

Summary of key points

- This chapter has introduced you to theoretical approaches to understanding the transition from a student to a newly qualified social worker.

- We looked at research into student work, transitions from other disciplines and explored some of the challenges involved in making such transitions.

- We have explored the concepts of sense-making (Weick, 1995) and Blair's (2000) process model for work role transition (preparation, encounter, adjustment and stabilisation) – and hopefully you will have considered how they might apply to your own particular situation.

- As you enter your first qualified post you are very likely to be entering your ASYE period, and this provides you with an opportunity to develop a personal development plan to support your transition from student to professional ASYE social worker. As part of this you may identify your own ongoing development goals, and the types of resources and support you need to achieve them.

- We have looked at the steps involved in securing your first qualified social work job, including searching for jobs, preparing applications and starting your first job. This has included consideration of the need to challenge feelings of uncertainty, while valuing the transferability of your skills to a variety of social work settings.

- Case studies from a recently qualified social worker, university tutors and an employer reiterate the importance of being prepared for job interviews, and being able to demonstrate that you are up to date with current practice issues.

FURTHER READING

British Association of Social Workers

www.basw.co.uk

The British Association of Social Work website is not only useful for hunting down jobs (**www.baswjobs. co.uk**) but also provides a good 'links' section and updates on the status of newly qualified social workers.

Careers services

Each university should have careers services, e.g. **www1.bournemouth.ac.uk/students/careers** – please make use of them.

Community Care

www.communitycare.co.uk/nqsw

This useful part of the Community Care website is informative for newly qualified social workers in that it gives a potted history of strategic developments alongside down-to-earth 'top tips' from managers in practice.

Health and Care Professionals Council

www.hcpc-uk.org

The regulatory body for health and social care professions in the UK contains useful information on the transfer of social workers to the HCPC, including a continuing professional development section here:

www.hpc-uk.org/registrants/cpd/

Chapter 5

Managing induction, probation and supervision

Ivan Gray with contributions from Mary (NQSW) and Karen (carer)

PROFESSIONAL CAPABILITIES FRAMEWORK

This chapter will help you to demonstrate the following ASYE-level capabilities:

1. Professionalism: identify and behave as a professional social worker, committed to professional development.

    - Be able to meet the requirements of the professional regulator.

    - Make proactive use of supervision to reflect critically on practice, explore different approaches to your work, support your development across the nine capabilities and understand the boundaries of professional accountability.

    - Identify your learning needs; assume responsibility for improving your practice through appropriate professional development.

5. Knowledge: apply knowledge of social sciences, law and social work practice theory.

    - Consolidate, develop and demonstrate comprehensive understanding and application of the knowledge gained in your initial training, and knowledge related to your specialist area of practice, including critical awareness of current issues and new evidence-based practice research.

7. Intervention and skills: use judgement and authority to intervene with individuals, families and communities to promote independence, provide support and prevent harm, neglect and abuse.

    - Build and use effective relationships with a wide range of people, networks, communities and professionals to improve outcomes, showing an ability to manage resistance.

8. Contexts and organisations: engage with, inform and adapt to changing contexts that shape practice. Operate effectively within own organisational frameworks and contribute to the development of services and organisations. Operate effectively within multi-agency and interprofessional partnerships and settings.

   • Proactively engage with colleagues and a range of organisations to identify, assess, plan and support the needs of service users and communities.

   • Understand and respect the role of others within the organisation and work effectively with them.

KNOWLEDGE AND SKILLS STATEMENTS

This chapter will help you demonstrate the following requirements:

Child and family:

9. The role of supervision.
10. Organisational context.

Adult:

8. Supervision, critical reflection and analysis.
9. Organisational context.
10. Professional ethics and leadership.

Introduction

Do I look like a newly qualified social worker? This was the question Mary asked a friend as she shopped for clothes prior to beginning her first job as a newly qualified social worker. We asked her to reflect on her first few weeks and months, and the following case study gives her reflections.

CASE STUDY 5.1

Mary's first job

For me, shopping for clothes was an important part of preparing for the job and not to be underestimated! Every workplace has a different dress code. Find out what is expected from your new employer – the last thing you want is to be wearing jeans when the dress code states no denim!

(Continued)

Clothes aside, after finishing my degree I had a phenomenal amount of literature, research papers, journal articles and leaflets from past placements. I could hear quite clearly my lecturers saying 'how can you link research into practice?' I must admit, half of me never wanted to see those papers again. I had often read them late into the night when studying for assignments, but as part of my preparation I filed any useful papers into a ring binder. This I found immensely helpful once starting the job. Access to research papers is critical with the growing culture of using research to underpin assessments.

Yet, this did not stop me experiencing losses in confidence and feelings of self-doubt in my first few weeks. My first week was very slow as I spent a lot of time in induction visits and shadowing colleagues. They would often ask for my thoughts following a visit but I would still be trying to understand the processes! I was fortunate in being given a mentor, who was always on hand to offer advice. If you can, ask your manager prior to you starting to appoint a mentor. When you are in a busy office and everyone is saying how stressed they are, you may feel like a burden asking repeated questions. Having someone to take responsibility as your mentor means that you can ask them questions knowing that it is okay to do so.

Working in a childcare assessment team requires you to hit the ground running. I had been in my team about three weeks when I had acquired a large caseload. I had been working for about two months when I had my first Child Protection Conference. I was seriously frightened. In an ideal world I should not have had one, but in the real world, if one of your cases reaches 'child protection' level, the likelihood is that you will have to continue working with it. My advice is to consistently and continually seek your manager's guidance and support and record all management discussions as case recordings.

I have now been in post for five months. My job is very pressured and I often start early and finish late. No day is ever the same though. And when things are good at work they are amazing . . . and long may they last!

Whilst recent initiatives such as the refreshing of the standards for employers (LGA, 2014) and ASYE (Skills for Care, 2015) have undoubtedly improved the induction of newly qualified social workers in general terms, it is still important that you take professional responsibility for and manage your own induction and probation periods. This is why the first two sections of this chapter, on induction and probation, seek to provide you with models of good practice. Tailored information on supervision forms the final part of this chapter. High-quality reflective supervision is at the heart of social care, and has been and will be crucial to the success of Mary's practice, including addressing much of the emotion she talked about.

Induction

The induction of newly qualified social workers can vary considerably (Bates *et al.*, 2010; Grant *et al.*, 2014). You may be warmly welcomed and provided with a well-structured, carefully planned experience that responds to your individual needs; or you may be offered a 'baptism of fire' that leaves you virtually to your own devices (Bates *et al.*, 2010, p21). There is some consensus on the value of a good induction and its key features (Fowler, 1996; Maher *et al.*, 2003; NSWQB, 2004; Moriarty *et al.*, 2011; Grant *et al.*, 2014); good induction processes have been found to allow workers:

- to become effective more quickly;

- to settle into their teams more quickly;

- to be less anxious in new roles;

- to create realistic expectations of the job and the organisation;

- to reduce misunderstandings and grievances;

- to have confidence in new employers.

There is even a likely correlation between the quality of your induction and how long you stay in your new post. Fowler (1996), in an Institute of Personnel and Development publication, suggests a strong link between induction and employee retention and identifies the heavy costs to an organisation of early leavers, in other words, those who leave in the first few months of employment. Two further studies on the induction experiences of social workers (Maher *et al.*, 2003, and an Irish National Social Work Qualifications Board study (NSWQB, 2004)) also note the importance of a good induction to retention. So it may well be that if you start happy, you stay happy.

Good reasons abound for you viewing induction as *your* professional responsibility, accepting that a good employer should meet you more than halfway.

- Even if organisational practices do improve there will always be some posts and small organisations where a newly appointed social worker finds themselves virtually on their own with little option but to plan and manage their own induction.

- Whatever the policy initiatives, organisational practices are still likely to vary. If you have your own model of good practice you will be able build on whatever is on offer.

- Professional social workers have considerable independence and responsibility in their work. Your induction sets the foundation for the effectiveness of your future practice and needs to be managed by you from the outset.

- Induction needs to be personalised so that it responds to your needs (Bradley, 2006). This is more likely to happen if you can take control and shape it.

This part of the chapter aims to ensure you are equipped to manage your own induction, even if organisational practices related to ASYE largely dictate your first year as a social worker.

Be clear

Be clear about what you want to achieve from your induction at the outset. This is best done by determining your aims and objectives. An aim identifies the broad purpose of an activity and objectives break this down into manageable 'chunks' that help both plan and review progress.

ACTIVITY **5.1**

Thinking about induction

Spend some time thinking about your induction. What are the aims and objectives for your induction period? One way of thinking about this is to see yourself as an explorer about to enter exciting new territory. You are on a journey to find out what you need to live in this new land. Most of your exploration will consist of locating and obtaining information from the people who already live here. But it is not just an exercise in data collection – it is an emotional experience as well. You want to be accepted by the locals. You are going to work with them and will probably want them to like you and your work. In turn, they are likely to want you to respect them and their work.

See how your aim matches up with our suggested aim of induction:

To determine your role, your responsibilities and the rules, procedures, expectations and goals of the organisation you have just joined, whilst building the relationships and identifying the resources that you will need to practise effectively.

Depending on organisational practice, your induction could last just a few weeks or, more likely with the ASYE, one year. In a broader sense, one could argue that your induction never really stops as you will be always finding out about your place of work. Nevertheless, remember the land of work is complex and well-populated. It is very common to feel overwhelmed and swamped by the number of people you meet and the amount of information you have to assimilate. Your first few days can be exhausting and chaotic. Some things might not make complete sense and you may even have doubts about how well you fit in. Recognise that this complex land, and your practice within it, will be subject to and affected by local and national political changes.

As such, your land of work is likely to have a formal and informal culture. For instance, there will be formal procedures that say how you *should* behave and then there will be the informal ways that people *actually do* behave and get things done. There will be some procedures you must follow to not put people at risk, but there is more choice than is often recognised around this essential core. It may be helpful to realise there will not be a fixed set of people you must know or a comprehensive set of procedures identifying the *right* way to do things. Build your own view of this land and your own way of doing things.

As with most journeys into unknown lands a guide is invaluable. During your ASYE year it is likely that your line manager, supervisor or assessor acts as one, working out with you who you need to see and the information you need to be given. Take any questions or clarifications to them for discussion – they might not be able to answer them immediately, but they should be able to identify others that can. You may find your guide has a structured induction plan waiting for you when you meet, clarifying your responsibilities in terms of caseload, your record of assessment or equivalent, appraisal, supervision and the ASYE process in general. You may, however, need to build your own induction plan, and agree it with your line manager and/or supervisor. If this is the case be mindful that corporate induction programmes tend to be very general and can too easily deteriorate into a tick-box experience. Check out what is expected and what is on offer and incorporate it into your plan. If you are managing your own induction you only need one initial contact to set the ball rolling. Once you have made contact with one key person in your network, find out from them their key contacts and what they view as essential information and then locate their contacts and arrange to meet them. Gradually, by following up on these 'threads', you will identify and make contact with everyone in the network. Either way – structured or unstructured – it is important for you to take responsibility for the process and be proactive, as induction is deceptively complex – and this is why we suggest you approach it methodically.

As you chart your passage through the land it can be helpful to take notes on the information and people you come across. You should be able to find time in your first few days and weeks to think, reflect and write notes. Keeping notes of who you meet, what they do, how you might work with them (e.g. how you make referrals) and their contact details can be invaluable. Also note any questions you have and/or points for clarification. Keeping an induction file that includes both your notes and the information you collect can help you gradually build a picture of your new land. This file can then be used as an ongoing resource. Just finding your way around can be important too. Some newly qualified social workers have found it helpful to buy an A–Z (or a satellite navigation tool if you can afford it) before their first day.

You will see by now that we view the process of induction as a creative space for you to fill. It is an opportunity for you to establish yourself and to shape your place in the organisation. We now explore in more detail the key dimensions of induction to help you do just that (Figure 5.1). You can, if you wish, use these four dimensions to structure your induction file and to organise your induction plan and experience. We have broken down each key dimension into its component parts and these constitute our suggested objectives of induction that you will need to achieve in order to meet our suggested aim of induction (see Activity 5.1). We will take each of the key dimensions in turn.

Key dimension 1: building relationships with those who support your practice

1.1: to identify, make contact with and build initial relationships with those within the organisation that will support your practice
Getting to know who in the organisation makes things happen and who to go to for advice is crucial. The best source of this information is your team or others

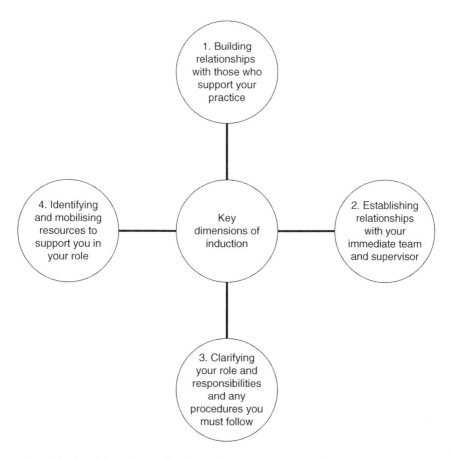

Figure 5.1   The key dimensions of induction

doing a similar job. Aim to meet the people they work with on a daily basis. Ask your team how they are best approached and the best way to work with them. Methodically build up a list of people in your file, make contact with them and introduce yourself. Sometimes a telephone call is enough but with really key players you may need to go and visit them. It may pay to build a map of crucial contacts – like the one in Figure 5.2 for example. This can be called a 'stakeholder map', as you are identifying all those who have a stake in your practice. Shadowing or a mini-placement can be useful for getting to know teams or sections you will work with on a daily basis, such as assessment or emergency teams. These methods can allow you to build relationships that can make a big difference to your effectiveness in the long term.

1.2: to identify, make contact with and build initial relationships with those outside of the organisation that support your practice

There may be as many people outside of your organisation that you will need to make contact and build a relationship with as within it. Health and social care provision is a complex network of voluntary, independent and private sector organisations,

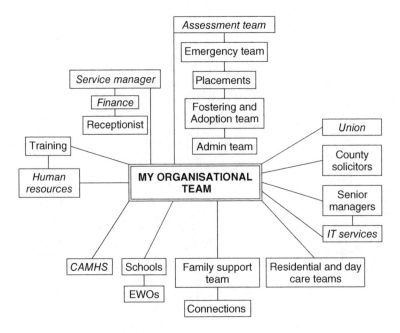

Figure 5.2   An example of a stakeholder map

groups and even individuals. Any care plan will inevitably demand that you mobilise this network and co-ordinate their activities.

As above, talk to your team about who they regularly work with and ask about how to get the best from them – perhaps even what sort of problems they experience and how they get around them. If there are any formal referral mechanisms, be sure you know what they are and check on waiting times. As within your organisation, visit any key organisations, groups or individuals and introduce yourself. Again, shadow or placement opportunities can be invaluable. It will be essential for you to talk to people who use services and carers too. Ask colleagues for advice about people who could help. Like Karen in Case Study 5.2, they often have the best local knowledge about support and resources.

CASE STUDY **5.2**

Karen's experience of meeting new social workers

G was our foster child and has lived with us for 27 years, since he was two weeks old. He has Down syndrome and autism, as well as a serious heart condition. As such we have presented an 'interesting case' for newly qualified social workers. For a period of about 10 years, when he was younger, we had a series of them. Even when they had left us, many of them would continue to ring me for advice and information for other clients.

(Continued)

CASE STUDY 5.2 *continued*

I have built a fair knowledge of local resources over the 27 years. I am always willing to be helpful, but I often wonder why this sort of knowledge is not recorded some-where central.

G loves meeting new people so it was never a problem for him to meet new social work-ers. He greeted everyone the same, climbing on their laps and giving them a sloppy kiss. Not all new social workers were prepared for this and had to work out how they would deal with it. One lady had very prominent teeth and G was transfixed by them and kept talking about them, much to my embarrassment, and hers. Be prepared for children to be frank and completely natural!

It is always refreshing meeting someone enthusiastic and raring to make a difference. They usually go away full of things to find out and ready to learn. The ones I appreci-ate most are the ones who are honest about both their own capabilities and the system within which they are working. Some promise the earth and deliver nothing. The one that impressed me the most was a lady who confessed to knowing nothing and went away on a mission to find out, always admitting when she failed and never forgetting to come back to keep me informed. She was always honest, modest and treated us as the experts in G's needs and habits.

I also remember being lectured in childcare by one new social worker. I had G and two other young children of my own. I was offended that she chose to speak to me in this way and discovered on asking that she had only a five-month-old baby! I did not appreci-ate her theoretical knowledge being delivered in this way. Theory is all well and good but there is nothing like a healthy respect for experience.

Key dimension 2: establishing relationships with your immediate team and supervisor

2.1: building an effective working relationship with your supervisor/s

It is worth noting at this point that at the heart of induction and probation is your interaction and relationship with your supervisor/s. In general terms the effective-ness of induction and probation, and your work generally, will be determined by the quality of your supervisory relationship. Although good practice around manag-ing supervision will be explored in more detail in the third and final section of this chapter, it is worth making some initial points here.

Find out about your organisation's formal supervision policy. Talk to managers about their expectations and ask colleagues for advice about what has worked (or not) for them. Try asking managers and supervisors how they like to work and establish the 'do's and don'ts'. Think about sharing a little about yourself as this can contribute to good working relationships. Tell them about what helps you most in supervision, what can cause problems for you and pinpoint any particular learning or other needs you have. Remember this relationship will be a different relationship from the one you had with your practice educator, but it will be similar in many ways. If there is no written contract to direct your relationship, at the very least you will need to determine when you meet, how regularly and for how long – who sets the agenda, who records it, what happens if it is cancelled and how emergency situations are dealt with. Help your manager or supervisor/s by identifying issues you wish to discuss in advance and making available any information they need. Use supervision to seek feedback on your performance and air any unhappiness and/or discontent.

Being supervised by several people, such as a team including senior practitioners, can be tough so find out how they co-ordinate activities. Try and meet middle and senior managers as well as first-line managers as their activities as a management team will impact on your work.

2.2: building effective working relationships with your immediate team

Your new team is the community of practice (Wenger, 1998) that will have the greatest impact on the effectiveness of your work and your happiness in the job. They are likely to be the greatest source of advice and support too, so good working relationships with them are vital.

Colleagues will want to be respected by you (also see Chapters 7 and 8), so make a point of seeing everyone. Even if people are busy, they usually appreciate being approached and can feel valued by you asking for their input. Start, don't finish, with your administrative and support team. They can have a considerable impact on your work and you will need to establish how to work effectively with them. Ask them directly what they like or don't like. Their personal support and goodwill can make a big difference to you in the longer term.

Find out from your social work colleagues what they are interested in and whether they have any particular specialism. Actively use their expertise, for instance, by asking your supervisor/s whose assessments are exemplary – try and get your colleagues to talk with you about what they do and don't do. And try not to forget those informal team arrangements that can assist in sustaining new relationships – they can be as simple as contributing to a tea and coffee or birthday fund.

Key dimension 3: clarifying your role and responsibilities and any procedures you must follow

3.1: to identify and understand any legal and organisational procedures you must follow

Having up-to-date copies of essential procedures for managing situations where people can be put at risk – such as child/adult protection – is vital for safe working. You may wish to print hard copies of these procedures and put them in your induction file. Discern any discrepancies between what the procedures say and your team actually does. If in doubt, get clarification from your supervisor/s and record it.

Some procedures, for example the timing of assessments, need to be followed as they will affect performance measures that can impact on your team or organisation. As with most procedures, you will be working with others in their implementation, so it may pay to visit and discuss them with, for instance, reviewing and finance officers.

It can really be helpful to shadow people following procedures or sit in on key events such as reviews, case conferences, etc. Written procedures are much more meaningful when you see them being applied and it may pay to create your own flow diagrams for common scenarios, critical events and/or emergencies to capture the essentials. Make sure you know who the experts are, so you can approach them when things come up.

3.2: be clear about your role and responsibilities

Your job description and person specification are a good place to start in determining your role and responsibilities – your supervisor/s should be able to clarify any questions you have. Make sure you are clear about what you can or can't do and what has to be authorised by others. Use your supervisor/s and colleagues to check things out and go out of your way to share what you are doing and brief people fully.

3.3: identifying any informal rules, processes and norms that shape behaviour in the organisation alongside formal procedures and processes

To be 'at home' in your organisation you need to know not only the formal rules and regulations but also the wider culture – *the way things are done around here* – and the unwritten culture. Take notice of the small things, for example, how people answer the phone and how they explain how the system works to people who use services. These hidden informal perspectives intertwine with the formal to make up the rich tapestry of organisational life. Listen, ask and look behind the formal espoused theory, in other words what people say they do, to the theory in use and what they actually do (Argyris and Schön, 1974). However, be slow to jump to conclusions or be over-critical if things don't make sense. You may either have misunderstood or important things may just not be said openly.

3.4: understanding the goals of the organisation and how it is structured

Try to gain a broader picture of what your organisation is trying to achieve by reading business plans and service strategies. Use any corporate induction opportunities you get to speak to senior managers. It is worth remembering that the plans of other organisations may also be important to you, since your practice will in part be dependent on and impacted by their improvement plans and direction. Remember there will be variation between employers – try not to make assumptions based on your placement experience.

3.5: be confident and motivated to do the job

Getting to know your new organisation and the people in it can be traumatic and emotionally draining. It is not uncommon to have periods when you can feel a bit 'down'. You can find yourself doubting your abilities and losing confidence. These are perfectly normal reactions and are a response to the changes you are grappling with; even if you are delighted with your new post and you are perfect for the job you can feel this way. These feelings should dissipate as you settle in.

In accepting the emotional aspects of joining an organisation, it is important to learn how to take care of yourself. Be grateful for the support people offer. Start off with 'comfortable' work you are familiar with, and enjoy transferring established skills. Move out from your comfort zone into areas of special interest over time.

Stress is an occupational hazard and workloads can easily be too high (Storey and Billingham, 2001; Gibson *et al.*, 1989). You should find that you have a protected caseload, but it is important that you take responsibility for managing your work-load. You may need to be realistic about what you take on and be assertive saying 'no' when you are at capacity, even if you would like to help out by taking on more. Workload management systems are never that accurate so try and establish an open dialogue with your supervisor/s about your workload. Chapter 6 of this book may also be an important resource for you as it looks at ways of managing yourself, stress and conflict. Use it to guide any difficult conversations you might have with your supervisor/s, e.g. about workload, induction or supervision. Prepare well for this type of conversation; keep to the facts and try to leave your raw emotions at the door. Personal 'out of work' support can be invaluable to discuss experiences and feelings but remember to keep confidentiality. Some organisations have started 'learning sets' made up of newly qualified social workers so that people can meet up to discuss their expectations and learn from experiences.

Key dimension 4: identifying and mobilising resources to support you in your role

4.1: understanding and completing essential human resource management processes and policies

There are essential human resource management processes that have to be com-pleted and processes that you need to know about. Often human resources personnel will find you, but if not they are usually happy to advise on the following issues:

- signing your contract and terms and conditions
- police checks
- hours of work and overtime arrangements
- flexitime and time off in lieu
- holiday entitlement and booking
- pension arrangements
- how you will be paid
- discipline and grievance procedures
- performance-related pay and pay progression

- appraisal

- severance procedures

- the probation period and the ASYE

- equal opportunities policy

- absence and sickness procedures

- paternity and maternity leave.

4.2: be aware of and access welfare and support services

In most organisations welfare and support services can be important to your work–life balance. Again human resources personnel may be helpful in the following areas:

- counselling

- employer's policies on well-being and stress

- occupational health

- trade union membership

- legal advice

- leisure activities

- staff associations and social clubs

- policies on 'whistle blowing'.

4.3: acquiring the essential tools and equipment you need to do the job

Having your own space and the things that you need to do the job such as a telephone, computer, diary and stationery can be important in supporting your role and ensuring you enjoy a successful induction. Colleagues, especially administration staff, are best placed to advise you on what you will need on an everyday basis. Check out ordering procedures and what is hard to obtain, but bear in mind that colleagues will have found ways around unhelpful formal procedures.

Although it can make you feel you belong to personalise your work-space, it may be that more 'flexible' working procedures and environments come with 'hot desks'. Wherever you are placed, work out where the 'heart' of team activity is, and make a point of spending some time in this environment. If you get a choice, think carefully about where you wish to sit and who you would like to sit with in the office, as it can affect your working life.

4.4: be aware and follow everyday operating procedures, including health and safety

A number of crucial procedures will be essential to the everyday operation of your organisation, including health and safety. Check out with supervisor/s and colleagues what these are for your particular organisation. They are likely to include:

- signing in and out of the office

- logging your location and movements

- safe interviewing procedures

- office security

- out-of-hours working and safe working procedures

- use of IT equipment and IT assessments

- transporting people who use services and carers

- fire safety

- first aid.

Find out too about everyday administrative procedures such as travel claims, allowances and receipts, timescales for arranging meetings and computer access. Find out what these are and obtain copies of any forms you are likely to need on a daily basis. Hopefully this gives you a useful start but you will find there is a lot to know. For instance, there will probably even be regulations to cover the gifts you may or may not receive from people who use services and carers.

4.5: access training and development opportunities and set the foundation for continuing professional development

This has already formed the subject of Chapter 2 so only a few brief points will be made here. Your induction may include some initial or core-training workshops; for instance, basic IT training. Find out what the organisation's personal development processes are by asking team members about the best resources and which ones they use regularly. Make contact with your staff or workforce development department to find out about how to access training, book places and any cancellation procedures. Check out any online training and other services such as library services (including the office library), help with research and so on. Finally, you should find it helpful to share your undergraduate personal development plan or skills analysis with your supervisor or line manager.

ACTIVITY **5.2**

Comparing

Now you have read what we think induction should be about, find out from your employer all you can about the induction period and think about doing a comparison of the two – ask yourself the question, where are the gaps and how can I fill them?

Probation

Where employing organisations have probationary periods, they are usually three to twelve months in length – if you are unsure about the policy of your organisation, ask your line manager or human resources personnel. Many employers have aligned their probation periods with ASYE completion. On the basis of this policy you will be able to determine your role within it and, as we advocate with the induction process, take responsibility for it. The experience of probationary periods of newly qualified social workers can vary considerably (Bates *et al.*, 2010) – the following aim of probation periods might therefore be helpful to you:

> *To jointly review and appraise with your supervisor the effectiveness of your initial practice and the suitability of the post for you; identify your future learning needs, the support you require and lay the foundation for your future performance appraisal and development planning.*

ACTIVITY 5.3

Probation

Find out whether your organisation or prospective organization has a probationary period, and if so, what is your role within it and how does it link to the ASYE?

Your probationary period is an opportunity for you to decide if the job is the right one for you and for your employer to decide if you are right for them. Ultimately, it is your employer's decision whether you pass or fail your probationary period. In the same way it is their decision whether you pass or fail your ASYE year. Probation and ASYE are linked though, in that good employers will be underpinning the ASYE year with a structured and supportive probation process. So, in order to remain employed in your first social work post, you will be required to pass both your probationary review period and the ASYE year. This serves as a reminder for you, as the newly qualified social worker, to check with any potential employer about their ASYE process and probationary systems, both in terms of the support you will receive and to assure yourself that methods of assessment are accurate, valid, robust and sufficient. It is after all your career – you will want to make sure you have every opportunity to demonstrate your capacity to practice as a social worker, and to complete ASYE and probation in a manner that will be acceptable to all potential social work employers.

Probation has three key dimensions (Figure 5.3). We will take each in turn and explore them.

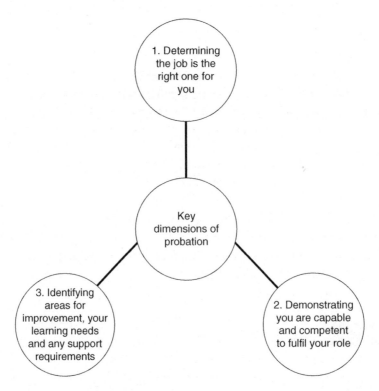

Figure 5.3   Key dimensions of probation

Key dimension 1: determining the job is the right one for you

A trial or probationary period works both ways – as we have already stated it can help you decide if the job is right for you, and the employer decide whether they think you are right for the job. Dialogue is important. A good employer will want you to be open about problems in the hope of resolving them. Above all, be realistic. It will probably take up to a year to feel established in your role. However, if you decide this is not the job for you, be clear why not and what you are looking for. Discuss these issues with your supervisor and human resources personnel – there may be transfer options that could be to your benefit and that of your employer.

Key dimension 2: demonstrating you are capable and competent to fulfil your role

The essential starting point in demonstrating your ability to fulfil your role is finding out what 'yardstick' your employer will be using to measure your performance. This will be the Knowledge and Skills Statements for social workers (DfE, 2014; DH, 2015) and the professional capabilities at ASYE-level across the nine domains that make up the framework (BASW, 2015). But there are also likely to be additional organisational requirements as part of any probation period. Employer practices will vary and in the past your contract of employment and job description have been key points of reference. Make a point of asking your employer early so there are no surprises.

As part of your probation period, your supervisor/s will be observing your practice, evaluating your records and reports, and listening and talking to team members and other colleagues. Although this can at times appear impressionistic, good practice is now much better defined and many managers are very good at judging performance. For example, ASYE assessments should be made by practice assessors and supervisors who have been specifically trained and assessed themselves to undertake this role. There is a useful online toolkit on the Skills for Care website so you can see how they have been supported: **www.skillsforcare.org.uk/Learning-development/The-ASYE-adults/Support-for-assessors-and-supervisors.aspx**.

It is advisable to make appraisal of your performance part of supervision and indeed a building block of your supervisory relationship. The final part of this chapter should help demystify the process of supervision. Do voice your concerns with your manager and/or supervisor/s if there is anything you are not happy about. If other issues arise, show you can take criticism 'on the chin', but make sure you are clear what the problem is and agree a way forward which should include support and help to develop your practice. These evaluations and the plans that arise from them should all be recorded in writing. If your probationary period is not completed successfully, your employer will follow formal procedures as laid out in their policies and your contract of employment.

Employment law is complex, so if you hit difficulties in your probationary period always seek advice from human resources personnel, a trade union, the Advisory, Conciliation and Arbitration Service (ACAS) or a solicitor. These last comments are not meant to frighten you – we can only offer very broad guidance and, if you need it, you must make sure you take qualified specialist advice.

Key dimension 3: identifying areas for improvement, your learning needs and any support requirements

Do ask hard questions about support and development opportunities, as it is important that you are able to develop your practice and career. Indeed, our advice is that you ask these questions at your interview for a potential social work post, so that you are clear before accepting any post about the support you will receive and the methods by which you will be assessed as capable, in order to pass your probation period. One of the first things you are likely to do as part of your ASYE period is complete and sign a learning agreement with your employer. This agreement will specify your workload, the frequency of reflective supervision, arrangements for protected development time, and so on. Importantly, it will also contain details of how ASYE reviews are linked to your employer's probation and appraisal processes. Just as you should ask for feedback on your performance if this is not provided, you should also say if you are not getting the help you need to develop your practice or you do not understand what is required of you. Seek advice from human resources personnel or your trade union if this is not resolved.

It does not mean that your performance is unsatisfactory if you have learning needs. On the contrary, it is good practice to work with your supervisor/s to evaluate your practice and improve it. These learning needs will ideally be discussed within the process of supervision – the final section of this chapter.

Supervision

Supervision in a contended profession

Professional supervision is at the heart of social care. As the Chief Executives of Skills for Care and the former Children's Workforce Development Council put it:

> *High quality supervision is one of the most important drivers in ensuring positive outcomes for people who use social care and children's services. It also has a crucial role to play in the development, retention and motivation of the workforce.*

(Skills for Care/Children's Workforce Development Council, 2007, p3)

Supervision is defined as:

> *An accountable process which supports, assures and develops the knowledge, skills and values of an individual, group or team. The purpose is to improve the quality of their work to achieve agreed objectives and outcomes. In social care and children's services this should optimise the capacity of people who use services to lead independent and fulfilling lives.*

(Skills for Care/Children's Workforce Development Council, 2007, p4)

Supervision, as highlighted in Chapter 3, is also a focal point where the key components of the service meet and all key activities and relationships are co-ordinated. Supervision requires commitment, respect and honesty from all participants if it is to be of benefit to the organisation and individual. Good supervision appears associated with effective job satisfaction, retention and effective professional practice (Carpenter *et al.*, 2012) although this evidence base is limited and is in places contested (Manthorpe *et al.*, 2015).

The Social Work Reform Board identified four purposes for supervision:

* to improve the quality of decision-making and interventions;
* to enable effective line management and organisational accountability;
* to identify and address issues related to caseloads and workload management;
* to help to identify and achieve personal learning, career and development opportunities.

(SWRB, 2012a)

The updated Standards for Employers document includes the expectation that newly qualified social workers should have access to regular, high-quality supervision by a registered social worker, and this should be weekly for the first six weeks and then fortnightly for the first six months and monthly thereafter (LGA, 2014). Alongside

Howe and Gray (2012), Skills for Care has also provided useful online guidance for newly qualified social workers here: **www.skillsforcare.org.uk/Topics/Social-work/Social-work.aspx**. The importance of preparation is emphasised here and it is suggested that this should allow workers to share and discuss appropriate topics with their supervisors:

- their reflections on their practice, including what's gone wrong;

- how they have accessed and used support in their work;

- their ability to implement personalised care and to maximise the participation and control that individual adults, families, carers, groups and communities have over their lives;

- how they have used training and development opportunities;

- their learning needs and how these will be met;

- the evidence they are collecting to demonstrate their achievement of ASYE-level capabilities.

(Skills for Care, 2011b)

Our services and profession are by nature contested. The management of service provision necessarily involves battling with dilemmas, ambiguity, conflicting interests, incompatible expectations, value issues and judgement calls where there may not be options that can be rationally chosen as the 'best' (Healy, 2000; Munro, 2011). It is at this crucial point of co-ordination, clarification and decision-making that these conflicts are identified and responded to. The final part of this chapter has begun by exploring the nature of supervision and moves on to why it is important (including the often overlooked emotional aspects to supervision), threats to its effectiveness and how you can evaluate the process.

ACTIVITY 5.4

Supervision

As a newly qualified social worker it is important that you take control of your own professional supervision. Think back over your previous experiences of being supervised and make some notes on:

- *what you valued most;*

- *what was least helpful;*

- *what you did to ensure that supervision was effective;*

- *what you might have done that undermined the effectiveness of supervision.*

If you can, share your thinking with your supervisor to help shape your new relationship.

Supervision as a forum for dialogue

Supervision is a crucial forum for dialogue in social care as it is where the professional and the organisation meet. In the past, professional reflection and personal development arguably dominated supervision at the expense of case and performance management and to the detriment of services and professional practice. More recently, it has been argued that case management and performance issues have come to dominate supervision and that professional needs and issues have been marginalised (Jones *et al.*, 2004; Manthorpe *et al.*, 2015). The Social Work Reform Board (SWRB, 2010), Munro Report (2011) and others stress the importance of moving away from top-down, target-driven management to enable social workers to learn from their experiences and have more freedom to exercise their professional judgement. However, it can be argued that supervision has never been entirely a professional domain. Supervision is also where managerial and organisational perspectives and needs meet and are resolved. Part of the tension that is endemic to supervision is competition for the space and the agenda that both you and your supervisor must respond to.

Managers and professionals have responsibility to ensure that there is a balance between competing but often mutual needs. The process of supervision must accommodate these needs to be effective. Figure 5.4 gives a personal illustration of your need for supervision.

There are also good grounds for approaching the process of supervision critically. If personal reflection and personal development are too easily lost from the agenda, opportunities to discuss social work values and the wider social and political effects of interventions may also be easily mislaid (Phillipson, 2002).

Time for supervision is undoubtedly a problem (Manthorpe *et al.*, 2015). It is very easy to make the shortage of it an excuse for unbalanced supervision. There is a danger that managers who are under pressure will undermine supervision by dominating it – rather than allowing time for exploration and reflection. What should be dealt with, and could be dealt with efficiently in formal supervision, ends up being dealt with 'on the hop' in informal supervision. This often does not allow for proper communication and joint consideration of the issues. Even in assessment or emergency teams where 'on the hop' supervision is unavoidable, formal sessions are still essential.

Supervision needs careful planning, review and plenty of time. To illustrate, one particular need in Figure 5.4 may dominate a supervision session. Future sessions may therefore need a different agenda to compensate. Keep an eye on the range of needs to ensure your supervision is balanced over time.

Supervision is likely to be your biggest training and development opportunity. Sometimes more powerful than activities such as training courses, supervision should allow you the space to ask questions, make sense of things and learn through your practice. With a good supervisor your personal growth and development will be enabled, and as you become more confident you will work in a more independent manner.

Emotional aspects to supervision

Whilst supervision is not counselling or therapy, it is very similar in that it requires sharing and openness, careful listening and challenge, joint problem-solving and joint

Figure 5.4 Why do I need supervision?

decision-making. It also reaches for personal growth and to address the emotion that is at the heart of our work. In short, it demands a trusting and enabling supervisory relationship which can be very hard to achieve if in every supervision session you find yourself working with somebody different, as can happen in some teams. If you work with more than one supervisor, your manager/s will need to be active ensuring consistency of provision. You too can contribute to the effectiveness of shared supervision by being sure to communicate as effectively as you can, and by briefing your supervisors properly. There is often opportunity to play one supervisor off against another and take advantage of breakdowns in communication and inconsistencies, so keep a reflective eye on yourself and try and be proactive in making things work. But if communication gets very difficult and issues are not being dealt with effectively, raise these issues with your manager.

Time pressures and a more procedurally driven and outcome-orientated service can mean that the culture of supervision changes to downplay the importance of emotion in our work. Managerialism is often represented as undermining the amount of supervision time devoted to the management of emotion, as well as the learning and development essential to practice. If the emotion of our work is not managed there can be a considerable impact on our effectiveness. We do not learn well if we are frightened, depressed, grieving or frozen; distress, if not responded to, can undermine our practice and our health (Hawkins and Shohet, 2007).

It is not just that our work involves traumatic and negative experiences, and sharing other people's grief and pain. The change process is also an emotional experience. The more fundamental the change, the more emotion (Holmes and Rahe, 1967). If you are going to be effective in improving the quality of life of carers and people who use services; if you are to respond to service changes effectively; and if you intend to develop your own practice, there will be a lot of emotion about. Chapter 6 should be a help to you here as sometimes we might feel manipulated or frightened by the people we work with. You will need to be able to discuss these issues openly in (and outside of) supervision to ensure you remain purposeful and objective about your work.

Leadership and supervision

As a newly qualified social worker, you will be motivated to do the work you have been employed for. You will have, at least, the basic knowledge and skills to do the job. An effective manager will recognise you (like us) have a lot to learn and allow you the space to do so. They may start by giving you lots of supervision time and guidance, gradually reducing this as they gauge the strengths and weaknesses of your practice and as you develop. You will need to play your part by taking more responsibility for your work and for supervision as time goes on. This chapter ends with two activities that you can employ to help you evaluate the development of your supervision.

ACTIVITY 5.5

Evaluating supervision

You can use the following questions to evaluate the development of your supervision practice over time.

- *Is my supervisory relationship changing as my needs change?*
- *Am I working more independently over time and developing my practice, allowing my manager to delegate?*
- *Am I taking more responsibility for supervision, increasing my contribution and exercising more control over the process?*

The Effective Supervision Unit

Until the publication of the Providing Effective Supervision unit (Skills for Care/Children's Workforce Development Council, 2007) there had been no national framework related to the supervision of social workers. Although this document has now been superseded by Effective Supervision in a Variety of Settings (SCIE 2013; see **www.scie.org.uk/**

publications/guides/guide50/index.asp) they join together with the recently refreshed Standards for Employers (LGA, 2014) to provide valuable reference points in evaluating your supervision with your supervisor. In particular, parts of the old Providing Effective Supervision unit can still be used as a detailed evaluative tool (see Tables 5.1, 5.2 and 5.3) leading to genuine, shared in-depth exploration of the quality of supervision you are receiving. So, it is worth giving these documents some time and attention.

ACTIVITY **5.6**

Supervision audit

This is the final activity of this chapter. Use this audit tool to evaluate the supervision you receive. It has been adapted from the Skills for Care and Children's Workforce Development Council (2007) Providing Effective Supervision unit of competence/ capability. There are three tables, each with a different focus. We provide a commentary on each of the performance criteria and space for your own notes.

Table 5.1 Implement supervision systems and processes

Performance criteria	Commentary	Notes
a. Implement supervision in the context of organisational policies, performance management and workforce development.	Locate and familiarise yourself with your organisation's supervision, appraisal, probationary and personal development policies and procedures.	
b. Develop, implement and review written agreements for supervision.	You will have an agreement that specifies supervision arrangements and responsibilities. They can be rudimentary, simply stating frequency, length and who has responsibility for setting them up. More complex contracts cover cancellation procedures, preparation and so on. Others may set ground rules for the relationship and identify such things as areas of interest or for personal development.	
c. Ensure supervision records and agreed decisions are accurate and completed promptly.	Keep a record, at the very least, of decisions made in supervision. Whoever has the responsibility for recording them will need to see they are signed off. Usually it is the supervisor/s' responsibility, but you should have a signed copy for your induction file or at least access to them. Areas of agreement should also be recorded.	
d. Enable workers to reflect on supervision issues and act on outcomes.	Your supervisor/s should encourage and give you space to reflect on your practice and identify your strengths, weaknesses and development needs and review your actions and care plans.	
e. Monitor and review own supervision practice and learning, reflecting on the processes and implement improvements to supervision.	There should be opportunity for you to comment on the quality of the supervision you have received. This could involve an exercise such as this one.	

(Continued)

Table 5.1 (Continued)

Performance criteria	Commentary	Notes
f. Identify wider issues and raise them appropriately in the organisation and with other stakeholders.	Your manager or supervisor should act as a broker identifying with you practice issues that need to be picked up on in the organisation more widely, so that the quality of services can be improved.	
g. Enable access to specialist supervision, support, advice or consultation as required. Specialist supervision can include peer, therapeutic or clinical supervision.	Specialist supervision can be an excellent way to develop your practice and can also be essential in some roles and situations that demand more support that your manager or usual supervisor/s can provide.	

Table 5.2 Develop, maintain and review effective supervision relationships

Performance criteria	Commentary	Notes
a. Create a positive environment for workers to develop and review their practice.	Supervision should challenge your practice but it should be a positive encounter that you value and where challenge is matched with encouragement and support. You should be encouraged to take responsibility and take control in reviewing and evaluating your practice.	
b. Clarify boundaries and expectations of supervision, including confidentiality.	It pays to review your previous experiences of supervision and what works or doesn't work for you. Good supervision contracts will cover these broader issues as well as clarifying confidentiality and what are (or not) suitable matters for supervision.	
c. Ensure relationships are conducted in an open and accountable way.	Both you and your supervisor/s are accountable for your practice so the relationship must be strong enough for you to share the details of your practice, including problems you are experiencing. Hidden practice can be dangerous practice.	
d. Help workers to identify and overcome blocks to performance, such as work conflicts and other pressures.	Effective practice is not just down to you. Others can influence your effectiveness in a positive fashion, as well as negatively. Chapter 6, in particular the section on dealing with conflict, may be of use here. Your supervisor/s should also be able to help with these broader issues.	
e. Assist workers to understand the emotional impact of their work and seek appropriate specialist support if needed.	It is a tough job – one that can affect us all deeply. The emotion of your work needs to be on the agenda for the sake of your own health, but also because it can impact on your practice. Some people who use services can be manipulative or frightening – openness about their impact on you will help ensure your practice is purposeful and objective.	
f. Ensure the *duty of care* is met for the well-being of workers.	Your employer has responsibility for your health and safety including safe working arrangements outside of the office, stress and workload balance.	
g. Recognise diversity and demonstrate *anti-discriminatory practice* in the supervision relationship.	Supervision should respond to your individual needs and actively seek not to discriminate against you.	

h. Give and receive constructive *feedback* on the supervisory relationship and supervision practice.	Both you and your supervisor/s need to reflect on and discuss the quality of your supervision and aim to improve it over time.
i. Audit and develop own skills and knowledge to supervise workers, including those from other disciplines when required.	Your manager should be seeking to develop their skills as a supervisor. You can help them do this by giving them positive and constructive feedback, identifying areas where supervision can be improved. Having good supervisory practice on the agenda is also useful as the supervision of others will become one of your responsibilities as your career progresses.

Table 5.3   Develop, maintain and review practice and performance through supervision

Performance criteria	Commentary	Notes
a. Ensure workloads are effectively allocated, managed and reviewed.	It is very difficult to come up with a definitive workload management system that determines fair workloads for all, as your work will be too complex and variable to be easily categorised and measured. Good dialogue that regularly addresses what you are being allocated, how, and whether it is manageable, is essential.	
b. Monitor and enable workers' competence to assess, plan, implement and review their work.	Your performance as a case manager should not only be evaluated, but there should be opportunities for you to develop and improve it.	
c. Ensure supervisor and workers are clear about accountability and the limits of their individual and organisational authority and duties.	Induction and supervision are the best places to clarify any areas of confusion that can arise. Job descriptions and procedures are often not definitive discussion works.	
d. Ensure workers understand and demonstrate *anti-discriminatory practice*.	Your qualifying course will have given a lot of attention to this topic, but do not let it drift – make it an explicit feature of your supervision agenda.	
e. Ensure work *with people who use services* is outcomes-focused and that their views are taken account of in service design and delivery.	Work with individuals needs to be achieving outcomes agreed with them. Supervision also needs to address the broader development of services and service quality and people who use services can be involved in this.	
f. Identify risks to users of services and workers and take appropriate action.	Risks need to be clearly identified, methodically assessed and actions agreed to manage them effectively. Any assessment and agreed plans should be recorded.	
g. Obtain and give timely feedback on workers' practice, including feedback from people who use services.	Both you and your supervisor have a responsibility to evaluate your practice and improve it. Actively seeking feedback on your performance (especially from people who use services and carers) and discussing and acting on it is a joint responsibility.	
h. Identify learning needs and integrate them within development plans.	It is important that you are clear about what areas of your practice you want to develop. Make sure your learning objectives and development plans are focused on these needs.	

(Continued)

Table 5.3 (Continued)

Performance criteria	Commentary	Notes
i. Create opportunities for learning and development.	You should be offered and take opportunity to make use of a range of on and off the job development opportunities. Their effectiveness in meeting your needs should be evaluated.	
j. Assess and review performance, challenge poor practice and ensure improvements in standards.	Supervision should encompass appraisal. Your performance should be evaluated jointly against agreed standards on the basis of readily identified evidence. The evaluation and agreed improvement plans should be recorded together with any differences of opinion.	
k. Enable multidisciplinary, integrated and collaborative working as appropriate.	This is essential to service quality and demands regular review and evaluation. Chapter 8 of this book will no doubt help here as multidisciplinary working is an essential element of practice. Many quality problems originate here and many quality improvements lie with more effective multi-agency and collaborative working.	

Summary of key points

- Your period of induction will be crucial in determining your role and responsibilities and the rules, procedures, expectations and goals of the organisation you intend to, or have just joined.

- High-quality reflective supervision is at the heart of social care and will be crucial to the success of your future practice.

- Evaluate the quality of your induction period and supervision processes.

FURTHER READING

Davys, A and Beddoe, L (2010) *Best practice in professional supervision: A guide for the helping professions.* London: Jessica Kingsley.

Written again by two experienced authors this book aims to be an authoritative guide to being an excellent supervisor – it will give you a heads-up around your potential future role as a supervisor. Also see their latest book (Beddoe and Davys, 2016) entitled *Challenges in professional supervision: current themes and models for practice* (London: Jessica Kingsley).

Howe, K and Gray, I (2012) *Effective supervision in social work.* London: Sage/Learning Matters.

Written by two experienced authors, this worthwhile book represents the development of their thinking about supervision over the past 20 years, in particular around the relational and organisation contexts of supervision.

LGA (2014) *What you should expect as a social worker?* London: LGA.

This is the sister document to Standards for Employers (LGA, 2014) and provides a short and helpful, four-page summary of what you should expect from your employer, including standards of induction. You can gain access to both documents here:

www.local.gov.uk/workforce/-/journal_content/56/10180/3511605/ARTICLE

SCIE (2013) *Effective supervision in a variety of settings.* London: SCIE.

A useful online guide containing practical help to develop supervisory practices in the workplace.

Available from: **www.scie.org.uk/publications/guides/guide50/index.asp**

Chapter 6

Managing the personal: from surviving to thriving in social work

Kate Howe with a contribution from Pru Caldwell-McGee (NQSW)

PROFESSIONAL CAPABILITIES FRAMEWORK

This chapter will help you to demonstrate the following ASYE-level capabilities:

1. Professionalism: identify and behave as a professional social worker, committed to professional development.

    *   Demonstrate workload management skills and develop the ability to prioritise.

    *   Recognise and balance your own personal/professional boundaries in response to changing and more complex contexts.

    *   Develop ways to promote well-being at work, identifying strategies to protect and promote your own well-being and the well-being of others.

2. Values and ethics: apply social work ethical principles and values to guide professional practice.

    *   Recognise and manage the impact of your own values on professional practice.

    *   Recognise and manage conflicting values and ethical dilemmas to arrive at principled decisions.

KNOWLEDGE AND SKILLS STATEMENTS

This chapter will help you demonstrate the following requirements:

Child and family:

1. Relationships and effective direct work.
9. The role of supervision.

Adult:

7.   Direct work with individuals and families.
8.   Supervision, critical reflection and analysis.

Introduction: the current context of social work

As a newly qualified social worker you probably know some of the effects social work practice can have on the individual. Making the transition from student to qualified social worker is often a larger shift than anticipated. Expectations and responsibilities are different, and the support mechanisms are not always obvious.

You may have experienced some feelings of stress, or witnessed colleagues reacting to stressful situations. Social work is no ordinary job as professionals engage with individuals who are at risk and invariably facing difficulties in their lives. Coupled with this, the working environment is beset with uncertainty through frequent changes in policies and practices, as well as staff turnover. A recent Community Care research report found that 73 per cent of their sample of 1359 social workers were emotionally exhausted (McFadden, 2015). The most recent Health and Safety Executive (2015) report finds that health and social care associated professionals have one of the highest rates of work-related stress, anxiety and depression. However, the evidence is not all negative as an earlier study found that 62 per cent of social workers were satisfied or highly satisfied with their current job (Baginsky *et al.*, 2010).

Organisational issues such as job demands, high caseloads and long hours contribute to the demanding nature of social work. Grant and Kinman (2014) also suggest that role stress is an important factor where the social worker not only feels overloaded with too many demands and expectations but also experiences conflict within the role. This is because the demands of one role make it difficult to fulfil another which can lead to ambiguity and contrasting expectations. Further factors such as the lack of control and professional autonomy coupled with constant change and little social support can cause a difficult work environment. The organisation clearly has some responsibility for taking steps to provide a healthy workplace culture, and this is to some extent explored in the following two chapters.

In this chapter though, my focus is on the individual social worker and therefore the 'personal'. You will also meet Pru, a newly qualified social worker, who is halfway through her ASYE year. Research has shown that stress does not always have to lead to negative outcomes. Some social workers are able to 'thrive' and demonstrate high levels of resilience during demanding times, managing to sustain good professional practice despite difficult circumstances (Grant and Kinman, 2014). Being a professional social worker in today's climate is clearly a complex task and requires you, the newly qualified social worker, to build the personal qualities and resilience to thrive in your work. So how can you be one of these thriving, resilient social workers in your first year?

Taking care of 'you' is a good start. Other professionals use a range of tools to practise; an artist has brushes and a nurse has medical instruments. For the social workers, the main instrument is **self**. So, just as other professionals will care for their instruments, you as a professional social worker need to care for yourself. A stressed, exhausted social worker is not able to offer the respectful standard of care that a service user has a right to!

So, the first part of this chapter is about understanding and managing the emotional impact of your evolution to a confident social work practitioner. Being aware of your emotions is a crucial part of this process as is the ability to manage them in order to develop professionally and address some of the opportunities laid out for you in Chapter 2. My view is that by looking after yourself, developing your personal and interpersonal competence and by managing your professional environment, you will be more able to work effectively with people who use services and carers, which incidentally is one of the key factors that motivates social workers to stay in the profession (Cameron, 2003; Huxley *et al.*, 2005).

Emotions and emotional intelligence in social work

It is easy to think that as a qualified social worker you have learnt to be 'objective', and maintain your professional boundaries even in the most difficult of situations. Indeed, there is ample anecdotal evidence of organisations discouraging and frowning on any emotional responses from their workers, dismissing them as unprofessional.

However, a growing body of knowledge is starting to acknowledge the role of emotions in practising social work effectively and reject the standard, rational approach to social work that is characterised by the managerial approach (Howe, 2008; Ingram, 2015). The essence of social work practice is the relationship that you can create with those who use services and so awareness and management of your emotions is crucial.

Harrison and Ruch (2007) distinguish between 'self-less' social work where the emphasis is on the *doing* of the tasks, and 'self-ish' social work that has self-knowledge and awareness at the heart of *being* a social worker. By rejecting the description of 'self-less', they challenge the traditional social work perspective of a distant, neutral and emotionless professional as lacking true focus on people who use services. To practise from a 'self-ish' perspective forces us to consider and understand the interpersonal dynamics of an interaction. Personal self-awareness as well as knowledge of others is at least as important as knowing 'what to do' and 'how to do it'. Developing this understanding leads to an appreciation of the unique relationship between yourself, the people who use services as individuals and our social context, and thereby a true personalised service. To attempt to reduce this understanding to standardised and rational behaviour patterns loses the depth and heart of the social work relationship.

The concept of emotional intelligence can help us to gain a depth of understanding, and it is simply defined as an individual's ability to be aware of their – and others' – emotions in any situation and manage their responses. Latterly, Goleman (2006) popularised the theory by claiming it was more important than cognitive intelligence in the development of successful leaders. Although some of these claims are contentious and some would argue that the many different definitions weaken its theoretical coherence (see Howe, 2008), it can give us a useful framework by which to gain insight into ourselves and our relationships with others.

Figure 6.1 is adapted from Goleman *et al.*'s (2013) model of emotional intelligence and shows the key aspects of each of the domains of emotional intelligence they identified. The construct of the four domains emphasises the intrapersonal and interpersonal aspects as well as differentiating between awareness and management. The arrows demonstrate that all domains are related and lead to the core aspect of managing relationships. Understanding this 'interrelatedness' is key to you being able to work in stressful and emotionally charged situations. As Shulman (1999, cited in Morrison, 2007, p251) points out, a social worker can only really understand and be in touch with the feelings of those he or she works with if they have the ability to acknowledge and manage their own emotions.

More recently the link between emotions and thought has been emphasised by Howe (2008) and others arguing that we need to understand how emotions can be used to

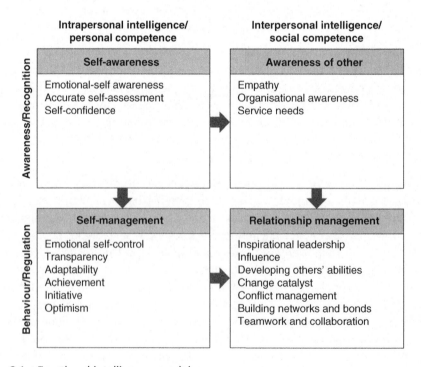

Figure 6.1   Emotional intelligence model

(Adapted from Goleman *et al.*, 2013)

improve reasoning and decision-making. Our mood and emotional state affects how we think and behave and, of course, how we think affects how we feel (Howe, 2008). It is probably not difficult to remember a time when a remark from a colleague triggered an angry response in you on a day when you were tired and stressed, and on reflection you recognised that it was a little 'over the top'. We know from neuroscience (Howe, 2008; Ingram, 2015) that being in an anxious state can seriously disrupt our ability to concentrate.

Our level of emotional intelligence can also affect and predict our ability to be resilient. Grant and Kinman (2014) found that the more 'emotionally literate' a social worker was, the more resilient they were. We will look at developing resilience later in the chapter, but for now read about Pru's experience.

CASE STUDY **6.1**

Pru's experience: part 1

I am halfway through my ASYE year and am slowly beginning to recognise my own emotional reactions to working in a frontline childcare team. I am gaining in self-awareness and sense of my own well-being through the quality of supervision I receive from my line manager and ASYE mentor. Through this, I am learning that with increasingly complex cases comes an increased strain on my emotional well-being. I am beginning to recognise the cases that will demand high levels of my emotional energy. For example, I am working with a family where there is suspected Emotionally Unstable Personality Disorder of the mother of four young children. In one visit I can be screamed at, thanked, made to laugh or provide comfort to her as she sobs while, at the same time, constantly assessing the impact she is having on her children and trying to focus the work on their needs. I can feel apprehensive before a visit and emotionally drained after so I now ensure that I plan visits that build in time to prepare, process, recover and recharge. The element of diary management plays an enormous part in being an effective practitioner and I am learning how to incorporate my own emotional protection into this.

With the benefit of supervision from two very different types of people, my critical reflection skills are constantly developing. My ASYE mentor is a CAMHS manager and my first two supervisions reduced me to tears. There are always going to be some cases that affect us more than others and one really got under my skin. It was a family with two boys where the older boy's behaviour was affected by the long-term emotional abuse he was suffering. Supervision helped me to unpick why this case had such an impact and allowed me to explore the emotion it evoked in me. I realised that I was comparing the life of this boy to my son's as they are similar in age and this therefore triggered an intense emotion in me. I felt embarrassed when I welled up during our conversation but my mentor reassured me this was normal and, perhaps more importantly, perfectly reasonable to expect. By being honest in supervision and open to exploring my own vulnerability, I was able to process it and build my resilience which in turn made me determined to improve the life of this young boy.

Have another look at Pru's account. Think about and identify the aspects of emotional intelligence that she identifies from Figure 6.1 before moving on to Activity 6.1.

ACTIVITY 6.1

Think of a time . . .

Think of a time when you know you worked well with a service user; when you were being a 'self-ish' social worker. It might be when you encountered an unexpected or difficult situation and were able to reach a positive outcome. Now look at the competencies identified in Figure 6.1 and reflect on which of them you were using.

Personal competence: building self-awareness

Goleman (1996, p46) defines self-awareness as the *sense of an ongoing attention to one's internal states*. In other words it is the ability to know how you are feeing and why, as well as identifying the impact they are having on your actions. This awareness of self is the first step to building emotional intelligence and your resilience.

Social work practitioners are emotional beings as much as people who use services. You may think it easy to recognise your emotions when faced with an angry user of services, but do you have the same level of awareness when completing the same care assessment paperwork for the hundredth time? Are you filling in a form or really listening to what your client is saying?

As already mentioned in Chapter 2, Daniel Kahneman (2011) brings an interesting perspective to this discussion by talking about our minds as having two systems. System 1 is fast, automatic and requires very little effort. It is the system that makes quick and very often unconscious decisions and can be the basis for our intuitive responses. It responds to our emotions. System 2 is slower, and requires energy and control to engage rational thought and understand the complexity of a situation. This can be linked to our understanding of how our emotions can be the basis for our actions knowing that the emotional part of the brain is the first to receive and react to an outside stimulus, with the more developed pre-frontal cortex always coming in second. One of Kahneman's assertions is that we often believe we are thinking rationally (system 2) when we are really reacting to events on an unconscious and intuitive basis (in system 1). This can lead to reactive practice and we need to grow our conscious awareness of how our mind is processing information. As Munro (2009) argues, we must be very aware of our emotional triggers and biases and their effect on our performance; we must not discount these system 1 thoughts, but be consciously aware of them. Developing reflective skills is clearly a method of increasing this awareness and making a regular time for critical reflection with your supervisor is important as Chapters 2, 3 and 5 have already pointed out.

Additionally, being able to assess your emotional state on a moment to moment basis increases emotional intelligence. In our busy lives we can often go through the day on 'auto pilot' and neglect to really get in touch with our 'self'. We know that how we are physically affects our feelings and Rosenberg's (2003) model of non-violent or compassionate communication suggests that our emotions are also inextricably linked to our needs. For example, we will have an emotional reaction if we need respect, or affection or even something to eat. However, we sometimes lack the awareness and breadth of language to express this. I have found using Rosenberg's feelings list as well as his needs inventory very helpful in identifying and understanding my emotional state. There are free and downloadable resources available from **www.nonviolentcommunication.com/aboutnvc/nonviolent_communication.htm**.

ACTIVITY 6.2

Checking in

(a) *Take a little time, stop what you're doing, and as you read this 'check in' by yourself:*

How are you feeling physically? Notice how you are sitting or standing, which parts of the body are more tense/relaxed than others? What might be the reasons?

How are you feeling emotionally? What might be the reasons?

What do you need at this moment to increase a state of well-being?

(b) *Take it one stage further: Commit to your own personal 'research' by writing down your feelings and needs over a period of time – say a week – where you take your 'emotional temperature' three times a day using the above questions. What patterns do you notice?*

(c) *As an extra perspective you might buddy up with someone in your team, swap notes and get some feedback from them. It could fit into a tea-break and give you some useful information.*

(d) *In preparation for working with a service user always ask yourself the question: What is my emotional state and what do I need? That 30-second space can make the difference between a productive or non-productive visit.*

Stress and burnout

Stress itself is not an illness – it is a state, and certainly in some instances some stress or pressure can be a motivator to get a task done. Collins (2008) talks of stress as being the individual's perception of a disparity between the demands being made and the ability to cope, i.e. high demand and low feelings of being able to cope result in stress.

The HSE's formal definition of work-related stress is *the adverse reaction people have to excessive pressures or other types of demand placed on them at work* (available here: **www.hse.gov.uk/stress/furtheradvice/whatisstress.htm**). However, if stress becomes too excessive and prolonged, mental and physical illness may develop and can result in what is called 'burnout'. McFadden's (2015) research project funded through the Stand Up for Social Work campaign examined the extent of 'burnout' in social workers, where it was defined as:

> *a syndrome of emotional exhaustion, depersonalization, and reduced personal accomplishment that can occur among individuals who do 'people work' of some kind . . . Burnout can lead to deterioration in the quality of care or service provided.*
> (Maslach and Jackson, 1986, p1, in McFadden, 2015, p4)

Each of these above components is now examined in turn. **Emotional exhaustion** is at the heart of burnout and leads to the other two. It is characterised by:

- a lack of physical energy, lack of energy; feeling tired all the time;

- emotional outbursts; feeling angry and frustrated, short-tempered and irritable;

- a low sense of low self-esteem where nothing seems to be going right, and you always seem to 'fail';

- disillusionment about work;

- being physically not well – having headaches and generally feeling run down.

Depersonalisation is when you have an unfeeling or impersonal response to the service users; they no longer seem real and are perhaps categorised by their problem rather than name. You become hardened to the work and everything is 'just part of the job'. Signs of depersonalisation can include:

- losing empathy with service users;

- creating physical and emotional distance between yourself and service users, avoiding visits;

- taking longer to do the 'easier' tasks;

- isolation from others (can include colleagues and friends) and feelings of being alone;

- leaving work early.

The theory is that combining these two factors can result in **reduced personal accomplishment** with feelings of no longer being able to work as well as you could, no longer being effective when working with service users and being dissatisfied with self. Interestingly, although McFadden's (2015) research found that the sample of 1359 social workers had high levels of emotional exhaustion and moderately high levels of depersonalisation, this had not resulted in reductions in feelings of personal accomplishment or satisfaction. Nevertheless, being aware of and watching out for early warning signs of burnout may help you to prevent their build-up.

ACTIVITY **6.3**

Watch out

Watch out for the early warning signs of burnout. The signs above can be distilled into four key areas:

- *Physical – such as aches and pains, frequent colds, digestive problems.*

- *Emotional – such as irritability, feeling overwhelmed, depressed, agitated.*

- *Cognitive – such as lack of concentration, predominantly negative thoughts, forgetfulness, lacking judgement and ability to make decisions.*

- *Behavioural – such as changes in appetite, increase in alcohol use or smoking, lack of sleep, isolating yourself.*

Take an honest and careful analysis of your current well-being. Do you have any areas of concern? If so, what might you do about them?

Personal competence: self-management

Good self-management is about being able to respond appropriately to a situation. It is not about denying or completely suppressing emotions – we have already shown how important emotions are – but being able to choose when, where and how they are expressed. To be able to do this consistently requires us to take care of ourselves and build our resilience.

Laming (2009) emphasised the need for social workers to develop emotional resilience, and it is one of the skills a qualifying social worker is required to demonstrate in the professionalism domain of the Professional Capabilities Framework. Recent work by Grant and Kinman (2014) has identified the need to focus on building resilient social workers and its relationship to improving professional practice. Munro (2011) and Mor Barak *et al.* (2009) have found that using strategies to increase our emotional resilience could provide some protection against the stress of work. As I mentioned earlier, Grant and Kinman (2014) suggest that social workers who have high emotional intelligence often having high resilience. There are so many definitions of resilience and lists of characteristics to be found within them (Grant and Kinman, 2014) that it is hard to be concise about its meaning. Collins (2007) offers a view that it is our general ability to develop flexible and resourceful strategies to external and internal stressors. An added dimension that I think is important to consider is that resilience cannot be acquired without some exposure to adverse situations; we need to be able to experience and understand our actions in difficulty to know how to act in future.

Hardiness

Research by Kobasa (1979, cited in Kamya, 2000) and Maddi *et al*. (1998) identified three characteristics of 'hardiness' or what we sometimes refer to as resilience, i.e. someone's ability to handle and manage problems or difficulties.

1. Having a strong characteristic of **commitment** that results in finding reasons for remaining involved in a situation and a way forward. You will have an active problem-solving approach and can find meaning in activities even when faced with significant adversity.

2. Believing you have some **control** over present circumstances which then enables an individual to think they can influence the course of events, rather than being a victim of circumstance. Control can either be a primary control, which is the ability to change a situation positively, or a secondary control, which is the ability to change how you think about a situation. Secondary control can also be called 'reframing'. By changing how you perceive a situation, you can change the meaning and thereby change your response to it (for further information, see O'Connor, 2001). For example, it can help you to accept areas that you know you cannot change and focus on the areas where you have some influence. Stephen Covey (1989, 2004) develops this characteristic and distinguishes between areas of **concern** and areas of **influence**. Within our area of concern are all the topics that we focus on ranging from health, family, climate change, global politics, organisational structure to how much we are being paid, and so on. However, many of these subjects are outside of our influence and control. It can be tempting to focus our energy (particularly our mental energy in the form of worry, frustration, irritation and complaining) on those things in life that most concern us. But if we have no influence over them that energy can be said to be wasted. By focusing your effort on what you are able to influence, you are likely to be more effective in your interventions and thereby increase your capacity for influence. Covey (1989, 2004) characterises those who focus on areas of influence and control as proactive and those who focus on what is beyond their control as reactive. People who are more reactive are more likely to feel a victim of circumstance and blame others for problems. Proactive people are more likely to be able to widen their influence as they focus on areas they can change or control.

3. Enjoying **challenges** and so seeking out opportunities for continual growth and learning, rather than staying in routine and safe comfort zones. This proactive attitude sees stress more as a challenge that is neither unfair nor unfortunate, but part of life to be accepted and worked with. Combining this with a realistic understanding of your own capabilities and limitations means that challenges can be perceived at an appropriate level.

Kamya (2000) highlights that younger social workers tend to have lower levels of 'hardiness' and fewer coping strategies and, therefore, may be more prone to stress and burnout. This is why it is so important to positively develop coping and management strategies which address the issues of workload, emotional stress and conflict.

ACTIVITY 6.4

Difficult situations

Think about a difficult situation you are currently facing. Ask yourself the following questions and write down some responses:

- *What reasons can I find in the situation that mean I can commit to being involved?*
- *How can I reframe the situation to regain a sense of perspective and control?*
- *What elements of control do I have?*
- *What can I accept as out of my control?*
- *What can I do to influence the outcome?*

Review what you have written and now consider:

- *What is my opportunity for learning in this situation and what can I do to develop and/ or improve my skills?*

Charles and Butler (2004) also offer a framework of control, influence and acceptance (out of my control) that is relevant to social work. It focuses on managing the tension between the ideals of social work (that as a newly qualified or about to qualify social worker are fresh in your memory) and the practice realities that often cause stress and dissatisfaction. It is worth considering Charles and Butler's (2004) distinctions between situations where you have control, those where you have some influence, and those where you have neither of these and need to reach a state of acceptance (Table 6.1). Focusing your energy on productive areas is likely to decrease stress levels, enhance job satisfaction and increase your resilience.

Table 6.1   Control, influence and accept

	Control	**Influence**	**Accept**
Personal	<ul><li>Allocation of time</li><li>Use of skills</li><li>Relationship building</li><li>Values</li></ul>	<ul><li>Team development</li><li>Express appropriate dissatisfaction about agency policies</li></ul>	<ul><li>Appreciation of own strengths and limitations</li><li>Preferred methods of working</li></ul>
Professional	<ul><li>Selection of working methods</li><li>Development of own expertise/ specialisms</li></ul>	<ul><li>Using professional credibility and research to influence other professionals</li></ul>	<ul><li>Uncertainty</li><li>What is possible to achieve and what is not</li><li>That small-scale changes can transform lives</li></ul>
Organisational	<ul><li>Skills in work/systems management</li><li>Your image at work of organised, professional worker</li></ul>	<ul><li>Collective action; participation in lobbying/union groups</li></ul>	<ul><li>Agency limitations</li><li>Benefits of work (e.g. plan holidays and take time off in lieu)</li></ul>

Adapted from Charles and Butler (2004)

ACTIVITY **6.5**

Control and influence

Take a few minutes to consider how much control and influence you have in your work or study. Then consider the following questions:

- *Do you agree with the contents of Table 6.1?*

- *What else might you add to these columns?*

- *Then consider whether the statements in the Accept column are accurate for you?*

- *What might you add or alter?*

- *How do these distinctions change your view of your work or study?*

Developing understanding of situations can bring emotional resolution

Using critical reflection and evaluation skills developed during your qualifying pro-gramme are good examples of how you can get to a place of letting go of negative emotions. Supervision is an obvious place to take time to 'unpack' difficult situations. Research has shown that *regular, extensive supervision, better informed and more sensitive supervision is likely to provide more effective support for social workers* (Collins, 2008, p1182). If you have not done so already, please refer to Chapter 5 – the last part of this chapter centres on supervision. Making space for reflection by yourself or with a team colleague can also help to bring about that important level of understanding. Arranging regular supervision sessions and attending sessions prepared with the issues you wish to discuss, including emotional issues, will be vital for your development.

Collins (2008) also stresses the importance to practitioners of developing support systems from colleagues, for example mentors and/or 'buddy systems' (Collins, 2008). Other types of support are also crucial to your emotional well-being: friends, partners and family can give you the opportunity to 'come up for air' and get a different perspective on life. Do make time for being with others to allow you to switch off from the pressures of work. Taking annual leave, switching off the work phone and work emails during the evening and weekends or when you are off duty are vital for the development of your emotional health. If this becomes increasingly difficult it is time to talk with your supervisor. Don't leave it until it is too late.

Developing good work strategies are important in enabling you to cope with pressures. As Pru points out in Case Study 6.1, managing your diary and allowing time to complete tasks is important. Ask yourself questions about how you manage your diary, for instance: is arranging a visit immediately after a particularly difficult multi-disciplinary strategy meeting really the best time? Could this visit be undertaken at a different time, thereby giving you time to address any practical or emotional issues that may arise from the meeting? While there are frequently deadlines to work to, ask yourself: are these imposed on me through statute, organisational guidance or am I putting pressure on myself?

Prioritise and be realistic – social work practitioners can have an overdeveloped sense of responsibility, leading to the setting of unrealistic goals. Also, be clear about what *must* be done now and what can be left until later. Covey (1989, 2004) has model of time quadrants that can help to identify where we might manage time better (Figure 6.2). Do take regular breaks – any you are entitled to during the working day, even if it is just ten minutes. Breaks are really breaks when you move out of your current environment, so a walk or even standing outside noticing the weather can be good enough. Read how Pru copes before completing Activity 6.6.

CASE STUDY 6.2

Pru's experience: part 2

I was fortunate to be offered a permanent position from my final placement setting so the transition from student to ASYE was relatively smooth. The biggest impact is the combination of increased complexity of my caseload and the adjustment of the reduced safety net of being a student.

I am continually assessing parents' capacity and emotional availability to their children but I now recognise that I must also do this for myself and my family. It would be easy to get caught up in trying to keep on top of the ever-demanding administrative aspects of the role by sitting at a computer till all hours of the night and never switching off but I have had to make a rule; unless it is something specific such as a report or assessment I do not work in my own time. I make sure this is the exception and not the rule as I am consciously not allowing my professional life to interfere with my personal life to protect myself and my family. I am encouraged to book admin days into my diary and have the flexibility of either working somewhere out of the office or, on occasion, working from home. This, for me, is an indication of working in a supportive and nurturing team which is fundamental if I am to thrive as a social worker.

ACTIVITY 6.6

Managing your time

Using the framework below (Figure 6.2), think about what you have done in the last week of work or study.

Identify which tasks fit into which quadrant.

The aim, i.e. to be most effective, is to have most working time in quadrant 2.

The tasks in quadrants 3 and 4 can be the places where time can be gained.

Where could you make some changes?

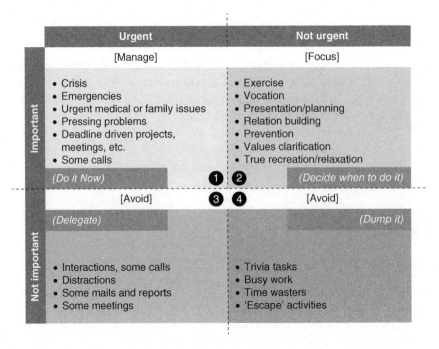

Figure 6.2   Covey's time management matrix (Covey, 1989, 2004, p151)

Image available from **http://takisathanassiou.com/wp-content/uploads/2013/03/Covey%E2%80%99s-Time-Management-Matrix.png**

Mind/body awareness and development

Understanding of how a situation is affecting your physical body is also a neglected area and, given that we know the body and mind are inextricably linked, it is an important gap to fill when considering how to look after yourself. For example, where do you hold tension after a difficult interview? Taking some time out to notice your reactions and then do some breathing and stretching exercises to help unblock those areas that are tense. Mindfulness is a growing area and there is increasing research demonstrating its effectiveness in improving mental health and concentration (Williams and Penman, 2011).

Popular resources such as Williams and Penman's (2011) book *Mindfulness: a practical way to finding peace in a frantic world* come with a very useful CD included to assist the development of mindful practice. The final link below is to a book by Steve Hicks – a social work professor in Toronto – where there are three free downloadable chapters:

www.bemindfulonline.com/

www.nhs.uk/conditions/stress-anxiety-depression/pages/mindfulness.aspx

http://lyceumbooks.com/MindfulnessAndSocialWork.htm

Another approach that may help develop positive self-management when faced with difficult situations is called 'anchoring'. This can be useful when giving evidence in court, or presenting a report at a case conference, or when you know you have a difficult interview to do. An anchor is a stimulus that becomes a trigger to make us respond in a certain way. It can be visual, auditory, a feeling, a smell or a taste. Existing anchors can set off emotions by remembering a particular experience. For example, hearing the first three notes of your favourite piece of music can create a warm feeling inside as you remember not only the rest of the music, but also any associated memories. A picture of your family by your desk can evoke a sense of joy. Equally, anchors can be negative. Certain places, people and events can make us feel upset, sad or afraid. For instance, just the smell of perfume worn by a critical teacher can bring back negative memories. You may be unaware of many of these anchors; in other words, they operate at a subconscious level. We can use positive anchors to improve our ability to work in difficult circumstances, exercise more control over our behaviour and actions and achieve outcomes we are working towards. Try the following activity.

ACTIVITY **6.7**

Anchoring

Find a quiet space where you will not be interrupted. You may need a pen and a blank piece of paper. Allow about ten minutes.

- *Step 1: think about the situation you are preparing for and decide on the positive emotional 'state' you want to be in. For example, you may write down 'confident' or 'assertive', but be specific about what sort of 'confident' or 'assertive' you mean. Add more precise words, so that you have a really comprehensive understanding.*

- *Step 2: decide on the 'anchor' that you want to use. This needs to be easy to apply in the situation you want to use it and has to be distinct, in your control, short and easily repeatable. It can be visual, auditory or kinaesthetic. Hand gestures may work well, such as clenching your fist, pressing your first finger and thumb together or pulling your earlobe. Visual or auditory ones can include looking at a picture or repeating a particular word.*

- *Step 3: think of a specific occasion when you remember being in the positive state you wrote down in step 1. It must be a positive memory and you need to be central. Then spend a minute remembering more about the situation. For example, think about the people who are also there and their movements and expressions; remember any colours, voices or other sounds. What were you doing, saying and thinking – were you walking around or sitting down, talking or listening, what were you saying to yourself?*

(Continued)

ACTIVITY 6.7 *continued*

- *Step 4: then, when the memory is really strong, repeat the anchor you decided upon in step 2, and hold it for a count of five. Let go and relax as your memory and feelings created in step 3 start to diminish.*

- *Step 5: then let go of that memory completely by doing something totally different for 20 seconds. Stand up, turn around and sit down again, look around the room or remember what you ate at your last meal.*

- *Step 6: repeat steps 3, 4 and 5 a couple of times to strengthen the anchor – and this can be repeated regularly to reinforce the feelings. Then 'fire' the anchor on its own and notice how your state changes to the one you identified in step 1. Some people find it helpful to close their eyes.*

- *Now think about the situation from step 1; imagine it is happening and use your anchor. Using your imagination and noticing what is happening will aid preparation substantially.*

You can use this and other anchors to recall positive memories and create a positive emotional state. You will find that the more you build these anchors, the more you will be in control of your actions and feel positively able to achieve your goals.

(Adapted from Henwood and Lister, 2007, p159)

CASE STUDY 6.3

Anchoring: an editor's tale

One of the editors (Jonathan Parker) remembers his first time giving evidence in court as a qualified social worker. Having observed court proceedings on a number of occasions and having taken and supported people at court hearings, the process and environment were well known. However, when it came to being responsible for giving evidence and ensuring the best outcome for those involved, it was a nerve-wracking experience. It were important to remain anchored to the reasons for being in court and to the planned approach determined beforehand. He had with him two well-worn pebbles that he held and moved around in his hand which allowed him to focus, take time, relax and concentrate on the task. There are, of course, many ways of anchoring and it is important to choose one with which you are comfortable and, if in court or other formal settings, something fairly unobtrusive.

You may recognise that these simple autogenic and 'self-talk' techniques derive from neurolinguistic programming (O'Connor, 2001; Henwood and Lister, 2007) and cognitive behavioural approaches. They can help you in your social worker role as well as being a process you may share with someone who uses services.

Interpersonal competence

So far we have considered the role of the personal and a range of intrapersonal activities that can help us acknowledge and manage our emotions in practice. We now turn to the management of difficult relationships and awareness of others in particular.

Management of difficult relationships

Good social work is conducted through effective relationships (Ruch, 2005) with anti-oppressive practice at its heart. Morrison (2007) believes that interpersonal intelligence is central to high-quality practice (see Figure 6.1). Throughout your qualifying education there will have been an emphasis on building communication and relationship skills. You will have developed a good understanding of the concept of empathy and its importance in understanding others. However, one area of relationship management that can cause much disquiet and anxiety for newly qualified social workers is working with conflict (Brown *et al.*, 2007). Conflict is an inevitable part of life arising from differences in needs, values and interests and is a state of discord or disharmony. What is important is how we respond to and manage it. We can respond constructively or destructively – often when we respond constructively we do not realise we have done so. When we view conflict in organisations or teams as positive it can:

- highlight underlying issues;

- motivate to deal with underlying problems;

- enhance a mutual understanding;

- stimulate a sense of urgency;

- discourage avoidance of problems;

- sharpen understanding of issues and goals.

However, when conflict is responded to destructively, it can take a tremendous amount of our energy and attention. We can resort to unhelpful strategies because of our emotional reactions.

ACTIVITY 6.8

Thinking about conflict

Pause for thought: think of a time when you responded positively in a situation of conflict and one where you think your response was more negative. Note down your answers to the following questions for each situation.

(Continued)

ACTIVITY *6.8 continued*

- *What were you thinking or feeling at the time?*

- *What did you do?*

- *What are the differences?*

The thoughts and skills you demonstrated may then help you next time you are in a situation of conflict.

Now compare your responses with the model of conflict resolution in Table 6.2.

Thomas and Ruble's (1976, cited in Huczinski and Buchanan, 2007) model of conflict resolution (Table 6.2) shows, in essence, that our actions in conflict can be understood by reference to two axes:

- how assertive or unassertive each party is in pursuing their own concerns;

- how co-operative or not each party is in meeting the needs of the other.

They distinguish five approaches to resolving conflict, which are explained below. No one style is perfect for each conflict situation and the table draws out some of the positives and negatives for each. However, for long-term effective solutions a collaborative approach is likely to be more successful.

Table 6.2   Thomas and Ruble's (1976) model of conflict resolution (cited in Huczinski and Buchanan 2007, p777)

Summary of style	When best used
Avoidance:	
This person ignores conflict and hopes it will go away. They will withdraw or evade conflict situations, feeling they are harmful. It is an ineffective approach because the situation is likely to remain unresolved and people will become frustrated.	when an issue is trivial or more important ones are pressing;
	when you perceive no chance of satisfying your concerns;
	when potential disruption outweighs the benefits of resolution;
	to let people cool down and gather perspective;
	when others can resolve more effectively;
	when issues seem tangential or symptomatic of other issues.

Accommodation:

This person is willing to meet the needs of the other at their own expense. They want to keep the peace and be friends with everyone. It can often result in conflict being resolved through submission or compliance without the views of others being considered.

when you find you are wrong – to allow a better position to be heard, to learn and to show your reasonableness;

when issues are more important to others than yourself – to satisfy others and maintain cooperation;

to build social credits for later issues;

to minimise loss when you are outmatched and losing;

to allow others to develop by learning from their mistakes.

Competition:

This person uses their power to force their views on others. They often believe that there is only one right answer and hurt feelings are unavoidable. It often results in conflict being resolved at a superficial level, but there is long-term damage to relationships.

when quick decisive action is vital (e.g. emergencies);

on important issues where unpopular action needs implementing;

on important issues vital to organisational or others' welfare, when you know you are right;

Compromise:

Often seen as the best approach and delivers an agreement that everyone can live with. This person believes that conflict is draining and so wants to reach a quick solution. But sometimes it leaves dissatisfaction on all sides and a better resolution might have been achieved with more time.

when goals are important but not worth the effort or potential disruption of more assertive modes;

when opponents with equal power are committed to mutually exclusive goals:

to achieve temporary settlements to complex issues;

to arrive at expedient solutions under time pressure.

Collaboration:

Time is spent listening to each person to find a way to meet everyone's needs. Conflict resolution is about reaching a good solution, and respecting each other's views. It is not about winning. Even if complete agreement cannot be reached, all parties feel the process has been fair. Collaboration is seen as being the 'gold standard' of conflict resolution, and is the outcome to be strived for, as it has much more chance of sustaining long-term resolution. However, each party will need to commit time to get there.

to find an integrative solution when both sets of concerns are too important to be compromised;

when your objective is to learn;

to merge insights from people with different perspectives;

to gain commitment by incorporating concerns into consensus;

to work through feelings that have interfered with a relationship.

It is clear that the most effective sustainable approach is collaboration and there are many reasons why this may not always be the approach used, and perhaps what is most difficult is being able to hold onto your own thoughts and feelings as well as those of the other. There may even be times when compromise and collaboration are both needed. The following four stage model of resolving conflict completes the chapter and can be useful in reaching good resolutions.

Step 1: in preparation

Here you might recognise that we have returned to Goleman *et al.*'s (2013) model of emotional intelligence (Figure 6.1) to give a preparation framework.

Self-awareness	Awareness of other
What are you thinking about the situation?	What is the other person thinking about the situation?
What are you feeling?	What is the other person feeling about the situation?
What do you need (look back at the needs list referred to earlier in the chapter) to resolve the situation?	What do they need?
	Step into their shoes to really consider these questions and understand their reasons.
What do you want to achieve?	*Can you accept these two statements about the other person?*
	• *that their behaviour is the best way they know of acting in the current context.*
	• *that their behaviour has a positive (although sometimes unconscious) intention.*
Self-management	**Relationship management**
How will you manage your emotions effectively?	How will you respond to the other's wants/wishes?
	How will you manage the emotional dynamics?
What do you need to do to be able to listen to the other?	What needs to happen to be able to reach a collaborative solution?
How will you communicate your needs and wishes in a way that the other can hear?	

Step 2: in discussion

- Be able to manage and express your emotions and views positively. Recognise when it will be useful to express your emotions. Techniques such as deep breathing, sitting back, taking time out, looking up at the ceiling for a count of 5 (or 10) are sometimes useful here.

- It is important that you say what you need to say, in a way that can be heard by the other person. You need to decide if this is at the beginning of the meeting or after the other person has spoken. It needs to be expressed when the other person can hear it and checked out with them.

- Listen to the other point of view and validate their contributions – this takes time. Listen and listen again. If they repeat the point they still feel that they have not been heard, so let them know that they have been heard. Paraphrase or summarise your understanding and ask them to say whether you have got it right.

- Find out what is important to them about their position and remember your own perspective. Consider whether there is any consensus. Any consensus will usually be at a higher level than the area of disagreement. For example, if you disagree about how many team meetings to hold in a month, then work out what you agree about the function of the meetings. This can develop a new understanding of the issue and help to open up different options. Take care to stay focused on this issue and to summarise at times throughout the negotiation.

- From this consensus position, you can now work on finding other solutions or alternatives to achieve a shared position. Identify a number of alternatives before deciding on which one is best. These may be a combination of your original positions, though it may be helpful to identify one that is distinct from them.

- Decide on which choice or combination of choices is going to be most effective and workable.

Step 3: resolving the conflict, even if there is no solution

If the conflict is not resolved in discussion, consider the following strategies.

- Time out – agree to disagree for the present time and plan to meet again later (it is often surprising how much can change during any interval).

- Mediation – use someone you both trust as neutral and impartial. Going to mediation is not failure – it is a courageous step that recognises it is important to find a resolution.

Step 4: looking after yourself

Resolving conflict is hard work whether you reach a resolution or not. If the conflict remains unresolved ensure you spend some time letting go of your emotions about the issue – try physical exercise, or a relaxation exercise, or talk it through with a *neutral* friend.

Summary of key points

- At the heart of social work is the 'personal'. Good practice is dependent on growing and valuing this perspective in all of the unique relationships you create.

- Thriving in social work involves development of your emotional intelligence which means paying attention to your intrapersonal intelligence and your interpersonal intelligence. This, as part of your continuing professional development, takes time and conscious effort. Reflection will assist your progress.

- Stress is part of the job – being aware of it and taking time to build resilience strategies will protect you against emotional exhaustion and help you to continue to enjoy the rewards, challenges and successes of your profession.

- Take time to look after all aspects of your 'self'. It is your most important professional instrument. And do not forget to celebrate your achievements!

FURTHER READING

Conflict resolution network: **www.crnhq.org/**

This website is a great resource for those considering any aspects of conflict resolution. It has a huge variety of downloadable free materials and an easily accessible self-study guide, which encourages you to develop confidence in conflict situations.

Grant, L and Kinman, G (2014) (eds) *Developing resilience for social work practice*. London: Palgrave.

Grant and Kinman provide an in-depth look at how resilience is an important subject for social workers to consider from a personal and organisational perspective.

Henwood, S and Lister, J (2007) *NLP and coaching for healthcare professionals*. Chichester: Wiley.

Although this book has originally been written for 'healthcare professionals' it is equally relevant to social workers. It is a self-help book that offers many tools and exercises designed to increase your self-awareness and self-confidence.

Howe, D (2008) The *emotionally intelligent social worker*. Basingstoke: Palgrave.

This book provides a readable and in-depth analysis of emotional intelligence and its uses in social work. Much of the focus and examples are related to social work practice and there is a helpful final chapter which considers the practitioner perspective and working under stress.

Ingram, R (2015) *Understanding emotions in social work: theory, practice and reflection*. Oxford: OUP.

A well-received, practical, up-to-date book that will enable your understanding of, and critical reflection on, your own emotions and those of others.

Marshall Rosenberg

The work by the late Marshall Rosenberg into non-violent or compassionate communication is a very accessible way of explaining how to build relationships with others. What follows is a website link and book reference: **www.nonviolentcommunication.com/aboutnvc/nonviolent_communication.htm**

Rosenberg, M (2015) *Non-violent communication: a language of life*. Encinitas, CA: Puddle Dancer Press.

Chapter 7

Joining and contributing to a team

Anne Quinney with contributions from George (carer), Liz Slinn (social worker), Marion Davis CBE (a former Director of Children's Services) and Greg Hind (team leader)

PROFESSIONAL CAPABILITIES FRAMEWORK

This chapter will help you to demonstrate the following ASYE-level capabilities:

2. Values and ethics: apply social work ethical principles and values to guide professional practice.

   - Demonstrate respectful partnership work with service users and carers, eliciting and respecting their needs and views and promoting their decision-making wherever possible.

5. Knowledge: apply knowledge of social sciences, law and social work practice theory.

   - Recognise the contribution, and begin to make use of, research to inform practice.

7. Intervention and skills: use judgement and authority to intervene with individuals, families and communities to promote independence, provide support and prevent harm, neglect and abuse.

   - Build and use effective relationships with a wide range of people, networks, communities and professionals to improve outcomes, showing an ability to manage resistance.

8. Contexts and organisations: engage with, inform and adapt to changing contexts that shape practice. Operate effectively within own organisational frameworks and contribute to the development of services and organisations. Operate effectively within multi-agency and interprofessional partnerships and settings.

   - Work effectively as a member of a team, demonstrating the ability to develop and maintain appropriate professional and interprofessional relationships, managing challenge and conflict with support.

KNOWLEDGE AND SKILLS STATEMENTS

This chapter will help you demonstrate the following requirements:

Child and family:

10. Organisational context.

Adult:

7.   Direct work with individuals and families.
9.   Organisational context.

Introduction

As a newly qualified social worker you will be joining a team in one of the many settings in which social work is practised. In this chapter, you are going to consider a range of topics that will help you to feel prepared for your new role as a newly qualified social worker, specifically:

- what you bring to the team as a newly qualified social worker; and

- what you need to know to help you work effectively in a team.

In this chapter you will also meet Liz, a newly qualified social worker in a statutory setting, and hear in her own words about her experiences of joining a team; Greg, a team leader in a local authority social services department; and Marion, a recent President of the Association of Directors of Children's Services.

But what do we mean by a 'team'?

Jelphs and Dickinson (2008, p8) offer a definition by Morhman *et al.* (1995, p4) which describes a team as:

> *a group of individuals who work together to produce products or deliver services for which they are held mutually accountable. Team members share goals and are mutually held accountable for meeting them, they are interdependent in their accomplishment, and they affect the results through interactions with one another. Because the team is held collectively accountable, the work of interaction with one another is included among the responsibilities of each member.*

The emphasis on shared purpose and interdependence is important. In this chapter, we will be looking at the things you can do to prepare for and enhance your contribution to the organisation and the team. It is highly likely that you will be working with people from other professional backgrounds. As is stated in domain eight

(Contexts and Organisations) of the Professional Capabilities Framework and in the social work subject benchmarks (Quality Assurance Agency (QAA), 2008, para 3.7):

social work increasingly takes place in an inter-agency context, and social workers work collaboratively with others towards interdisciplinary and cross-professional objectives.

The Climbié Report (Laming, 2003, para 17.112) highlights the importance of working closely with people from other professional groups and agencies:

It is clear that the safeguarding of children will continue to depend upon services such as health, education, housing, police and social services working together.

However, the following statement from the report into the death of Peter Connelly provides a note of caution that is important to remember:

Yes it is evident that the challenges of working across organisational boundaries continue to pose barriers in practice, and that cooperative efforts are often the first to suffer when services and individuals are under pressure.

(Laming, 2009, para 4.3)

When teams work well this can impact on the satisfaction of people who access services and their carers. Research undertaken by Borrill *et al.* (2003) and Brown *et al.* (2003), which is still relevant today, indicates that good team working involving participation, support for innovation, reflexivity and support from team members can impact positively on the satisfaction of people who use services. So what can you do to contribute to good team working?

CASE STUDY **7.1**

What do I bring to the team as a newly qualified social worker?

Liz describes some of the important qualities that a newly qualified social worker brings to a team:

- *fresh enthusiasm and energy;*

- *a head bursting with lots of theories but wanting to put them into practice;*

- *high standards and expectations of yourself and other professionals;*

- *hopes and aspirations for people who use services and carers;*

- *a willingness to share ideas and new research;*

- *different ways of approaching work;*

(Continued)

- *a willingness to learn and absorb as much information as possible;*

- *a willingness to challenge practice, thinking and attitudes;*

- *up-to-date IT skills;*

- *a range of knowledge and skills gained from working with other agencies on placement.*

Liz (in Case Study 7.1) clearly captures the qualities of openness to new situations, the capacity for contributing new ideas and a readiness to learn and develop. These can all make very positive contributions to your new team, but you will need to be careful at first that you do not appear insensitive to the established culture of the team. Your team will already have established relationships and ways of working so you will need to gradually gain people's trust and find a place for yourself. So how do you build the trust or cement that Greg talks about in Case Study 7.2?

CASE STUDY **7.2**

Greg, a team leader in a local authority team, shares some advice for newly qualified social workers on joining a team.

1. In any work role, confidence and being open to learning are always important.

What is often critical in your new role as a newly qualified social worker is the way information is shared with other agencies and doing this in a timely way whilst maintaining appropriate confidentiality. Whilst trying to do this, if you make some mistakes along the way, don't 'beat yourself up'. You will make some mistakes, we all do. It's how you cope afterwards and what you learn from the experience that counts.

2. One of the key attributes I value in a newly qualified social worker is that they see processes with a fresh pair of eyes.

In any team there are ways of doing things which may have outgrown their usefulness and need challenging. Fresh comments from newly qualified social workers are nearly always well received. Don't be shy in raising questions about established practices. Doing so will help you feel ownership of what your team does and cement your relationship with your colleagues.

Implicit in the cement that Greg talks about in Case Study 7.2 is the development of trust.

Developing trust

Trust is an important dimension of working collaboratively, described by Stapleton (1998, p12) as an essential attribute which depends on the *support, honesty and integrity* of all concerned. So what does trust involve and how might you as a newly qualified social worker develop this quality? Thomas *et al.* (2009), building on the work of Stapleton (1998) and Lawson (2004), tell us that trust involves:

- valuing other people;
- building relationships based on mutual respect;
- explicitly acknowledging each person's unique contribution;
- being explicit about policies that you have to work within;
- seeking to understand the constraints on another person;
- being honest and realistic about what you can do.

And that the following behaviours are likely to break or undermine trust:

- not doing what you have agreed;
- 'free riding' or leaving other people to do the work;
- offering more than you can deliver;
- alluding to policies in a vague way to give excuses for taking action;
- moaning about another professional;
- exploiting the difficulties of others in order to show yourself in a more positive light;
- working on the assumption that unresolved difficulties encountered in previous contacts will re-emerge.

Keeping (2014), drawing on the work of Sellman (2010), emphasises that trust and mutual respect are important in effective team working, particularly in an inter-professional setting, and that trust in an individual can develop into trust of the professional group. Conversely distrust can be engendered in the same way. Holroyd (2012) provides some useful information about how verbal and nonverbal communication skills underpin the building of rapport. In building trust with your team it is also worth bearing in mind that informal time spent with colleagues is important as it allows people to get to know each other better. Spending time chatting over coffee or a team lunch is not time wasted.

ACTIVITY 7.1

Reflecting on developing trust

Set some regular time aside, say over a week, to reflect on the strategies that you are using to develop and sustain trust in working relationships with colleagues and with carers and people who use services. Keep some notes and think about strategies to develop and sustain trust, for example, helpful rather than hindering strategies.

Beyond trusting relationships what are the other factors that can contribute to good team working? It is a good idea at this point to remind yourself of the group work theory that you may have studied as part of your qualifying training, e.g. Preston-Shoot (2007) and Doel and Kelly (2014). The concepts that underpin our understanding of groups can all be applied to team working. So, for instance, you may well remember the stages of group development: forming, storming, norming and performing? Like groups, teams are seen to go through a number of distinct stages from the point of formation until their termination. Each stage is part of a progression that leads towards increasingly better performance (Tuckman, 1965). As a team member you will be seeking to help develop your team so that it develops and becomes more effective, improving its performance over time.

Developing team effectiveness

What are the advantages of effective team working?

You will be able to have an impact in your day-to-day work in improving the way in which the team works. In Figure 7.1 you can see that improved team working can have an impact on the satisfaction of people working in the organisation and on the outcomes for people who use services and carers and on their satisfaction with the service. In turn, these can influence the performance of the organisation and generate further positive outcomes.

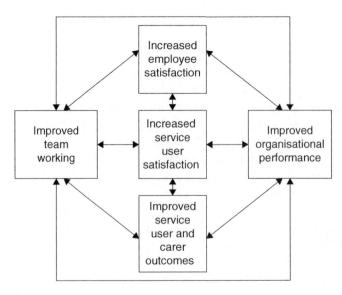

Figure 7.1   The impact of improved team working

(Adapted from Jelphs and Dickinson, 2008, p16)

> ## ACTIVITY 7.2
>
> ### *Auditing team development*
>
> *Spend a few moments considering what you know about group process dynamics and its place in social work and social care. Note the similarities to team development and consider how you might use your learning to understand your place within the team and the potential contribution you can make to its development.*
>
> *Use the team development audit tool in Table 7.1 to structure and document your reflections on your team, informed by your understanding of group work skills and group dynamics.*

Table 7.1   Team development audit tool

	Reflections	Team attributes
A purpose, value base and sense of direction that is meaningful to its members		
Objectives that integrate with the plans of the wider organisation and are regularly reviewed		
Trusting relationships between its members and positive regard		
A climate where problems can be raised and practice challenged		
Responsive and flexible leadership that encourages participation		
A good range of personalities and roles		
Procedures and ways of working that allow it to work effectively including resolving conflicts		
Good relationships and established working relationships with co-providers		
Good relationships and established working relationships with the rest of the organisation		
Continuous team development and improvement		
Good communication within and outside of the team		

Auditing team effectiveness

Some other useful questions for you to consider are:

- Could the team be seen in any way to be 'stuck' in unhelpful behaviours?

- What might I do to help them move on?

- Is there a team development plan that has been discussed and agreed with the team?

Team meetings

Teams often hold formal meetings in order to share information, plan, problem-solve and learn. Most of us interact with our teams on a daily basis outside of these meetings, but sometimes if a team is dispersed and people work very independently it can be the only time you can get together. In either case team meetings can be important events. They can make a significant contribution to how effectively a team carries out its tasks and how good its relationships are. You may find it useful to reflect on your role in the team, and to consider your contribution in team meetings. Try using this checklist to help you reflect on your contribution to team meetings.

How do I behave in team meetings?

- Am I happy with my contribution to the team so far?

- Do I help others to express their ideas? Am I willing to support other people's ideas?

- Do I listen well? Am I sensitive to other people's feelings?

- Do I communicate my ideas well?

- Do I avoid conflict when I shouldn't? Do I give in too quickly when challenged?

- Do I tend to hold on to my own opinions without taking account of the views of others? Do I tend to stick to my own views despite criticism? Am I tolerant of opposing viewpoints?

- Do I take on a leadership role? Do I try to dominate the conversation?

- Am I too quiet? Can I tolerate silence?

(Thomas *et al.*, 2009a)

Your team as a source of support

So far we have explored how you might contribute to the effectiveness of your team. However, it is important to remember that your team is also a crucial support for you. Being part of a team can be very rewarding personally, but it can also offer you some crucial practical help. Let's return to Liz, the newly qualified social worker.

CASE STUDY **7.3**

Support and encouragement

Cycling without stabilisers: the experiences of Liz, as a newly qualified childcare social worker in a statutory agency

I completed my three-year social work degree through the employment-based route. I already knew the team that I joined as a newly qualified social worker as I worked in the team during my course when I wasn't on placement. When I returned at the end of the

(Continued)

CASE STUDY **7.3** *continued*

course as a newly qualified social worker there had been a high turnover of staff so I didn't know as many people. I was the new girl, although fortunately I knew where the toilets were, whose cup not to use and where the stationery cupboard was!

The team members were very welcoming but I didn't have an induction and from day one I had my own caseload of real-life families and children in need. I had previously been a family support worker so working with families wasn't too daunting. However, it was a big transition to discover what my role as a newly qualified social worker really was. I had been a confident, maybe even a bit arrogant, social work student who was doing and learning new things every day on placement, writing about theories and practice, knew the law inside out, and was supported every step of the way by lecturers, practice educators and placement supervisors. Suddenly I was a newly qualified social worker with a supervisor who was really supportive but drowning in paperwork and procedures and squeezing in supervision where she could. It was like someone had taken the stabilisers off my bike. Although it was exciting to start 'real' cycling, I kept falling off and there weren't people right next to me to pick me up. I had to look around to find someone. I found the biggest support came from family support workers and professionals from other agencies like health visitors and teachers. Suddenly I was the newly qualified social worker who they welcomed as part of their team.

ACTIVITY **7.3**

Who might offer support?

Liz uses a powerful analogy of learning to cycle and found that she needed people to 'pick her up' when she fell.

Take some time to consider who might be able to offer support and encouragement to you in your team and how you might build a relationship with them.

As Liz described, these people may not be other qualified social workers, but colleagues working alongside or nearby in other roles. They may well not even be in your organisation. Adams (2005) and Vatcher and Jones (2014) remind us of social work's distinct and sometimes unique contribution to working with other professions in multidisciplinary teams and it is not just the effectiveness of our immediate teams but also these wider teams that have an important impact on service quality. They are often described as interprofessional, multidisciplinary or inter-agency teams. This important theme of interprofessional and inter-agency collaboration is explored in more detail in Quinney and Hafford-Letchfield (2012), Quinney *et al.* (2009), Thomas *et al.* (2009, 2009a) and Whittington *et al.* (2009, 2009a). However, these wider teams not only have a lot to offer us both personally and as practitioners, they also present us with their own challenges. So what do we need in order to be an effective member of a multidisciplinary team? A good starting point is a strong sense of professional identity.

Professional identity as a newly qualified social worker

An important aspect of surviving and thriving in your new job is that of professional identity. Although you may have recently qualified as a social worker you might not be clear about what distinct contribution you will be able to make to any team you have joined (see also Chapters 6 and 8). You may have asked yourself how other people in the team see you as a social worker and also how people who use services, carers and the general public see you. You may be feeling apprehensive as well as feeling excited and relieved to finally be working as a social worker after the demands and rigours of the qualifying course you have recently completed. This will be particularly so when you are practising in an interprofessional or inter-agency context (Quinney and Hafford-Letchfield, 2012). The study by Keeping (2006) identified several things that social workers can do to sustain their professional identity when working in interprofessional and inter-agency settings. You may find these helpful in overcoming initial uncertainties about your new role and your status as a newly qualified social worker as they are still pertinent today.

These are:

- staying connected to your professional community – through regular contact with other social workers;

- staying connected with your practice and sense of purpose – through a reflective approach to your work and the values that underpin it;

- seeking clarity about your role and validation of your contribution – through discussions with colleagues and in supervision;

- enlisting the help of managers – through acknowledging and challenging appropriately when organisations' policies or procedures have a detrimental impact on professional practice.

Keeping (2006, p33) uses extracts from interviews with social workers, some of them reflecting back on their experiences of being newly qualified social workers, to illustrate her findings.

> . . . one of the difficulties with social work itself is that its aims are quite diverse, so it's quite difficult to describe to outsiders what you do exactly . . . just thinking back to when I started, I guess in my first jobs I didn't have a very clear idea of what I was doing.

and

> social workers need to be clear about what they are doing . . . they need to be clear about their own aims as a profession. When I first started out, I remember there being a big discussion about what social workers do within mental health teams

and somebody reeling off a big thing about social workers don't take referrals from psychiatrists, they don't do X, Y, Z . . . I don't think you can define yourself by what you don't do.

(Keeping, 2006, p33)

CASE STUDY 7.4

Liz's top tips for developing your professional identity

- *Find yourself a mentor, whether this is a senior social worker, someone in senior management, a lecturer or practice teacher. Someone who you respect, who understands the nature of social work and can give you direction on a wider scale. I approached an area manager who had been with the local authority for over 20 years. He gave me insight into the organisation, encouraged me to think beyond just being a social worker and recommended other things I could get involved in as well as encouraging me with the skills I already had.*

- *Don't be scared to ask for help. If you look as though you are coping that's what people will think.*

- *Look after yourself. Easier said than done, but really important for those who want to be a social worker for the long haul. Establish clear boundaries. Turn your work phone off and don't look at work emails when you get home. Establish good habits right at the start; if you start off planning to have a lunch break you are more likely to have one.*

- *Establish a good work pattern, so if you're rubbish in the mornings then don't try completing an assessment at that time. Just because a colleague may prefer to get in at 8am you may work better till 6pm.*

- *Don't compare yourself. Just because your colleague always gets their assessments completed on time and you struggle to, it might be that you manage a crisis situation well or are good at establishing good relationships with people who use services and other agencies.*

- *Get organised. Your diary, whether it is an electronic or a traditional diary, is an important tool and if you learn to manage it you will be more flexible when things don't go as planned. Book in future appointments and meetings in advance. That way you will have a clearer picture of how much time you have left.*

- *Learn to prioritise, or ask someone to help you, particularly when everything seems important.*

- *Establish good working relationships with other agencies. Book in time before or after meetings to discuss your roles so differences can be ironed out.*

The points being made by Liz in Case Study 7.4 are very important. It is important to prepare for interactions with other professionals and people who use services and carers by being clear about the remit, services and powers of the agency you work for, your role and the role of others and to be able to explain this positively. This will help you and them feel better informed and enable others to have confidence in your interactions with them.

It can be helpful to refer to the International Federation of Social Workers' (2014) global definition of the social work profession when you want to feel engaged with a sense of purpose for social work that has resonance in many countries across the world:

> *Social work is a practice-based profession and an academic discipline that promotes social change and development, social cohesion, and the empowerment and libera-tion of people. Principles of social justice, human rights, collective responsibility and respect for diversities are central to social work. Underpinned by theories of social work, social sciences, humanities and indigenous knowledge, social work engages people and structures to address life challenges and enhance well-being.*

> (International Federation of Social Workers, 2014)

The extent to which social justice can be realised, if at all, through the efforts of individual social workers in the UK is contestable. Arguably, however, it is this politi-cal dimension which distinguishes social work from other professional groups. It is also important to hold on to the importance of values in social work practice. *Values determine who we are and how we practise: what we do, how we do it and why we do it* (Warren, 2007, p71).

In order to stay connected to your sense of purpose, you may also find it helpful to reflect on what it was that led you to become a social worker in the first place. In a review of the literature and study of people wanting to become social workers, Moriarty and Murray (2007) found that the opportunity to **make a difference** was the main reason for people wanting to work in public sector services and that life experiences, altruism and idealism are other influencing factors. In another study, Gilligan (2007) looked at how social work applicants see the origin of and solution to social problems. Values are inherent in motivations and how people define social problems. Also, people's responses to situations are influenced by them.

If you are interested in reading more about the career paths and motivations of social workers you may like to read the collection of accounts of social workers across the globe engaged in practice, management and education settings (Cree, 2013). These narrative accounts will help you to consider the range of possible routes within social work and may inspire you in your future career path.

If a clear sense of professional identity and purpose is essential to being an effective member of a multidisciplinary team, what else can help?

Professional differences and similarities

In exploring professional differences and similarities, Whittington (2003) suggests that what can help is trying to understand:

- what we have in common;

- what we can each contribute distinctively;

- what is complementary between us;

- what may be in tension between us.

Using the above bullet points together with Table 2.2 in Chapter 2 will help you maintain a critically reflective approach to your professional identity and practice. What else might help?

Creating networks and making alliances

Developing networks and alliances with colleagues and other significant people and the importance of working in a learning organisation (Williams *et al.*, 2012; Gould and Baldwin, 2004; Social Work Task Force, 2009) are important aspects to support your ongoing professional development.

Both formal and informal networks which cross organisational boundaries can contribute to transforming practice. The aim is to not only have the support of the frameworks and line management systems within the agency or organisation, but to be able to establish and draw on a wider range of people through local networks and contacts whose skills, experience and local knowledge can be drawn on to make services more responsive to individual and local need.

Adams (2009) points to a study in the USA by Sarason and Lorentz (1998) in an education setting. The study identifies *people with a flair for boundary crossing as the key to more effective co-ordination* (Adams, 2009, p29) and this continues to have important messages for newly qualified social workers. Adams (2009) also highlights social work qualities and skills in their findings, that contribute to effective boundary crossing, partnership working and creative and transformational practice. These are:

- developing real and authentic knowledge of the locality or subject area, driven by 'curiosity' and a proactive approach to learning;

- being readily alert and recognising commonalities, using imaginativeness;

- a strengths-based approach which recognises assets;

- being able to appropriately use power and influence and selflessness.

Brechin *et al.* (2000, p37) urges critical practitioners to create connections with other professionals *through which real communications can occur, bringing opportunities to learn about others' views and perspectives and discovering ways of talking constructively about differences of opinion.* Good communication, therefore, is also crucial in co-ordinating services to ensure that they meet the needs of people who use services.

Good communication: the key to effective interprofessional practice

Several research studies have drawn attention to the obstacles experienced by people who use services and carers, of ineffective collaboration between professionals and agencies. They highlight recommended improvements, for example:

> *Many [service users and carers] valued good communication, both between members of staff, and between staff and service users . . . Users and carers commented on the importance of knowing that staff shared information, and therefore had a better understanding of the user, viewing them as a 'whole person'. They were more confident of receiving the right care if staff were communicating with each other.*
>
> (Miller and Cook, 2007, p64)

Case Study 7.5 is a first-hand account by a carer of some of the problems encountered when working with several professionals and agencies involved in the care of his wife.

CASE STUDY 7.5

A carer's experience

I have cared for my wife over the last 16 years and especially since she was diagnosed with a personality disorder. We have four children.

My experience of multidisciplinary teams in this example is based on the last nine months and many of the issues I talk about below have yet to be resolved – it's an ongoing saga shall we say!

A few years back my wife admitted herself into hospital and stayed in for about two weeks. Towards the end of her stay there was a discharge planning meeting with the consultant, a ward nurse and the two of us – there was no community mental health team member, even though it was planned to discharge her later that day. My wife had asked for the follow-up meeting not to be during school finish time, but nobody listened – they arranged the meeting when our children were coming back from school.

My wife's GP, child and family social worker, community mental health nurse and consultant were invited to a follow-up meeting to discuss her care. Neither her GP nor the allocated social worker could attend. My wife was then referred to a new consultant, one who is an expert in personality disorders. He met with her, compiled an in-depth report on the basis of this meeting and her notes, and set up a multidisciplinary review meeting.

(Continued)

Letters were again sent out to her GP and the child and family social worker. By ringing the child and family social work team up, I found out that they had not been informed that she had been discharged from hospital! Her social worker had also changed. Her GP didn't attend or reply to the invitation letter. Nevertheless the outcome of this review meeting was that they gave my wife three options – and needed another meeting to discuss them as my wife would not attend the meeting.

This is where we are today. It's been hard work – we are getting somewhere but what we've been through highlights the need for, and the importance of, good communication. The care co-ordinator, whoever that might be, plays a crucial role as a broker between a person who uses services, their carer and other professionals.

ACTIVITY *7.4*

What are the challenges and opportunities for you as a newly qualified social worker if you were to find yourself in this situation?

Accepting that, as in this case study, some obstacles will be hard to overcome, think about different techniques or strategies you might use to enable clearer communication between colleagues in different organisations and between professionals, carers and people who use services.

Managing the tensions created by interprofessional practice

Sometimes there can be real tensions and conflicts in interprofessional practice that are about more than effective communication and demand from us different stances and different skills.

- Being calmly assertive is an important skill to practise. There will be occasions when you will need to ask for clarification about the views and activities of other professionals in order to improve the experiences of people receiving services, and your knowledge about working with other professionals will help you do this with more confidence and authority. For example you might be in a situation where you need to question the attitudes of another professional or a colleague about age or race or about a judgement that may appear to place a person who uses services at risk. Perceived or structural hierarchies of status and power need to be recognised and overcome to promote clear and open communication.

- Whittington *et al.* (2009) point out that several studies (Hudson, 2002; Lymbery, 2006; Townsley *et al.*, 2004) have shown that historical differences in professional status and the ways in which services are organised can lead to territorial attitudes to professional boundaries. The relative status and power of different professions can also lead to tensions and inflexibility. Lymbery (2006) highlights the importance of social workers challenging the 'dehumanising' aspects of other services that older people may experience.

- Working with other professionals and agencies can also be time-consuming as additional time has to be allowed for reaching a consensus in decision-making, and for co-ordination (Penhale, 2007). From the viewpoint of carers and people who use services, the discussions between professionals may take place over their heads and exclude them (Turner *et al.*, 2003; Beresford, 2007), so you may need to be very active in order to include and empower them.

- In addition to clear communication, a range of studies have pointed to the need for good leadership, management, supervision and staff development to support effective collaborative working (Whittington *et al.*, 2009, 2009a). As a newly qualified social worker you will have limited levels of influence in some of these areas but it is important that you are assertive about your development needs in supervision meetings and that you participate in formal and informal staff development opportunities.

- When working with other professionals we have to ensure we understand each other's viewpoints as well as those of the people who are the focus of the assessment and their carers. Sometimes the perceptions of needs, strengths and risks by people who use services and carers can be in opposition to one another and may also conflict with the views of professionals (Quinney *et al.*, 2009). Effective care management demands that you attempt to reconcile some of these differences and broker a way forward.

- These experiences will inevitably be compounded by wider structural inequalities, for example, in relation to gender, class, race and disability. So you may need to actively challenge discriminatory behaviour.

ACTIVITY 7.5

Take the assertiveness quiz in Thomas et al. (2009) and make a note of and take action on the feedback from your score. This quiz can be found in the 'Building relationships, establishing trust and negotiating with other workers' module on the SCIE website: **www.scie.org.uk/assets/elearning/ipiac/ipiac03/resource/flash/index.html.**

Look under the 'Tools for disagreement' and 'Conclusion' sections of the module. Remember, the person with the widest range of behaviour options is likely to be the most successful in any communication (McBride, 1998, p7).

Before finishing the chapter let us just remind ourselves of a particular strength you will bring to your new team.

Helping your team develop research-mindedness

Remember Liz, the newly qualified social worker at the start of this chapter who identified the many strengths that she took to her new team? Several of these related to the fact that she was an effective and up-to-date researcher. This 'research-mindedness' can be really important to a team, as practice on qualifying courses has often got ahead of practice in the field. So as a newly qualified social worker it is an area where you may be able to make a valuable contribution. What is research-mindedness? It has been described as:

- a faculty for critical reflection informed by knowledge and research;

- an ability to use research to inform practice which counters unfair discrimination, racism, poverty, disadvantage and injustice, consistent with core social work values; and

- an understanding of the process of research and the use of research to theorise from practice.

(Centre for Human Services Technology, undated)

Your experience of having developed research skills and awareness during your qualifying course of how research can inform or transform practice should continue to be built on and applied in your practice.

As Dominelli (2005, p226) tells us, research has many purposes in social work as it can be used to:

- *enhance the status of the profession in both the field and the academy;*

- *improve services by finding out what people who use services think about those that have been delivered to them;*

- *evaluate the extent of their use and who uses them;*

- *highlight issues;*

- *elucidate depth and complexities in practice;*

- *explore problems;*

- *raise additional questions; and*

- *enhance critical reflection.*

These ideas are still current. As a social work student you will have been familiar with the importance of accessing and evaluating research and applying it to practice situations in your assignments; and as a newly qualified social work practitioner you will be able to extend these skills and knowledge in order to apply research findings to your everyday practice, but also to undertake research into practice and to more systematically evaluate your own practice. Humphries (2008) reminds us of the need for commitment and passion underlying being research-minded when this involves enquiring into the inequalities and injustices that people who use services experience.

How is the use of research promoted and encouraged? According to Walter *et al.* (2004, p13) this involves:

- *ensuring a relevant research base;*

- *ensuring access to research;*

- *making research comprehensible;*
- *drawing out the practice implications of research;*
- *developing best practice models;*
- *requiring research-informed practice; and*
- *developing a culture that supports research use.*

It is useful to take time to find out about the culture of the team or organisation in relation to research-minded practice. Talk to people who are doing research, find out what practical support there is to undertake research and find out about the facilities for accessing research information.

One of the things you will have relied on, and possibly taken for granted, while at university was the vast range of materials a modern university library provides you with access to, in many cases by using an Athens password. You will have been able to borrow library books and access the contents of peer-reviewed journals in addition to the learning resources available through the course's virtual learning environment. Unless you are registered on a programme of study, perhaps a post-qualifying programme, you are unlikely to have access to a university library (either physically or electronically), so you will need to be resourceful and search more widely for material. It will also be important to 'make friends' with your computer terminal – you'll spend a lot of time together. These computer and information technology skills will be important not only for searching for information and research, but also for inputting data into computer systems, which takes up a large part of a social worker's time.

ACTIVITY 7.6

Publicly available sources of research and literature to inform practice include resources available electronically from the following:

- *Social Care Institute for Excellence:* ***www.scie.org.uk*** *and* ***www.scie-socialcare online.org.uk***
- *Joseph Rowntree Foundation:* ***www.jrf.org.uk***
- *Your agency may have access to Research in Practice:* ***www.rip.org.uk*** *or* ***www.ripfa. org.uk***

Did you know? As a member of the British Association of Social Workers (BASW) you are eligible for a preferential personal subscription to peer-reviewed BASW journals, the *British Journal of Social Work* and *Practice: Social Work in Action.* A subscription will enable you to remain up-to-date with academic and practice-based research and ideas.

Summary of key points

- Remember the many strengths you are bringing to your new team.

- Actively seek to build trust with your new colleagues.

- Reflect on how effective your team is and try and contribute to its development.

- Work on improving your contribution to team meetings.

- Multi-professional working presents many challenges. Develop your sense of professional identity and work on understanding, collaboration, communication and assertiveness.

- Your 'research-mindedness' is an important asset that you bring to your team.

I would like to end the chapter with some positive encouragement from Marion, Children's Services Advisor and former Director of Children's Services who has a wealth of experience as a social worker, manager and head of service.

CASE STUDY **7.6**

Marion's advice

Even though the reality is that you will be working with chaotic and difficult families, focus your energy on the things that are known to produce the best outcomes for children and young people, making good use of the support and expertise of your team and other professionals. Despite what you might read in the newspapers, social work is still a fantastic job.

FURTHER READING

Payne, M (2000) *Teamwork in multiprofessional care*. Basingstoke: Macmillan.

Payne provides a useful resource for learning more about working in teams.

Research-mindedness: **www.resmind.swap.ac.uk**

To learn more about being research-minded in social work visit the above 'research-mindedness' website. The aims of this very user-friendly learning resource are to:

- help you understand what being research-minded means;

- assist you in assessing your current level of research-mindedness;

- provide you with a range of resources for improving your research-mindedness;

- support you in developing research-mindedness amongst fellow students, colleagues and other stakeholder partners or collaborators.

SCIE: **www.scie.org.uk/publications/elearning/ipiac/**

To learn more about interprofessional and inter-agency collaboration visit the website of the Social Care Institute for Excellence (SCIE) and view or download the published series of e-learning resources devoted to interprofessional and inter-agency collaboration written by Quinney *et al.* (2009), Thomas *et al.* (2009/2009a) and Whittington *et al.* (2009/2009a).

The resource titles are:

- *An introduction to interprofessional and inter-agency working.*

- *Professional identity and collaboration.*

- *Building relationships, negotiating trust and negotiating with others.*

- *Assessment of risks, needs and strengths.*

- *A model of practice and collaboration.*

- *Working collaboratively in different types of teams.*

- *The practitioner, the agency and inter-agency collaboration.*

Chapter 8

Contributing to service quality and development

Ivan Gray, Jonathan Parker and Marion Macdonald with a contribution from Angela (person who uses services)

PROFESSIONAL CAPABILITIES FRAMEWORK

This chapter will help you to demonstrate the following ASYE-level capabilities:

1. Professionalism: identify and behave as a professional social worker, committed to professional development.

    *   Identify and implement strategies for responding appropriately to concerns about practice or procedures, seeking guidance if required.

2. Values and ethics: apply social work ethical principles and values to guide professional practice.

    *   Demonstrate respectful partnership work with service users and carers, eliciting and respecting their needs and views, and promoting their participation in decision-making wherever possible.

6. Critical reflection and analysis: apply critical reflection and analysis to inform and provide a rationale for professional decision-making.

    *   Show creativity in tackling and solving problems by considering a range of options to solve dilemmas.

7. Intervention and skills: use judgement and authority to intervene with individuals, families and communities to promote independence, provide support and prevent harm, neglect and abuse.

    *   Select, use and review appropriate and timely social work interventions, informed by evidence of their effectiveness, that are best suited to the service user(s), family, carer, setting and self.

8. Contexts and organisations: engage with, inform, and adapt to changing contexts that shape practice. Operate effectively within own organisational frameworks and contribute to the development of services and organisations. Operate effectively within multi-agency and interprofessional partnerships and settings.

- Taking account of legal, operational and policy contexts, proactively engage with your own organisation and contribute to its evaluation and development.

- Be able to work within an organisation's remit and contribute to its evaluation and development.

9. Professional leadership: take responsibility for the professional learning and development of others through supervision, mentoring, assessing, research, teaching, leadership and management.

- Show the capacity for leading practice through the manner in which you conduct your professional role, your contribution to supervision and to team meetings.

- Take steps to enable the learning and development of others.

KNOWLEDGE AND SKILLS STATEMENTS

This chapter will help you demonstrate the following requirements:

Child and family:

7. Analysis, decision-making, planning and review.
10. Organisational context.

Adult:

9. Organisational context.
10. Professional ethics and leadership.

Introduction

As a newly qualified social work practitioner you may sometimes feel alone in your role. In reality, of course, you are always part of a bigger team, including all the people in your organisation that support your work and the network of interrelated services with whom you work in partnership. This is even the case for people practising as independent social workers or when you are the only social worker in the team. The quality of your individual practice, and the way people who use services experience it, will always be affected by this broader context in which your work is set. This impact can be experienced as positive or negative. So, for example, if you set up a care planning meeting and the administrative team get the invitations out too late and key people do not attend, the quality of your practice is diminished, and ultimately, those who use services lose out. If you put together a care package with people who use services but their day-care provision is poor, your assessment work and the rest of the plan may be undermined. Where services do not work together, people who use services may experience an inadequate and fragmented service that not only does not respond to their needs but can even confuse or damage them. On the other hand, good systems, relationships and service provision can greatly enhance your practice. For instance, an effective family support service or a specialist assessment can much enhance your work. Volunteers and supportive local leisure facilities can greatly improve a care package and ready access to training and developmental activities can improve the quality of your practice.

Individual practice is often integrated within organisational practices. We are perhaps best seen as members of a *community of practice* (Wenger, 1998, 2015), in which our individual perspectives, aspirations and actions form part of these wider systems and relationships. In social work, these are underpinned in England by our explicit and shared value base that holistic practice is influenced by all professional capabilities (BASW, 2015) and the new skills statements (DfE, 2014; DH, 2015). For social workers in Northern Ireland, Wales and Scotland, these are still underpinned by the National Occupational Standards for Social Work (e.g. see **http:// www.ccwales.org.uk/national-occupational-standards/**). Together they make influencing the broader context in which your practice is set central to high-quality professional practice. It starts with helping the different systems communicate and work together, i.e. *build and use effective relationships with a wide range of people, networks, communities and professionals to improve outcomes, showing an ability to manage resistance* (BASW, 2015). However, to demonstrate in your practice the capabilities and statements identified at the start of this chapter you need to reach beyond these relationships to make a more direct contribution to developing service quality.

On placement it is often hard to be able to contribute to developing service quality, especially over the long term, and it is not unusual to find that social work students tend to focus on developing their own practice and take, as given, the broader context in which it occurs. So, as a newly qualified social worker, contributing to service quality and development is likely to be identified as a key area for personal development and for this reason it is the subject of this chapter. Before exploring this important area of work it is worth making a few observations.

Learning cultures and 'collective leadership'

Chapter 2 has already explored how important it is to services that you continue to develop professionally throughout your career. Your effectiveness as a practitioner is dependent on your effectiveness as a learner and it is fundamental to the ASYE and beyond. Yet your practice will always be dependent on the resources, systems, procedures and relationships of the organisation in which you work, and the network of provision in which it operates. Personal expertise is not enough, so that beyond your continuing professional development lies the issue as to whether organisations are continually 'learning'. Do they seek continually to improve the quality of the services they provide or do they simply repeat past mistakes and failings? The likely importance of developing a learning culture has been recognised in the literature (Senge, 1990, 2006; West *et al.*, 2014).

Yet the biggest block to developing a learning culture is perhaps the power relationships that stop people contributing to problem-solving and decision-making. This has led to the development of the concept of 'collective leadership', often referred to in the literature as 'distributed leadership' (Watson, 2002; Mehra *et al.*, 2006; Gray *et al.*, 2010; Gray *et al.*, 2013; West *et al.*, 2014) where responsibility for the leadership and management of services is distributed as widely as possible within the organisation, mobilising the full expertise and the abilities of all staff to innovate and lead. In effect, in an organisation practising collective leadership, everyone is a leader or manager, including the newly qualified social worker. Regardless, every one of your actions will indeed shape the existing and emerging culture of the organisation (West *et al.*, 2014) – this can be a sobering thought.

Collective leadership is more readily practised in organisations employing social workers because they will have developed expertise and responsibility for the effective leadership and management of their cases, so it is not as hard to reach beyond this and engage them in the broader endeavour of effective leadership and the management of services. This perspective, of collective leadership, determines the aim of this chapter – to *start* the process, if it has not started already, of you developing your leadership and management skills so that you can *show the capacity for leading practice through the manner in which you conduct your professional role, your contribution to supervision and to team meetings* (BASW, 2015) and in doing so can *take steps to enable the learning and development of others* (ibid) and contribute to the development of a learning culture.

But will I be allowed to get involved?

Perhaps a big question you may ask is: will my agency or organisation allow me to be involved in service changes and development? Your contribution to the development of service quality may not be fully facilitated by your organisation. A criticism of current service provision is that we suffer from 'managerialism' (Jones *et al.*, 2004) which is viewed as the imposition of centrally determined agendas that do not allow for the involvement of staff in service development and improvement. Other commentators (e.g. Munro, 2011) have also picked up on this and the need to develop a more creative and flexible approach to service provision that enables social workers to learn from their experiences and have more freedom to exercise their professional judgement (Williams *et al.*, 2012; Gray *et al.*, 2013; Rutter and Brown, 2015).

It might be the case that you will find all your contributions encouraged, welcomed and implemented and you are already part of an organisation with a culture of learning. Most of us though will be part of a work in progress, so that contributing fully to service quality and development is aspirational. This schism between managerialism and collective leadership constitutes a polarity that needs bridging (Johnson, 1996). Managers need to offer social workers more scope to contribute and professionals also need to reach out and embrace some managerial perspectives and issues so that they can contribute to service developments. You may find this challenging as it requires grappling with the acknowledged resource constraints and demanding policy initiatives, such as the personalisation agenda (DH, 2007; Gardner, 2011), that may require significant changes in your practice. One key piece of sound advice is to ensure good alignment between your organisation's strategic objectives and your own.

Whatever your circumstances, empowered or struggling against the system, it may not be possible to promote our social work values that commit us to providing services that are as responsive as possible to the needs of people who use services, without addressing the issue of service quality and improvement. If we sometimes find our circumstances to be daunting, and the impact we might have limited, it is encouraging to remember that small changes can make a big difference. Tom Peters, the 'managing for excellence' champion, once suggested that some of the biggest service improvements can be small ones (Peters, 1989). He uses the example of a significant service improvement resulting from a team moving a filing cabinet, having worked around it for the last two years. He suggests it was a massive step forward – not in the least because the team had at last felt empowered enough to do it.

It is also worth remembering that as an agent of service improvement, a social worker is particularly well positioned. Apart from people who use services and their carers (who are the closest to the issues), you are well placed to identify and respond to problems. You will also be gaining understanding of your organisation, how the system works (or not) and how to influence teams, managers and other groups that make up the service. You are a crucial 'broker' between management, the wider organisation, networks of service provision and those that use them. You not only negotiate and secure an individual's care package; you also have the potential to broker available services and their quality (see Figure 8.1).

Herein lies an important point: if collective leadership suggests that leadership should be diffused as much as possible within an organisation, it raises the question as to whether it should be distributed to people who use services. This is the thrust of the current personalisation agenda, allowing users to lead and manage their own services (DH, 2007; Gardner, 2011). As a social worker you will play a key role in engaging both people who use services and carers in service improvements through identifying problems, designing improvements and implementing solutions. For example, this can be achieved by evaluating the effectiveness of services they receive or working with representatives of people who use services, using their expertise to bring about service improvements (see Angela's Case Study 8.1). To ensure this involvement is genuine will require you to challenge, question and change your practice and seek to change the way your organisation does things.

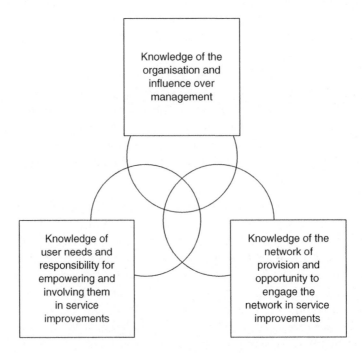

Figure 8.1   The role of the social worker as broker for service improvements

CASE STUDY 8.1

Angela's involvement in service development

Involving the public, users of services and carers, in health and social care development initiatives has been increasingly promoted in government policies in the UK and is high on the agenda of regulatory bodies (DH, 2002; DH, 2006; DH, 2007; Lowes and Hulatt, 2005; Gardner, 2011).

My own experience of involvement has developed over many years, from being a silent voice at a formal strategy meeting, to participation as one of many stakeholders, and now to an expert in my own field. As a user of mental health services, I wanted to do something positive to 'make a difference'. Initially, I was thrust into an alien environment which excluded me through its structures and jargon. The professionals did not know what to do with me. I sat at a meeting and then left. To continue, I had to question my purpose and function.

Through a user forum, I began to accept invitations to speak about my experiences. I spoke to others so that I could offer a balanced perspective of how people experienced services. I came to conclude that often what people were offered was 'service-led' rather than 'needs-led'. I wanted to communicate that the voice of the 'consumer' was key. Receiving a service appropriate to individual need made sense and was surely more cost

(Continued)

effective? My aim was not to be critical, but to simply report 'how it is' and offer constructive input on how it could be better – for both the practitioner and person using services. The practicalities of being involved proved to be a challenge. These included:

- *being required to attend meetings at 9am which involved a long journey by public transport;*

- *having no prior discussion/training to be able to participate from an informed perspective;*

- *waiting months to receive any payment for expenses;*

- *finding myself sat next to my own psychiatrist at a service review!*

It is only by voicing these difficulties that change can occur. It is not always easy when fluctuating mental health can bring periods of acute anxiety and withdrawal. In spite of this, I have worked hard to gain respect and credibility in my involvement activities and have begun to engage in meaningful dialogue with all stakeholders. I am encouraged when I have tangible evidence that I have been heard and taken seriously.

The gains of involvement are rarely financial, so what motivates me? I want services to be of a high quality and to provide good outcomes for those who use them. I want to use my years in the system in a positive way; to give something back. Through this, my confidence and sense of self-worth have significantly increased.

I started out as the token user of services – wheeled in and out at the appropriate time and my involvement was meaningless. This has developed into what I would describe as inclusive and productive partnership working.

So what are your options: how can you get involved in developing services?

There are a number of options open to you as a newly qualified social worker to become involved in the development of your organisation and service. What you need to beware of is being used either because more senior team members no longer have the capacity to develop and drive change or as a 'straw man' used to show up an inadequacy of the service.

- In your everyday work you can seek, with your team, to make immediate improvements in working practices when dealing with individual cases or systems that affect service quality.

- You can take responsibility for championing a particular aspect of a service, developing particular expertise and sharing this with your team.

- You can identify, in your everyday work and in supervision, quality issues and solutions to them that would enhance services or even new ways of working – and then get these on the team agenda.

- You can be a member of a project team or working party designing or implementing a service development that has been delegated to you.

- You can contribute to team development planning or business planning initiatives to generate improvement plans.

- You can review and evaluate a case with colleagues to learn from what went well and what went wrong, in order to improve the service (SCIE, 2012).

All the above options are dependent on how effective you are as a problem-solver. Taking a problem-solving approach to your work is the key to contributing to service improvements, to the development of your team and the wider organisation. So, what is effective problem-solving?

A problem-solving approach

Charles Handy (1993) describes managers as 'organisational GPs' – they diagnose and then prescribe treatment plans that deal with organisational disorders. They investigate problems with service quality, and formulate and implement solutions. In a collective leadership approach everyone seeks to improve service quality and contribute to organisational problem-solving, but how can we maximise our effectiveness as problem-solvers? The problem-solving process is outlined in Figure 8.2.

This cycle of activities is a logical and rational approach that brings order and control to any process. Central to the management of any task, the problem-solving process appears in many guises. It can also be called the decision-making process or the planning process – there are many variants. In social care we might re-badge it as the case planning or assessment process, while in other professions it appears as the teaching or the nursing process. The challenge is not to develop a completely new

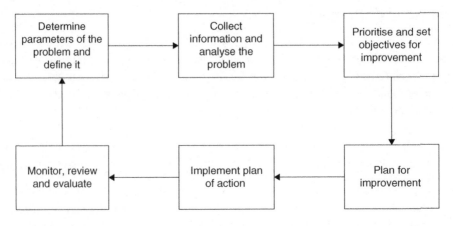

Figure 8.2   The problem-solving process

set of knowledge and skills but rather transfer knowledge and skills you already use as a case manager and apply them to services more generally. This process can be applied to just about any activity area to improve service quality; for instance, slightly re-framed it becomes the 'team development planning' or, if you like, the 'business planning process' (see Figure 8.3).

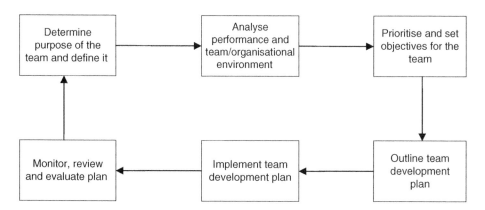

Figure 8.3 The team development planning process

An important aspect of problem-solving, as illustrated by Figures 8.2 and 8.3, is that the process is 'iterative'; there is a feedback loop that allows progress to be reviewed and changes made to problem definition and analysis. Sometimes this process is presented in a linear fashion (see Figure 8.4).

Although the lack of a feedback loop in this linear representation is a disadvantage, it does have its uses. It offers a logical structure to a written report, and could shape any recommendations you might make if you are leading or contributing to a working party exploring a quality issue. This way of working may be quite familiar to you

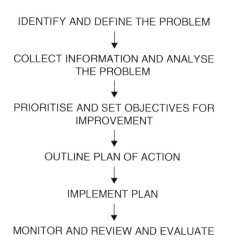

Figure 8.4 A linear representation of the problem-solving process

as a newly qualified social worker, and similar to the processes you are involved in when working with cases. Transferability of learning and skills is something that you will be become quite adept at (see Case Study 8.2).

CASE STUDY 8.2

James and the day centre

James had been discussing the services provided at a day centre attached to his office with members of that centre. They were requesting more overt involvement and a users' forum. James discussed with centre members what that forum would be like and took his ideas to his next supervision with his manager. James agreed to consider what happens in other day centres and to use his research skills from his degree to search for information on similar projects, and to take a view from those who used the day centre on the best way forward. After discussing a range of options he took a plan back to his manager and set up a forum in which all who wished to could be involved and have a say in addressing issues of concern, feed back on services offered and present ideas for future activities and projects to develop. James's manager supported him by acting as a facilitator and conduit for people using the day centre to develop the service. When his manager suggested to him he was involved in project management and developing the service, James said he simply thought he was working with those using the day centre to enable them to make choices. He had not thought that the two could be the same.

This problem-solving process can also be used more proactively, such as the basis for project management (see Figure 8.5). Rather than identifying a problem with the delivery of an existing service, it can be used to introduce new service developments.

The problem-solving process, like most models, is necessarily a simplification. Reality and application can be more complex and more problematic. Hamm (1988) describes the different levels of problem-solving as a cognitive continuum (see Table 8.1).

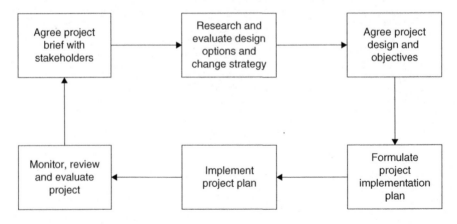

Figure 8.5   The project management process

Table 8.1   Levels of problem-solving

Judgement	Problem-solving
Individual judgement	You apply problem-solving process to a case or situation using your professional knowledge and expertise to determine a response.
Peer-aided judgement	Your assessment is agreed by your supervisor or your report and proposals become the basis for a care plan as the result of a multidisciplinary planning meeting.
Systems-aided judgement	You follow a process determined by experts and organisational/professional experience that helps you problem-solve (e.g. child protection and risk assessments, and flow charts used by advisors at a single access point).
Quasi-experimental	Pilot projects and action learning groups where a group methodically analyses a service issue and adjusts activity on the basis of findings.
Scientific research	Problem-solving where there is a clear systematic research methodology, structured information collection, verifiable analysis, and the presentation and dissemination of findings and/or outcomes.

Based on Hamm (1988)

Accepting that you may get involved in problem-solving at all levels, let us explore each of the problem-solving stages in turn and then discuss some of the broader issues.

Problem identification and definition

Applying the problem-solving process can take up a lot of resources. Therefore, direct your activity towards priorities. A useful rule for thinking about this is Pareto's 80:20 rule (MSH and Unicef, 1998). This suggests that 80 per cent of breakdowns in service quality lie with 20 per cent of the problems. Try to identify these *key* problems, rather than those that will actually have little impact on overall quality. Quality assurance systems can help identify and quantify service quality problems; business plans can generate priorities for improvement; and risk analysis can also be used to determine priority problems. Many organisations have also developed complex risk assessment processes that can help identify where services might break down (Bostock *et al.*, 2005; see also Munro, 2011).

The clearer the problem definition the more focus can be given to problem analysis, objective setting and planning. The greatest clarity comes from being able to iden-tify the problem. Performance measures may help as they quantify organisational and agency priorities; however, because they are often set top-down, they may not represent what professionals would consider to be the key performance and quality outcomes. Sometimes teams have set local performance measures that capture what they consider to be the important dimensions.

Collecting information

It has been suggested that in war and in management, the easier information is to come by, the less useful it is. A problem needs researching thoroughly, including identifying and agreeing on what constitutes evidence-based practice and sometimes interviewing stakeholders. Information collection and exploration in social work and social care can be as complicated as full-blown social research and, as such, it is time-consuming and expensive.

Often, we will operate with insufficient information, having to make judgements on the basis of what is available at the time. This can prove more costly in the long run, but in a crisis we often have little choice. In general, however, planned and methodical information collection impacts positively and directly on the effectiveness of problem-solving. It is worth remembering that the crucial information you may need to solve a problem could lie in the experiences of those stakeholders who are involved in the problem. Engage them in problem-solving and you immediately improve the quality of your information collection.

Analysis

Problems vary in their nature and demand different approaches to analysis. So, for instance, it may be possible to accurately measure and use statistical analysis to identify the causes of some problems. Yet, many problems faced by social work practitioners and managers cannot be analysed in this way and demand qualitative approaches. A combination of approaches is often necessary. To illustrate: if you want to improve the percentage of assessments completed within a timescale set by a performance measure, you may wish to interview a small number of staff to identify possible causes for delays. Then you might carry out a survey across the service so that you can target the dominant causes. Analysis can embrace a number of activities and can be very multifaceted, especially in complex social situations. Some options are shown in the box below.

Options for analysis

- *Applying social science – social science provides us with a range of different explanations for human behaviour. Each can cast a different light on an issue and also suggest a different response (Cunningham and Cunningham, 2008; Ingleby, 2006).*

- *Applying social work methodologies – different social science approaches have generated different social work methodologies and interventions. These can readily be mobilised to help you analyse management problems and interventions (see McLaughlin, 2012).*

- *Applying models of good practice – sometimes there are models of good practice that can be used to compare current practices against – e.g. see **www.skillsforcare. org.uk/Learning-development/The-ASYE-child-and-family/Case-studies.aspx**.*

- *Using standards and benchmarks – it is increasingly the case that desirable behaviour is defined by the production of detailed standards. An example of this*

---

is the national management standards from the Management Standards Centre (MSC, 2015). These can be used to judge not only individual performance but the general performance of a particular activity.

- *Analysing the change environment – analysis needs not only to address the problem but the capacity of individuals, work teams and organisations to implement change and how the change might be managed effectively and successfully (e.g. see SCIE, 2015).*

- *Systems analysis – if organisations or services are viewed as interacting social systems, then analysis should approach problems as multidimensional and caused by the interaction of several systems, all of which may need to be addressed. The impact of an intervention in one part of the system might be explored on the system as a whole. Otherwise a solution in one area may create a problem elsewhere (Fish et al., 2008).*

- *Action learning and appreciative enquiry – it is possible to work with a team helping you analyse a problem and identify possible causes or build on strengths and capabilities to bring improvement (Hart and Bond, 1995; Bryman, 2015). Working with the multidisciplinary team reviewing a case to both identify what has gone well as well as what might be improved on, as recommended by Munro, is an example of this (Munro, 2011; SCIE, 2012).*

Setting objectives

A common approach to objective setting and planning is that they should be SMART.

- S – specific;

- M – measurable;

- A – achievable;

- R – realistic;

- T – timely.

(See Parker and Bradley (2014, pp78–88) for an application to social work planning.)

This is a popular formulation which was and still is contrasted with a tendency in social care to be inexact, or to focus on the 'art' rather than the 'science' of social care. As a mnemonic it has value but should not be used slavishly, as 'process' as well as 'outcome' objectives do matter, particularly in a value-orientated activity like social care. To demonstrate, an objective such as: *To ensure that stakeholders are committed and motivated in implementing the change* is not 'SMART', but it might be crucial in determining the success of the service improvement. One could argue that it could be made measurable, but this might be an unnecessary effort that does not do justice to the qualitative nature of the objective. It certainly will not be hard to reach for evidence that stakeholders are engaged and motivated.

It is important to remember that objectives serve two crucial purposes. They structure both planning and evaluation. Each objective should have a plan of action consisting of the actual steps that will be taken to achieve it, and monitoring may focus on the implementation of this plan of action. Evaluation should involve a review of each objective. Objectives can have different priorities. Some may need to be identified as 'success criteria' and can be separated out, as such, to provide the crucial measures against which a problem-solving activity or project can be evaluated.

Plan of action

As we noted previously, it should be possible to link each element of a plan of action to an objective or objectives. A simple plan identifies what will be done, who will do it and when they will do it by. However, there are more complicated planning tools such as bar and Gantt charts (e.g. see **www.businessballs.com/project.htm**) that can assist with planning more complex implementations and facilitate monitoring (also see Walker *et al.*, 2008 for a review of useful management tools in practice education). There are also opportunities here to identify creative ways of achieving objectives, rather than relying on standardised responses. Involving your team and other stakeholders in planning can often generate creative options and build commitment.

Risk analysis can be used to identify and gauge the possible causes of breakdown in an improvement project. Sometimes, when a risk is judged to be considerable a contingency plan can be developed that can be quickly put in place when a problem is identified. When broad, alternative options for achieving an objective are identified, techniques such as a decision-making matrix can be used to try and make an informed judgement about the best way forward.

It is good practice to include an objective that encompasses the monitoring and evaluation of any implementation. This should be planned for in advance to avoid the tendency to leave evaluation to the last minute and to do it badly, thereby excluding any huge gains that can be made from learning from mistakes. As a newly qualified worker, the more time spent on planning, the better. It will help you to identify success and see where things do not always work as planned. In this way, you can monitor your progress and development.

Monitoring and evaluation

It is all too common *not* to monitor and/or evaluate. This can have a number of unfortunate outcomes, including the stalling of any implementation. It is essential to determine who will monitor, and how. Early identification of difficulties in implementation can often lead to timely resolution. Disruption or re-thinking should be planned into the work.

Monitoring can be aided by establishing milestones. These are key dates along the 'journey' of implementation that pinpoint when crucial activities will have been completed. This gives a welcome structure to monitoring, and a project or development team can use these 'way marks' to meet and consider progress and respond to problems.

Evaluation is a review of a project's effectiveness. It should explore each of the objectives in turn, as well as asking whether the problem as a whole has been responded to or whether the aim of the project has been achieved. Any evaluation can raise insights to inform other developments within an organisation. In other words, it is as essential as the problem-solving process is to the functioning of learning organisations. As implementation or work on the problem or project is likely to be ongoing it can allow for re-analysis and the iterative setting of new objectives and a new plan. In effect, it allows us to learn from experience and continuously improve services. Activity 8.1 considers how you monitor and evaluate your own work.

Going beyond objectives and performance measurement: evaluating service outcomes

It can be argued that while it is important we try and measure activities, perhaps by target setting, success criteria and performance measurement, a potentially negative impact may be that the real purpose of changes and improvements are lost. This has led to services attempting to reach beyond measurable outputs to 'service outcomes'. This can be at an individual, community or societal level and demands thinking further than whether a child's needs assessment was carried out on time and according to the relevant performance criteria to evaluating the impact of the assessment in respect of meeting their needs and improving their long-term quality of their life. The next stage beyond this would be to ask if the range of services provided were having a wider social impact in enhancing the quality of life of a community.

Evaluating service outcomes is much harder than identifying if project objectives have been achieved or measuring outputs (e.g. how many assessments were provided). Going back to Table 8.1 and the different levels of problem-solving, determining service outcomes can involve us in complex, long-term and expensive social research. Yet it is important that we try and reach beyond the numbers to the features of a service that really determine its quality.

ACTIVITY 8.1

How do you monitor and evaluate your own work?

Think about your own work as a newly qualified social worker. Write down some of the ways you monitor and evaluate your work. Consider what you have learned when you evaluate your work and what you have learned when you have not evaluated your work.

(Continued)

Remember, effective evaluations:

- *are planned;*

- *evidenced;*

- *explore the overall aim of the intervention, each objective and any success criteria;*

- *involve key stakeholders;*

- *are the basis for personal and organisational learning and development;*

- *try and evaluate service outcomes.*

If you are interested in learning more about service evaluation and the political and partici-patory functions it can have, try reading Ovretveit (2014), Everitt and Hardiker (1996), Rossi et al. (2004) and/or Unrau et al. (2007). In respect of evaluating your own work, which can then be applied to your organisation's services, consider the work of Ashencaen Crabtree et al. (2012, 2015) and Parker et al. (2012, 2014) in exploring the learning and practice of cultural competences and reflective development of social work students on placement in unfamiliar places.

Some issues arising from the problem-solving process

The problem-solving process is not, of course, a panacea. It will not solve all problems you may face in contributing to the development of services and improving service quality, although it is an essential tool and method. Thinking critically, some of the issues with it are:

- *It oversimplifies*: it can be argued that the basic model (Figure 8.2) oversimplifies reality and that in practice actual problem-solving is very different. For instance, things don't happen stage by stage. Information comes in all the time leading to changes in analysis, plans and objectives – in an altogether much more fluid process.

We argue that it is important to use a simple model to help order our thinking and actions, and of course we accept that all models by their nature simplify to provide structure. Accepting that the actual process of assessment is more complicated, with a practitioner moving flexibly around the cycle, does not mean that formal analysis, objectives and agreed plans are not necessary.

- *It's too positivistic and too individualistic*: the approach can be seen as assuming a knowable objective reality that can be analysed and changed rationally. An alternative interpretation often cited in social care is that meaning is created by people, so that the process of negotiating the definition of a problem, agreeing objectives and a plan of action are more important than 'scientific' analysis.

This may be the case in public services, where there could be several stakeholders with different problem definitions, analyses and objectives that have to be recognised and reconciled. However, the importance of mobilising groups and communities as problem-solvers could be seen as the pathway to effectiveness in any organisation. Senge's (1990) formulation of a learning organisation emphasises the importance of group problem-solving as does total quality management and theories of Communities of Practice (Wenger, 1998, 2015). Case planning meetings, reviews and case conferences can all be seen as exercises in group problem-solving. For instance, a good chairperson is likely to consciously try and follow the problem-solving process, encouraging people to share information and analyse it rather than jumping straight to a possible plan of action.

- *Need for criticality and creativity*: A problem for a professional wanting to contribute to the leadership and management of the service by improving service quality is, to use the language of the Professional Capabilities Framework, how you *show creativity in tackling and solving problems, by considering a range of options to solve dilemmas* (BASW, 2015). Argyris and Schön (1978) suggest the need for a double feedback loop to achieve critical problem-solving (see Figure 8.6). That is to say, the culture of an organisation influences the problem-solving process so that everyday identification of problems and responses to them are standardised and based on hidden assumptions that define culture – *the way we do things around here.* A double feedback loop challenges these value assumptions and power relationships, e.g. who defines the problem; how it is defined; how causes are identified; how objectives are prioritised;

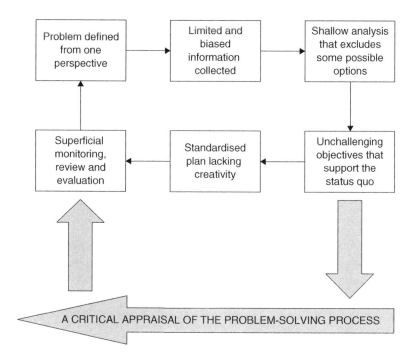

Figure 8.6   A double feedback loop

which systems are not challenged; which plans are eventually adopted; and whether carers and people who use the services have been consulted and involved. Although limited resources can restrict options considered in the plan of action, the feedback loop can also be used to challenge the efficacy of the process itself, e.g. was the definition of the problem clear enough; were enough sources of information used; and to what extent was the analysis critical?

We have already discussed some of the other options for developing creative problem-solving involving people, particularly with service users and the multidisciplinary team, learning from successes as well as problems. Another option is researching and learning from what others have done. This can involve identifying evidence-based practice, e.g. SCIE's (2015) latest organisational change resource (see **www. scie.org.uk/publications/elearning/organisational-change-in-social-care/**) but can also involve learning from other disciplines. For instance, NHS Improving Quality (see **www.nhsiq.nhs.uk/**) and the Institute for Healthcare Improvement (see **http:// ihi.org**) in the USA have an excellent range of quality and service improvement tools on their websites that you will find very helpful.

- *Learning styles and problem-solving*: According to your learning style (see **www. talentlens.co.uk/develop/peter-honey-learning-style-series**), you might be seen to emphasise different parts of the problem-solving process to the detriment of others. For instance, a theorist might enjoy the analysis, a reflector review and evaluation, a pragmatist the planning and an activist the implementation. Effective problem-solving, and therefore effective leadership and management, may demand a balanced style. This critical self-awareness can be seen as an extension of the double feedback loop and encompass questioning how your personal history and value base might influence your approach.

Applying the problem-solving process to your team or unit

Team development involves developing the ability of the team to respond to whatever it might be faced with and to improve its systems, processes and relationships. Or if you like, it is about building the capacity of your team. Although we have already touched on this issue in Chapter 7 it is worth noting that team development planning is often now called business planning and is about determining the objectives the team seeks to achieve.

The problem-solving process can underpin any methodical approach to managing an activity. What often varies is the analysis. So if we explore team development or business planning, and refer again to Figure 8.3, the second box, 'analyse performance and the team/organisational environment', will probably be your biggest challenge as a newly qualified social worker. The factors you can draw on in this analysis are outlined in Figure 8.7.

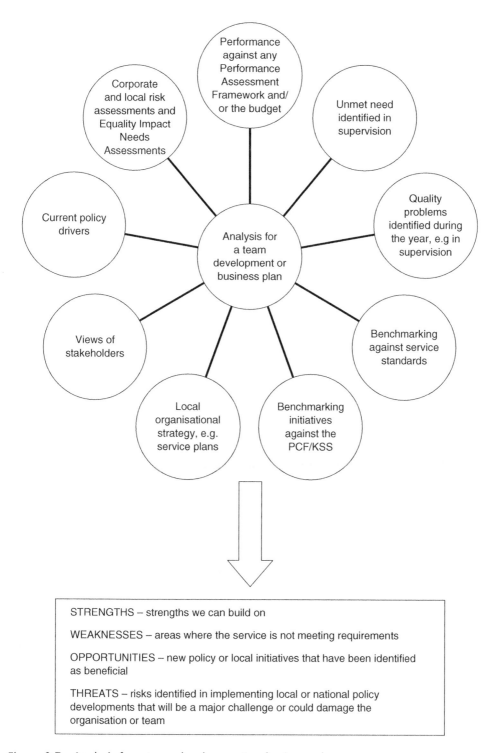

Figure 8.7   Analysis for a team development or business plan

There are a number of things to note in how we have represented Figure 8.7.

- We have emphasised the involvement of all stakeholders. Each has a part to play in the service, either as contributors or beneficiaries. Not only are they the best source of information but are crucial in agreeing and implementing any future plans. People who use services are the most important stakeholders.

- Making judgements about previous organisational performance involves collecting information. Some information is readily available as performance measures but others will need collecting as they arise, e.g. out of supervision.

- As a team you will need to keep abreast of national policy initiatives.

- Your manager will play an important role of feeding you organisational information to which you may not have ready access. There may be local organisational strategies and service plans that you need to incorporate into any business planning.

- You will probably need to carry out some benchmarking activity such as reviewing team performance against the service standards for your area of work.

- Some 'good practice models' are worth considering (see following section on learning organisations).

- We suggest that the different factors feed what is often called a 'SWOT' analysis to identify key objectives that, as in Figure 8.3, are translated into the detail that becomes the team's development or business plan.

- If you and your team are not ready or able to get involved in a full team development/business planning process then try and identify a simple team service improvement which you all agree is a priority and can all contribute to (see Case Study 8.3). Sometimes, once you start reviewing some aspects of service provision and thinking about options that might better meet need, it can become part of how a team works and can develop over time.

CASE STUDY 8.3

A carer's support group

Karla was concerned that her new team never really looked at the gaps in locally available services, but based care plans on what was assumed to be there. She believed there could be a much wider range of services and that some big gaps could be filled. In supervision, she began to identify what she thought were unmet needs and talking about projects she had become involved in on placement as a student, or knew colleagues had been involved in. Her team manager started exploring this in supervision with others, and after discussion in a team meeting it was suggested that a carers' support group would be valuable. Karla and others pointed out that it was important to be sure what carers wanted and she started working with a colleague to talk to carers about what might be developed locally to offer them more support.

Learning organisations

As we move toward the end of this final chapter, it is important to address an issue we raised earlier. Another approach to contributing to service quality is to develop your team and organisation via continual learning, i.e. one that mobilises its resources to continually learn and develop itself. In 2004, the Social Care Institute of Excellence designed an audit tool to help us develop our organisations as learning organisations (SCIE, 2004). There is an adapted version of this audit presented in the box below, after the final case study. Although this self-assessment pack is classed as 'out of date' by SCIE, we believe the questions it raises are still relevant and it may be worthwhile using them with your team. You may, as Zoe found out (Case Study 8.4), draw different conclusions in analysing your team compared with the wider organisation. You may also end up with an improvement agenda for your team that includes the need to influence the wider organisation. Remembering the importance of aligning your personal objectives to those of your organisation, reflect on how your development needs might contribute to organisational and agency development.

CASE STUDY 8.4

Learning cultures

Team meetings had got rather 'flat'; the dynamism had gone and people began to miss them. Zoe's manager mentioned this in supervision and said she was looking at ways of 'livening them up a bit'. Zoe suggested they use the SCIE learning organisational audit to review how they worked as a team. They accessed the SCIE website and used the materials to generate debate in a team meeting. The discussion got a bit heated, but the team were reminded of the many things they did well, as well as finding some areas where they could make improvements. They concluded that they were more of a learning community than the wider organisation. Her manager thought she might take these findings to the management team meetings despite being a little unsure how well they would be received.

ACTIVITY 8.2

Learning organisation audit

On a five-point Likert scale ranging from strongly agree to strongly disagree, rate how the following statements apply to the information systems used in your organisation.

- *There are effective information systems for both internal and external communication.*

- *The organisation makes good use of IT to improve information exchange and management.*

(Continued)

147

ACTIVITY *8.2* *continued*

- *Information is freely available.*
- *Where possible, information is shared openly with people who use services and their carers.*
- *Policies and procedures are meaningful and understood by all.*

Using the same Likert scale rate how the following statements apply to the structure of your organisation.

- *Feedback and participation of people who use services and carers is actively sought.*
- *Team working, learning and utilising all staff skills are integral to the organisation.*
- *There is cross-organisational, collaborative and partnership working.*

Again, using the same Likert scale, rate how the following statements apply to the culture of your organisation.

- *There is a system of shared beliefs, values, goals and objectives.*
- *Development of new ideas and methods is encouraged.*
- *An open learning environment allows the opportunity to test innovative practice.*
- *New evidence and research are considered and incorporated into practice.*
- *Ideas and proposals can come from any part of the organisation – not just 'top-down'.*
- *People who identify problems are not blamed.*

Again, using the same Likert scale, rate whether the following statements are present in your workplace.

- *There is a commitment to continuous personal and career development for all staff and by all staff.*
- *Individual learning styles and learning needs are responded to.*
- *A good range of formal and informal learning opportunities are open to all.*
- *A high quality of individual supervision and support is offered.*

And finally, using the same Likert scale, rate whether the following leadership strengths are established in the organisation you work for.

- *The organisation develops and improves services wherever it can.*
- *Leaders model the openness, risk-taking and reflection necessary for learning.*

(Continued)

- *Leaders ensure that the organisation has the resources and capacity to learn, change and develop.*

- *Learning and development opportunities are linked to organisational objectives.*

These statements have been adapted from the SCIE website and are used with permission within this book (see SCIE, 2006a).

Summary of key points

- We hope the perspectives we have presented in this chapter will help you build on your professional skills and increase your influence over service quality and development by being able to contribute more to the leadership and management of services. We know that some of you will find that your organisation does not encourage you to play a full part in this, but you will always be able to make some improvements and may find some ways forward by which you can help them change features of their culture that are unhelpful and move towards achieving the features of a collective leadership culture, one where continual learning is welcomed.

- Whatever your experience, we hope you share with us the perspective that service development and quality improvement cannot, and should not, be separated out from professional practice. This means that leadership and management skills are part of professional capability and skills development, and that they should feature strongly in your continuing professional development.

- The essence of empowerment and collective leadership is, perhaps, best seen as not just professional involvement and leadership but also the involvement of people who use services and carers in the leadership and development of services. At the very least this should involve opportunity to play a part in leading their own care plan, but their potential and the potential of our services will only be fully reached when they are enabled to contribute to building service quality and determining the future of services more generally.

FURTHER READING

Everitt, A and Hardiker, P (1996) *Evaluating for good practice*. Basingstoke: Macmillan.

This small book offers a critical and value-based approach to evaluation of social work services and individual practice in the UK. It recognises the complex political settings in which social work is practised.

Ovretveit, J (2014) *Evaluating improvement and implementation for health*. Maidenhead: OUP.

If you are looking for a book outside the social work zone to expand your horizons and knowledge in terms of evaluation then try this text.

Walker, J, Crawford, K and Parker, J (2008) *Practice education in social work: a handbook for practice teachers, assessors and educators*. Exeter: Learning Matters.

This is a book written specifically for practice educators. It examines contemporary theories and knowledge in practice learning, teaching and education, with a clear emphasis on developing the skills and practice of individual social workers performing these roles.

Williams, S, Rutter, L and Gray, I (2012) *Promoting individual and organisational learning in social work*. London: Sage/Learning Matters.

Offers help in leading and enabling others and contributing to the development of communities of practice and learning organisations.

Appendix 1

Writing towards ASYE: advice from an experienced lecturer

Melanie Forsyth-Smith

PROFESSIONAL CAPABILITIES FRAMEWORK

This appendix will help you to demonstrate the following ASYE-level capabilities:

5. Knowledge: apply knowledge of social sciences, law and social work practice theory.
6. Critical reflection and analysis: apply critical reflection and analysis to inform and provide a rationale for professional decision-making.
7. Intervention and skills: use judgement and authority to intervene with individuals, families and communities to promote independence, provide support and prevent harm, neglect and abuse.

KNOWLEDGE AND SKILLS STATEMENTS

This appendix will help you demonstrate the following requirements:

Child and family:

7. Analysis, decision-making, planning and review.

Adult:

8. Supervision, critical reflection and analysis.

What follows is a summary of the hints and tips I have amassed from almost 15 years of supporting thousands of practitioners who have risen to the challenge of completing post-qualifying training programmes – mostly, I must say, with the dedication, goodwill and optimism that I believe epitomise the unique qualities of our profession. Most of these have been students completing the first stage of a professional development programme, e.g. a Consolidation or Graduate Certificate in Professional

Practice programme. In my experience, the vast majority have enjoyed these programmes as a positive professional development opportunity. Although previously some may have viewed the post-qualifying framework as yet another imposed and demanding hurdle to jump in order to remain credible, or even employed, the value of these programmes has been widely recognised by practitioners and employers alike as being essential to support and encourage the ongoing development of practitioners, and to reinforce a culture of lifelong learning within practice that will support them throughout their careers.

Academically assessed professional training places demands on practitioners, who are in effect engaged in 'work-based learning'. Newly qualified social workers are not, after all, like the average student, responsible only for meeting the demands of an academic programme. In recognition of this, the development of the ASYE programme has been a positive step in providing newly qualified workers with an appropriate environment in which to consolidate and develop their capability and skills, offering a well-supported and carefully structured framework within their workplace, in which to embed their early continuous professional development.

The recent review and revision of the ASYE programme (Skills for Care, 2015) has attempted to strengthen this scheme into a well-structured and consistent process that provides all newly qualified social workers with the opportunity to further develop skills that will significantly enhance their professional practice. Some of these skills I intend to focus on in this appendix, as I believe they are skills that are essential to good practice but tend to be undervalued in the process and procedure-driven world of everyday social work, and therefore can be the easiest to lose sight of. The four main topic areas of this appendix (critical reflection; reflective writing; what and how to write; and the use of theory) have been chosen specifically to support you through the demands of the world of the ASYE and your early development as a professional.

Critical reflection

Critical reflection can be seen as a challenging and time-consuming activity that is not often facilitated within normal working environments; the workplace appears to be becoming more and more procedure and regulation-based (Fook and Askeland, 2007) demanding that practitioners must be *ready for, not critical of, practice* (Preston-Shoot, 2000a, p88). This helps to explain why I have often found that students on post-qualifying training programmes approach reflective writing and its demand for critical reflection and self-evaluation with trepidation. Critical reflection, to any useful depth, requires time and space which is not readily available to the busy practitioner – nor is it often encouraged. A sense of confusion about what critical reflection means is also not uncommon as there appear to be as many interpretations of the term. Perhaps some helpful interpretations include:

- *working through for oneself, afresh, a problem* (Kneale, 2003, p3);
- *weighing up the arguments for and against* (Cottrell, 1999, p188);
- *a sustained and systematic process of examination* (Moon, 2005, p5).

These readily make sense when applied to reflecting on practice situations. However, critical thinking is a developmental process in itself (Moon, 2005). So, your social work degree should have enabled your first steps in this direction and the ASYE will certainly help you to develop your skills further. There are many models of critical reflection encouraging the questioning of practice to differing levels of analysis (e.g. Johns, 1998; Gibbs, 1988), and just as many textbooks which discuss them (many of which will be listed within this book's references for your future perusal). These can be very helpful in familiarising yourself with the wide variety of reflective tools on offer. However, I encourage practitioners initially to adapt one model that works for them, within their own context of practice experience, which may be a model that they have used and found helpful in the past.

I like to simplify and have used my experience of working alongside practitioners on our programmes to devise a simple starting process for analysing own practice to help identify the relevant factors for fuller reflection. This model uses simple questions starting with 'What', 'Why' and 'How' and repeats them, providing a series of questions with each one prompting a different focus for a fuller discussion of the factors identified.

- *What* did you do? This prompts **description** – to introduce the scenario for analysis with brief relevant background information, the actions taken and decisions made.

- *Why* did you do it? This prompts **explanation** – identifying what informed your understanding and decision-making – consider your role and responsibility, reasoning and rationale, professional ethics and values and the knowledge you applied.

- *How* did you do it? This prompts **examination** – a critical review of your activity, the methods, models, skills and anti-oppressive practice that you applied.

- *How* did it go? This prompts the **evaluation** process – evaluating the effectiveness of practice relating to desired or expected outcomes, leading to an honest, objective appraisal and self-evaluation – what went well and what went wrong?

- *Why* did it go like that? This prompts **critical reflection** – a deeper review of the effectiveness of practice, asking why did things go well or not so well? Reviewing initial reasoning, understanding and decision-making, the relevance of methods used and your own application of knowledge and skills, to identify strengths and areas of weakness.

- *What* did you learn from this? This prompts **conclusions** – how future practice will be strengthened/changed from the deeper or new understanding gained from the process of reflecting in depth, and why?

These questions encourage an examination of your own practice, encouraging you to explain and evaluate your own actions and decisions rather than evaluating and reflecting only upon the events. This reflection entails self-evaluation; a process that I find can elicit a state of nervous anxiety from even the most efficient and competent practitioner, yet to evaluate the effectiveness of your own practice is one of the essential skills of a good practitioner as well as an expectation of many current programmes, including the ASYE.

I acknowledge that it can be daunting for the newly qualified worker to actually admit, through self-evaluation, to not knowing something or to acknowledge any area of weakness. After all, if you have just completed two or three intensive and demanding years of university training you will have had to extensively prove your capability to qualify as a social worker. Of course, it is always said that qualification is just the start of the development of a practitioner and this is never truer than in the field of social work. Indeed, this is clearly acknowledged through the introduction of the Professional Capabilities Framework, outlining the increasingly higher levels of professional capability required as practitioners develop throughout their careers (BASW, 2015). It is therefore essential that the newly qualified social worker becomes comfortable with the need to critically and honestly self-evaluate at a very early stage of their career. However, thinking critically must not be about feeling threatened or inadequate (Rutter and Brown, 2015) – quite the opposite in fact. And as I usually stress within workshops when encouraging practitioners to critically reflect upon their own practice, we cannot be called upon to work perfectly, as there are no perfect solutions out there to find (Rutter and Brown, 2015). Good practice is about recognising uncertainty and working with it.

Conversely, I have found that practitioners are often reticent to recognise their own strengths and practice competence. In my view, this is partly due to an organisational culture of professional evaluation that only responds publicly after high profile media cases, and which otherwise lives quietly with widespread misunderstanding and misinterpretation of what social workers are and do. This has led to a profession that evaluates defensively rather than positively. As a result we can be slow, reluctant even, to acknowledge our own strengths and skills. Also, a practitioner's skill base develops gradually and can therefore go unnoticed. The many skills that are required for day-to-day practice become a part of a practitioner's professional 'self', in that they become second nature, being honed and developed through experience – in essence, being practised in practice. For instance, skills such as those involved in communicating, engaging and developing relationships are, I believe, particularly prone to being unnoticed and undervalued, often by everyone except the recipient of them. I personally find it very interesting that I regularly see many areas of skill – such as communicating, reflecting, negotiating, valuing and respecting others – being very ably demonstrated by the practitioners that attend my workshops, through their engagement with our discussions. Indeed I cannot help but notice, appreciate and be constantly reassured by the high calibre of these skills that I witness during these sessions.

Trevithick (2012, p46) provides a lexicon of 80 skills and interventions reflecting the expectations of competence and capability, and revisiting this and other such textbooks is strongly recommended to help you in the process of identifying your own skills that may have already become embedded in your day-to-day practice. Such texts will also remind you of the variety of practice approaches that may have become a part of your tacit toolbox and will help you revisit and identify your use of these approaches that are often, again, intuitively but very skilfully melded together to meet the needs of your service user(s) and their situation.

Discussion with your supervisor, line manager, and colleagues can also help this self-evaluation process. Most post-qualifying professional development programmes require a 'third party' assessment of competence which will involve others in a positive evaluation process to highlight your strengths, and it is often easier for others to identify and name your areas of strength, knowledge and capability than it is for you yourself. The ASYE assessment process will therefore hopefully encourage and support your own ability to self-evaluate. Recognising, acknowledging and valuing your own professional progress is, I believe, a very important part of developing as a competent and confident practitioner. So, this critical reflection and self-evaluation needs to be recorded and discussed in written form, and this is where my next topic, reflective writing, comes in.

Reflective writing

Writing about practice and for practice are not unfamiliar skills for social work practitioners, but the term 'reflective writing' introduces another skill level. As Jenny Moon (2005) acknowledges, reflective writing is an important developmental exercise, enabling the writer to literally take another look at practice, using the processes involved in transferring thoughts to paper, to clarify, decipher and gain a deeper understanding. Reflective writing refers to the processes involved in writing that can be utilised as means in themselves to help us learn from our experiences (Rolfe *et al.*, 2011, p55). As already identified, critical reflection in practice has become an expectation of current qualifying programmes, and is now firmly embedded in the expectations of career progression through the capabilities framework. This has undoubtedly contributed to a stronger culture of critical reflection as a basic and essential requirement for today's social work practitioner. The writing of critically reflective assignments has thus *become commonplace as a means to verify the achievement of competence in practice arenas* (Rolfe *et al.*, 2011, p52), but it is important to recognise that reflective writing is not only a means for assessment, but also an opportunity to learn. In fact, it is acknowledged that critical reflection can be developed through the process of reflective writing (Rolfe *et al.*, 2011). The current structure of the ASYE programme expects the newly qualified social worker to reflect upon their experience and development through specific reflective writing tasks, as outlined for instance in the critical reflection log introduced by Skills for Care (2015a). Therefore, writing about your own practice to support the critical thinking process is not a new idea. I agree with Moon (2005) that the production of a paper version of your thoughts is the starting point for a review of the critical thinking process. Early on, I encourage practitioners to start writing down some of the ideas they may wish to discuss as they begin to analyse practice in relation to programme requirements – my mantra being *to get something down on paper*. The use of tools such as Bruce's Spidergram (2013) mentioned in the final section of this appendix in more detail really come into their own here. These jottings help the practitioner to begin the exploration process necessary for critical reflection, e.g. deciding what is important enough to be written down, identifying themes, choosing the areas for deeper examination, and beginning the analysis and organising the often overwhelming amount of potential material that most practitioners find when they start to think critically about practice. It is a process where *writing most clearly interacts with thinking and learning* (Moon, 2005, p13). So, reflective writing reflects and supports the development of skills in critical reflection. Now I turn to 'what to write and how to write it'.

What to write – and how to write it

The assignments that are generally expected within assessed work for the ASYE and other professional development programmes are often in the form of reflective evaluations of your own practice, and these mostly require the practitioner to write in the first person. This is, of course, not the norm for many academic assignments, but is relevant, in my opinion essential, for demonstrating the self-awareness, analysis and critique required in writing reflectively about practice (Rutter and Brown, 2015).

Exemplars of written work from previous successful portfolios (often provided with university programme documentation) will show that there are different styles of reflective academic writing, each one personal to the author. Your own style will develop as you practise. Personally, I prefer a writing style that allows me to grasp the meaning of the sentence upon a first read – preferably without the use of a dictionary. Academic-speak has its place, of course, but my advice to the ASYE practitioner is to keep your writing simple, keep it focused and state the obvious. Identify early on what you are going to write about, and, equally importantly, what you are going to leave out. An analysis of practice, the type of assignment often required to evidence post-qualifying development on a professional development programme, is not a 'case study'. Instead, the focus is on providing a detailed examination of an example of your professional practice, rather than writing a more superficial overview of many events. As Fook and Askeland (2007, p521) observe, these examples are normally 'critical incidents'; a specific and concrete example of some piece of practice which was significant for the participant. The bulk of the account should consist of the in-depth examination of why and how you did what you did, your recognition of the influences and constraints upon your actions and an evaluation of your practice and its outcome. But where does theory fit in?

Theory? What theory?

The skills and knowledge base used, incorporating methods, models, legislation, policy, theory, research, values and professional ethics, should automatically be identified through the reflective process described above. It still surprises me how often I am met by an uncomfortable silence from practitioners confronted by the requirement to link theory to practice – a requirement that, although running explicitly through the social work education framework, is still often met with a response of 'I know it, but I can't tell you exactly what it is'.

This reaction is understandable in as much as the theory base for social work is extraordinarily wide. No one theory, method, study, model, paradigm, perspective or approach 'fits all' in social work practice – or even comes close, as we have to make sense of *multiple perspectives gathered from a range of different sources* (Trevithick, 2012, p27). This is why as a profession we draw on many areas of knowledge from a variety of disciplines, particularly those that align with our own professional value base. But although we use theory as a starting point, we adapt and develop our ideas in response to changing scenarios. This type of learning tends to be known as practice wisdom (Trevithick, 2012) or more intuitive, tacit knowledge (Gabbay and le May, 2004) which is related to the *knowledge gained from watching what colleagues do, trial and error, reflective practice, peer approval, client satisfaction and so on* (Pawson *et al.*, 2003, p11). This to me sounds very close to the learning that takes place very early on in the newly qualified practitioner's career, so perhaps it should not be surprising that many practitioners find that *much of this experiential knowledge and theory-in-use is extremely difficult to articulate* (Rolfe *et al.*, 2001, p12). To do so requires us to take the time to stand back from our practice and reflect on it at a deeper level, asking: 'What do I know about this situation/person/issue? How do I know that? How does that knowledge guide me in my actions and decision-making?' in order to identify our own personal knowledge base. The developmental supervision process inbuilt within the ASYE year should provide the opportunity for this type of reflection, which is so important but often lost in the murky waters of day-to-day practice.

There are several tools which can help in the teasing out of the many and varied areas of knowledge that often merge together in a sometimes seemingly vague but nonetheless powerful perception of what is going on and what we should do next in a practice situation. For instance, Pamela Trevithick, (2012, p33) provides a very clear and coherent *practice knowledge framework* which I recommend as a useful tool for identifying and evaluating the many differing areas and types of knowledge that can contribute to the understanding of a practice scenario. Alternatively, Bruce (2013, p90) offers a spidergram to guide the identification and organisation of the knowledge that we most rely on in a particular practice situation. Such tools for exploration can be very useful in enabling the often seemingly impossible process of identifying and evaluating the impact of our considerable ways of 'knowing' in practice.

Once you have identified it, and are examining and explaining your use of knowledge in practice, please do not leave the reader to make the links between what you have done and why you have chosen to do it – make this very clear. For instance, if you have chosen a certain method of assessment, communication or intervention over another because it is more empowering, respectful or more likely to enable the client to have their thoughts and wishes heard, then clearly say so. Where you have compared and anticipated the consequences of using one method of working over another before deciding what to do; or have considered one branch of knowledge or research to be more applicable in the specific situation in question than another, then clearly explain this thinking process. Where you have recognised, in revisiting and evaluating your practice, that you did some particularly good value-based work, used strong and well-developed skills or extended your knowledge of theory or research – again, please say so. Don't assume that the reader will automatically recognise this – tell them yourself! This type of writing, with clear explanation and evaluation, will significantly enhance your ability to show how your critical thinking is guiding your practice and will hopefully lead to your gaining both the increased respect and possible awe of your supervisor/manager, and a higher grade in your written assessment!

In summary, you need to make sure that you clearly and fully explain your practice, as there is no place for subtlety in reflective writing.

Summary of key points

- The main encouragement from this appendix is that critical thinking and writing about this thinking is not as daunting as it may seem. Actually, you are always thinking critically as you practise. Writing about this thinking is just another way of expressing and acknowledging how critical reflection supports your practice.

- And you are always using theory too. This might be so embedded in your thinking and responses that it has already become 'tacit knowledge' or 'practice wisdom' – but with a bit of gentle exploration and relating these thoughts to sources of learning, you should be able to appreciate just how much theory you are applying.

- You are constantly learning and this does not end with qualifying, ASYE or years of experience. As a practitioner, you will take something from every practice experience. It may take time and effort to uncover this, but it will be there. The more you explore this learning, the more valid and valuable it will be to you. Make it a habit to self-evaluate and be willing to acknowledge the good and the not so good of your practice – it will really support your career development.

- Through my work on CPD programmes, I am very aware of the high quality day-to-day work that is going on as practitioners provide an excellent service to a huge number and variety of individuals in need. One of the joys of my role is the ability to acknowledge this in my feedback and to congratulate practitioners on a job well done. I sincerely hope you enjoy your early career development.

FURTHER READING

Rolfe, G, Freshwater, D and Jasper, M (2011) *Critical reflection in practice: generating knowledge for care*, 2nd edn. Hants: Palgrave.

This provides an excellent discussion of how to develop critical reflection and, in particular, reflective writing skills, through models, methods and reflective writing exercises.

Rutter, L and Brown, K (2015) *Critical thinking and professional judgement for social work*, 4th edn. London: Sage/Learning Matters.

This provides not only a very readable overview of the practical application of thinking skills, but also excellent guidance on writing reflective academic assignments.

Trevithick, P (2012) *Social work skills and knowledge: a handbook for practice*, 3rd edn. London: Sage.

This provides an excellent review of the knowledge and skills base of practice and a very useful series of appendices summarising social work models and approaches.

Appendix 2

Using written skills: translating your learning from university to practice in developing case recording

Jonathan Parker and Angela Parker with Emma Crawford (NQSW)

PROFESSIONAL CAPABILITIES FRAMEWORK

This appendix will help you to demonstrate the following ASYE-level capability:

7. Intervention and skills: use judgement and authority to intervene with individuals, families and communities to promote independence, provide support and prevent harm, neglect and abuse.

KNOWLEDGE AND SKILLS STATEMENTS

This appendix will help you demonstrate the following requirements:

Child and family:
2. Communication.
6. Child and family assessment.
7. Analysis, decision-making, planning and review.

Adult:
3. Person-centred practice.
6. Effective assessments and outcome based support planning.

Introduction

Hopefully having recently completed your initial social work qualification, whether at undergraduate or postgraduate level, you may have breathed a sigh of relief at having finished with writing academic assignments, essays, case studies, developing presentations and other written work associated with study. However, your use of the written word and construction of reports, profiles, presentations and overviews has not ended, but it has changed and now, potentially, it has a significant bearing on the future of those people with whom you are working.

Before reflecting gloomily on this prospect, the translation of writing skills from academe into practice is something that you can use effectively to advocate, record, argue, negotiate and rely on if it's done properly and viewed as an integral part of your role. Don't forget, much of your academic work acts as training for this important aspect of social work. If, on the other hand, you see the use of writing skills as an additional burden and one that is not considered as important as directly working alongside people, you may find that a lack of attention to good written skills is letting you, your organisation and, most importantly, those who use your services, down. A review of serious case reviews highlighted poor recording as a significant factor in contributing to poor outcomes for children and also presented difficulties in reviewers being able to piece together the 'story' of a case (Brandon *et al.*, 2008). This concern continues to be expressed by those responsible for providing social services to the public. However, the Munro report (Munro, 2011) adds an important caveat here that an over-emphasis on prescription of practice may equally detract from the outcomes desired. It is important to maintain a balance. The demand for high quality written skills by employers is clear (Nelson and Weatherald, 2014), an issue that transfers across the world (e.g. see Nkateng and Wharton's 2015 discussion of written social work skills in Botswana). Therefore, this area of practice is one that needs to take its place alongside other interpersonal and communication skills for good social work practice.

Writing skills and social work

It is worth considering for a moment the kinds of written work important in social work practice. The written word records work that has been undertaken, is being offered and/or will be done. It is something that can be referred to justify, explain and review actions. This is important not only as a means of protecting yourself and your agency if things were to go wrong, but as a means of improving on your practice by systematically reviewing what was done, what worked and why (see Musson, 2011). Rai and Lillis (2013) emphasise the centrality of honing your academic writing skills to enhance your practice, but see that currently there is little linkage between writing in academia and transferring this into practice. You may think of your recording as a means of evaluating your work. Social workers operate in a wide variety of roles and fields and some written tasks will be more appropriate in some areas than others. However, it is likely that you will be involved in constructing some of the following in the course of your work:

- case recording (including key information sheets, contact records, closure summaries);

- chronologies and case histories;

- referral documents;

- assessment reports;

- intervention reports;

- case reviews and evaluations;

- court reports and conference reports;

- communication and letters/emails (with service users and carers, other professionals and internally);

- using the written word and your skills as a means of intervention.

Social work can use the written word in many ways. For instance, written skills facilitate and/or form a main plank of intervention as reflective, narratives or letters (Roscoe and Marlow, 2013), creative writing for self-enhancement (Gilzean, 2011) or writing for recovery in mental health (Taylor *et al.*, 2014). They can introduce critical social work perspectives to report writing (Weiss-Gal *et al.*, 2014), or participatory paradigms into child protection work (Roose *et al.*, 2009).

Case recording

If we focus on case recording as a central skill and task we note a problematic history. In 1999, Goldsmith prepared a report for the Department of Health aimed at improving case recording in then social services departments. Inspections of case recording demonstrated a lack of attention to case records and promoted good practice in terms of access, sharing records, using IT and developing checklists to improve standards. Unfortunately, case recording was one element of the inquiry into the death of Victoria Climbié that was noted as seriously inadequate (Laming, 2003, 7.28–7.30).

Recognising the shortfall in practice, the Department of Health commissioned the development of a set of training materials to account for these inadequacies (Walker *et al.*, 2005 – see **www.writeenough.org.uk**) by offering interactive exercises, drawing together messages from research, inspections and inquiry reports relating to children's services, although the basic principles are shared across all social work areas. This set of training materials put centre stage the importance of case recording as a means of improving the quality of practice. If we look at the current Cafcass web-based case recording policy we can see how the lessons from past inadequacies are being applied to current social work (Cafcass, 2015). Previous documents (e.g. Cafcass, 2008) set out the reasons for case recording, the particular practice associated with it at Cafcass, legislation issues and its quality. The current version stresses data security. When considering quality issues, it is interesting to note that those issues with which you will be familiar from your qualifying education were also stressed in earlier iterations:

- case recordings should be of high quality, i.e. structured, analytical and proportional to the requirements of the case;

- case records should be legible;

- attention to ethical principles are identified – facts are distinguished from opinions, respect of service users is central;

- reflection and analysis can also be included.

However, these are now more focused on process. This makes it more important to emphasise the quality of written work. Often your employing agency will have guidance on record keeping or case recording (also see our Further Reading section for a SCIE e-learning module). If you have recently joined a team, search out your organisation's case recording policy – increasingly these are on the web, but it will be written down if not – and familiarise yourself with it. It is sometimes worth comparing the policy of your agency with one or two others. This will give you a good idea of the common features; those core elements of recording that are necessary wherever you work and in whatever field you practise.

However, it is important to remember that increased prescription in practice can skew practice away from what is required, seeing compliance to procedures and record keeping as the end goal rather than improving the lives of people who use services (Munro, 2011). It is important, of course, to remember that Munro was not arguing against good record keeping or against its centrality in good practice. Rather, it should be seen in the context of the Professional Capabilities Framework as a tool and resource for good practice as opposed to systems compliance. However, it is worth reflecting on Roets' (2015) examination of power issues in report writing that can assist in developing your reflective approach to the task (also see Rai, 2006).

General issues in writing for practice

Reflection point

Think back to your social work qualification and the written work you undertook on placement, the notes made for essays and other assignments.

- *What skills can you use from your social work education to enhance the quality of your written work now?*

- *What's similar or different and why?*

- *How can you allocate time and energy in an efficient and effective way that recognises the importance of the task and its skilled completion?*

In answering the question: 'What can you transfer from your social work education?' you may have identified some of the following core elements in Table A2.1.

Table A2.1 Transferring writing skills

Planning	Considering carefully the purpose of what you are about to write, and setting out what to include, how to gather information and how to complete it.
Structure	Making sure your work is organised and focused, introduces the issues, debates them and offers a clear and logical analysis.
Presentation	Being careful to maximise immediate visual impact, proof-reading to identify 'typos' and sentences that are not as clear as they could be, and ensuring readability and accessibility.
Evidenced and sourced	Ensuring that fact and opinion are distinguished and that the source of evidence for your statements, conclusion, recommendations etc. is clear and accessible.
Logical argument and analysis	Developing a style that weighs up and evaluates arguments and alternatives, that is balanced and based upon knowledge and research evidence where appropriate.
Theoretical	Analysis and evidence should be theoretically informed to enable a conclusion to be drawn.
Timeliness	Ensuring that reports are lodged with relevant bodies (funding, other agencies, courts) in good time, making sure that case records are up-to-date and completed as near to the event as possible and that communication with others is timely.

These are, no doubt, areas that were commented upon when undertaking your qualifying education. They indicate that consolidation of your learning and transfer of your skills and competences (meta-learning) is the name of the game now you are qualified. It is not, as more cynical workers may suggest, time to leave behind your education but to hone and develop its use for working alongside and with people to effect change, make a difference and safeguard. A key question now is, how do you find, preserve and honour time for continually updating your knowledge through reading?

Consider the following case study from a newly qualified social worker.

CASE STUDY A**2.1**

NQSW experience

I don't have time to read much at all. After a month in the job I had a caseload of over 30 where an ASYE should have 15. I have kicked up a fuss and it's has gone down to 20, however, I was on duty on Friday as TEN S47s came in. The amount of work at the minute is unbelievable, and coupled with an 'inadequate' inspection report it's pretty hard times here at the minute.

The barriers need to be acknowledged as does the 'anti-intellectual' push that many new social workers may experience from more seasoned colleagues where theory, reading and university fade into a stark background of immediate concern and calls for action. Social work action has developed over many years and a large body of practice-based evidence has been collected. The importance of research, reading and continued updating is recognised and promoted but not always facilitated within stretched teams. There are three things that you can do to assist:

a. Gain the backing of your manager and team;

b. Focus on the values of social work to give the best possible service to the people you work with;

c. Consider yourself and your development in the longer term and demand the time.

These might be easier said than achieved but there is a range of ways in which reading and updating can be made easier. One of the best ways is to engage with your local university at a range of levels, for example:

• Developing podcasts;

• Working with a university to develop practice updates – distillations of recent research and case descriptions;

• Using supervision to ensure practice is underpinned by knowledge and agreed evidence;

• By team recognition and management recognition of the importance of updating to best practice for people who use services;

• By drawing on the practices of other professionals – medical doctors, nurses, psychologists etc.

In many situations, case records will be used to inform decisions made in relation to the allocation of limited resources and it is therefore important to ensure that reports are concise, factual, evidence-based and with analysis of the situation that is reflective of needs. This will enable readers to make an informed decision about the case and will ensure the fair allocation of resources.

The following case study shows how important the transfer of learning about record keeping can be.

CASE STUDY A2.2

Learning from record keeping

A case was recently presented to a panel for decision in relation to a request to accommodate a young person. The young person, James, has autism accompanied by severe learning disabilities and challenging behaviour. The behaviour included threatening behaviour towards his parents and siblings (including holding a knife to his mother's throat), inability to sleep for longer than three hours, tantrums, switching lights on throughout

(Continued)

the night, screaming and so forth. He is also incontinent and requires constant supervision and, during tantrums, two-to-one care.

In order to make an informed decision in relation to this case, the social worker presented the panel with a report that initially described James's behaviour, placing it in the context of his home, school or residential respite unit. She described how his autism impacted on his ability to understand his actions and interpret the behaviour of others. She used evidence from her experience and others, and clearly stated her opinion of the situation based on factual evidence.

She described in her report the impact that this behaviour was having on each member of the family and the effect this had on the family to function as a 'system', e.g. the mother's inability to perform her role as mother to James's siblings due to his high level of need. Her arguments were theoretically based, helping to clearly set out all the relevant information in a concise, understandable and readable way.

She then went on to analyse the information – for example, looking not just at 'what' behaviour James displayed in which setting but 'why'. She analysed the reasons why James's behaviour was more manageable in the structured environment of a residential respite unit than in the home and how the stresses of coping were impacting on the family. She explained and analysed the risk factors of the situation versus the protective factors of the situation and how these impacted on the family's ability to cope with James.

Along with a comprehensive discussion of previous interventions and support offered to the family the social worker was clearly able to identify that this was a family that had been in severe difficulty for some time and to detail James's needs in terms of the need for stability, consistency and attachment. She was also able to clearly state the needs of the family to access support and therapy in order to help them continue to care for James in the future. This enabled the panel to make a decision to accommodate James, with a view to achieving the outcome of his eventual return home.

The panel were also able to identify that, had intensive behavioural support been offered earlier, James may not have needed to be accommodated in order to safeguard and promote his welfare and may well have been able to remain for longer within the family home.

So, we can see that high-quality written work or now more commonly web-based written work is central to good social work practice. It will be helpful to briefly identify what are the valuable aspects of written work. The earlier principles for case recording identified by Cafcass (2008) provide a clear agency perspective on key elements constituting written work. These include writing only what needs to be recorded and not duplicating material where possible (*proportionality*), writing in accordance with the law, especially the Data Protection Act 1998 (*accountability*) and ensuring records are shared with service users wherever possible (*transparency*). Case records and files should be *accessible* and kept *safe*. It is useful to add the following key points important to case recording:

- ensure that you write in a clear, simple and accessible style free from jargon and ensuring that any specific and technical/professional language is explained in plain English;

- write in a decisive way that distinguishes between fact and opinion;

- make sure you set out the evidence base you have used and where the information can be consulted if appropriate. In some reports it will help your case if you use appropriate references and source material. It allows your work to be subject to challenge and scrutiny and this is only fair when dealing with sensitive situations and potentially vulnerable people. If a case goes to court, the court will expect that you have based your arguments within a theoretical framework, so it is important to be clear about WHY you have reached a particular conclusion;

- like the skills transferred from your qualifying education, organise and structure written work in a way that sets things out in a logical order and sequence.

Summary of key points

- In this short piece we have focused predominantly on case recording.

- However, what we have discussed applies equally to the development of informative literature and media advertising the services your agency offers, in developing a bid for funding for your agency and in more formal report writing.

- High-quality writing skills will assist you in providing the best possible service to people with whom you are working.

- It also concerns you being able to continue reading for social work practice and dealing with some of the complexities and difficulties of managing this in a busy and pressured job.

FURTHER READING

Healy, K and Mulholland, J (2012) *Writing skills for social workers*, 2nd edn. London: Sage.

This book aims to raise the profile of writing skills in social work practice, and to enhance social workers' written communication skills.

Hopkins, G (1998) *The write stuff: a guide to effective writing in social care and related services*. Lyme Regis: Russell House Publishing Limited.

A plain English guide design to develop effective written work.

O'Rourke, L (2002) *For the record: recording skills training manual*. Lyme Regis: Russell House.

A useful training pack providing material that details the importance and principles of recording.

Parker, J (2010) *Effective practice learning in social work*, 2nd edn. Exeter: Learning Matters.

An excellent guide for placements, as one commentator puts it. Aims to tackle anxieties and explain the ways in which the placement experience can deliver a unique learning opportunity for the student.

Prince, K (1996) *Boring records? Communication, speech and writing in social work*. London: Jessica Kingsley.

Katie Prince has written a practical book on the central role and importance of record keeping.

Rutter, L and Brown, K (2015) *Critical thinking and professional judgement in social work*, 4th edn. London: Sage/Learning Matters.

This is a highly recommended text that contains practical, down-to-earth guidance in an easily digestible format.

Records and report writing

Training available from:

www.scie.org.uk/assets/elearning/communicationskills/cs01/resource/index.html

Click on the practice tab and number 5 is entitled 'Records and report writing'.

Appendix 3
Court skills

Clare Seymour

PROFESSIONAL CAPABILITIES FRAMEWORK

This appendix will help you to demonstrate the following ASYE-level capabilities:

5. Knowledge: apply knowledge of social sciences, law and social work practice theory.
7. Intervention and skills: use judgement and authority to intervene with individuals, families and communities to promote independence, provide support and prevent harm, neglect and abuse.
8. Contexts and organisations: engage with, inform, and adapt to changing contexts that shape practice. Operate effectively within own organisational frameworks and contribute to the development of services and organisations. Operate effectively within multi-agency and interprofessional partnerships and settings.

KNOWLEDGE AND SKILLS STATEMENTS

This appendix will help you demonstrate the following requirements:

Child and family:

8. The law and the family and youth justice systems.

Adult:

9. Organisational context.

In our research the key issue that stands out above all others in the advance of newly qualified social workers' learning needs is the development of court skills (Bates *et al.*, 2010). The following article describes a model to support the development of these skills and is written by Clare Seymour. It is reproduced with her kind permission and that of the original publisher, copyright Whiting and Birch, from the *Journal of Practice Teaching and Learning*, volume 7, pages 70–81, in 2006/07. Although the article was originally written with practice assessors or educators in mind, its excellent, now updated, content is equally pertinent to newly qualified social workers. In fact, this content is based on a much more detailed text published by Learning Matters in 2011, *Courtroom and Report Writing Skills for Social Workers* by Seymour and Seymour, 2nd edition. This book contains useful advice, research summaries, case examples, websites and further reading sections and is strongly recommended as the starting point for this demanding aspect of a newly qualified social worker's journey.

A model to support the development of courtroom skills

There is widespread interest on the part of social work degree students in developing their courtroom skills within a framework of learning about social work law, but it is often not until they qualify and are 'thrown in at the deep end' that anyone gives any serious thought to the need for preparation and skills development in this area. As a result, students and newly qualified social workers are frequently apprehensive about court work, which means that they do not always do themselves, or the people who use social work services, justice when faced with court involvement. This article offers a model for practice assessors to use with students in agencies where court work is undertaken, and encourages skills development against a foundation of critical analysis and reflection. The term 'practice educator' has been adopted in preference to the previously widely used term 'practice teacher' to describe the person responsible for facilitating learning and supervising and assessing social work students in practice and, indeed, most of the suggested learning activities primarily involve a facilitative or educative, rather than an assessment, role.

Keywords: social worker, social work students, courtroom skills, model for skills development, observation and shadowing, reflection, evidence, cross-examination, values.

Introduction

Law is a key area of teaching and learning in the social work degree. Knowledge of legal rules and skills in their application are included in the social work benchmark statement (QAA, 2000) and in the PCF. However, most commentators agree that the relationship between social workers and lawyers in practice is often strained, characterised by antagonism and distrust, and that social work students frequently approach learning the law with fear and lack of confidence (Preston-Shoot *et al.*, 1998, cited in SCIE, 2005). Many qualified social workers also experience court work as extremely stressful, which can result in defensive practice in which the values of their profession appear to become side-lined or obscured. The courtroom is an arena where preparation and rehearsal is difficult, and yet frequently court work is where the robustness of social workers' practice, professional confidence and knowing the rules can make a key difference to the experience of people who use social work services (SCIE, 2005, p174).

Preston-Shoot (2000) suggests that competent practitioners are those who are:

- confident (to challenge);

- credible (in presenting the rationale for decision-making);

- critical (to make their practice and legal rules accessible to those with whom they work, to assess the impact of policies on people's lives and to navigate through questions of ethics, rights and needs);

- creative (in order to exploit the possibilities that legal rules present and to manage the practice dilemmas and conflicting imperatives that the interface between law and social work practice generates).

Cull and Roche (2001) further argue that health and social welfare professionals do not need to learn to *think like a lawyer*, but instead to engage with the complexity of the law–practice interface. This encompasses factors such as the values and principles which shape the two professions, and the motivation and personal attributes of their respective practitioners. Also important are the differences in the nature of the relationships which lawyers and social workers have with their clients and in the structure and regulation of law and social work, and the frequently negative influence of preconceptions and stereotypical assumptions. The comprehensive SCIE review on the teaching, learning and assessment of law in social work education (2005, p49) emphasised the need for social workers to develop the conceptual tools to understand law, rather than simply learning what the law says. These principles can only be developed against a practice framework in which students feel able to question, challenge and debate issues which arise in the legal context of social work.

The SCIE review found that courtroom skills were, for the most part, not identified specifically in social work education, but tended to be included in generic learning objectives, such as *being confident in using the law* and *understanding the legal system.* Despite, or perhaps because of, apprehension about court work, there is evidence of considerable interest on the part of social work students in developing their knowledge and skills in this area. When Anglia Ruskin University introduced an elective module on courtroom skills as part of its social work degree, the module was heavily oversubscribed and well-received. However, as with any area of learning, knowledge, skills and values have to be applied to be effective, and practice assessors in agencies where social workers regularly undertake court work can play a key role in helping students develop and apply relevant skills, such as keeping up-to-date with changes in law and policy, advocacy, communication, fact-finding and research, writing and presenting reports, presenting an argument, using facts to formulate an opinion, problem-solving, negotiation and responding to challenge. There is evidence, too, that learning about the law is often not retained (Preston-Shoot *et al.*, 1998, cited in SCIE, 2005), and it is suggested that this may be because academic learning is *insufficiently linked to practice, failing to connect the law and social work, or to engage students on a personal level with the context of what they are learning* (SCIE, 2005, p30). It follows, therefore, that practice assessors are in a key position in which to maximise the effectiveness of students' learning.

It is possible for students to undertake academic preparation for court work, by, for example, researching the historical development of the courts, the structure of the legal system, court rules, legal language and concepts, and there are many accessible texts available to facilitate this. However, without practical application, such information is likely to prove difficult to understand and retain. This model offers a framework with which to support students in developing confidence and competence in court settings.

Reflecting on attitudes to the law

As preparation for professional involvement with courts, students should reflect on their own experiences and consider how these may influence their current attitudes to courts and lawyers, and their understanding of the legal system. Sitting on a jury, ending a marriage or partnership, being convicted of a motoring offence or having to wind up a relative's estate will each shape perception and understanding of legal processes and the people involved, which in turn can influence professional behaviour. Comparing their attitudes towards lawyers with those they have towards other professionals will help students identify the preconceptions they hold, and form the basis for devising creative ways of overcoming the barriers which can impede effective professional relationships.

Law reports appear in *The Times* on most days when the High Court is sitting. Other newspapers usually publish them weekly, and they are available on various websites (**www.iclr.co.uk**). Encouraging students to keep any cuttings which relate to decisions in cases within their particular areas of interest will give them a flavour of legal decision-making and provide a framework for professional debate in the context of the ways in which opposing views are determined.

Values and principles

Key aspects of the relationship between social work and law are the values and principles which shape the two professions. This is highlighted in the SCIE report as an area which is neglected by many social work degree programmes, and yet one which worries many social workers, despite the shared commitment of both professions to social justice. Critical analysis of how lawyers are governed and the principles which underpin their profession, including fairness, honesty, transparency, confidentiality and anti-discriminatory practice encourages students to see themselves as entitled to be regarded as equal players when in a professional role in court, and therefore in a unique position to make a difference to the experience of service users faced with court involvement. The General Social Care Council as the former regulator of social care services in England (with companion organisations in Scotland, Wales and Northern Ireland) produced the first codes of practice for social care workers and their employers in 2002. These codes have now been replaced by the Health and Care Professions Council's standards of proficiency, conduct, performance and ethics (see **www.hcpc-uk.org**) and describe the standards of professional conduct and practice required of social care workers. Whilst student social workers are learning to work in accordance with these standards and develop their understanding of the nature of professional relationships and boundaries, it is also helpful for them to consider service users' expectations of different professionals. This can be facilitated by means of structured exercises or reflections on personal experiences.

Observation and shadowing

Observation or shadowing can reduce anxiety by increasing knowledge of unfamiliar processes, but most importantly from a practice learning perspective, it is a means of developing self-awareness and providing a framework for reflection.

> *The observational stance requires social workers to be aware of the environment, the verbal and non-verbal interaction; to be aware of their own responses as a source of invaluable data, provided that they are aware of what comes from them and what comes from their clients; and to develop the capacity to integrate these and give themselves time to think before arriving at a judgement or making a decision.*

> (Trowell and Miles, 1996, in Knott and Scragg, 2007, p43)

Most courts, even those whose hearings are not open to the public, will permit people with a professional interest to attend a hearing, and many judges and magistrates are willing to have informal discussions afterwards, if approached through their clerk. Dickens (2005, 2006) has explored the tensions which can arise between local authority lawyers, social workers and managers, and Brammer (2010, p92) suggests that barriers to effective relationships between social workers and lawyers would be reduced by, among other things, the clarification of their respective roles and responsibilities. Students can be supported in developing their understanding of the legal/social work interface by being offered the opportunity to meet with and, if possible, shadow other professionals, for example in-house lawyers, children's guardians and independent advocates, which is particularly beneficial if it occurs away from the tensions of actual proceedings. In addition to using supervision to encourage reflection on the opportunities and constraints of multidisciplinary working, practice assessors could devise a mini project as a framework for learning, such as preparation of an information leaflet for a particular client group on roles and responsibilities in legal proceedings.

Careful observation in the course of everyday activities will support the development of students' presentation skills, which are an important component of effective court work. Watching people presenting their views, or answering questions, in a variety of settings, such as a television discussion programme, church service, lecture or party political broadcast, enables students to identify what seems to support effective communication and what creates barriers between speaker and listener.

Observation of interprofessional decision-making forums is also helpful, particularly if combined with an activity such as compiling a diagrammatic representation of group processes. It also helps students to understand the challenges of individual decision-making in the context of different cultures and priorities, and differing perceptions of professional duty, power, responsibility and autonomy.

Giving evidence

Students should be familiar with the concept of gathering evidence which relates to learning objectives, and the criteria put forward by Parker (2004, p96) specifically to evidence practice learning, with the possible exception of the last element, can be transferred to the process of presenting evidence to court, thus further demonstrating that courtroom skills can be developed within a generic professional framework.

- Is it valid?

- Is it sufficient?

- Is it relevant?

- Is it based in social work values (and, I would add, codes of practice)?

- Is it reliable?

- Is it clear?

- Is it agreed?

Simple memory exercises, process recording or comparing different assessments of the same trigger will demonstrate the influence on evidence of shortcomings in memory and errors in perception, judgement or estimation and consequently the vital importance of comprehensive, accurate and fair recording.

Although courts need to know what professional opinions are being advanced, they are, if anything, more interested in how they were formed. In other words, what facts informed the analysis and how they were interpreted. Through their academic training, social work students should be developing an ability to move from description to the formulation of a rationale for their actions and opinions. This can be supported by practice assessors acting as 'devil's advocate' in suggesting alternative views, and encouraging students to incorporate four further Rs into the process.

- Reading (about relevant theories).

- Research (about 'what works').

- Resources (what are needed and, more importantly, are available to support any proposed plan).

- Reflection.

It is worth remembering that the best way to be a helpful witness is to understand the task facing the court, and so role plays (as in, for example, a planning or review meeting) can provide the opportunity to practise advancing, or defending, different professional judgements and opinions.

In relation to the sufficiency of evidence, an important aspect of court work is the need for social work evidence to include everything which might be relevant to the decision, even that which might be prejudicial to an individual's performance or the result they are hoping for. Also important in the context of collaborative and inter-disciplinary working is for students to learn to work with the fact that once in court, social workers are required to give evidence of their own knowledge and opinions, not those of anyone else. They do not have to support the line of the party on whose behalf they are giving evidence if, on professional grounds, they do not (Seymour and Seymour, 2011, p139). This is potentially difficult, since it requires professional confidence which usually only develops with experience. However, practice assessors can encourage students to question proposed courses of action, seek out and analyse alternatives in terms of the work they are doing, and also to identify and reflect upon things that, with hindsight, they might wish to do differently in the future. All of these activities will encourage the open-mindedness and fairness that courts, and also people who use social work services, seek (ibid, p90).

Report writing

In most situations in which social workers are involved professionally, their evidence will be presented to the court in writing, and consequently it is through their written work that their practice will, initially at least, be exposed to the scrutiny of others. Thus, reports and records are an important factor in determining the image of social work from the perspective of other professionals and potentially hold enormous power in the minds of service users.

There have been too many instances of social work reports to court failing to reach expected standards; specific criticisms have included lack of focus, failing to distinguish between fact and opinion, reproducing large sections of case records with little structure or editing, and, worst of all, failing to address the best interests of the child (Cooper, 2006, pp1–2). Dickens (2004) found that a major complaint of local authority lawyers was the amount of time they had to spend on overseeing the quality of social workers' written statements. They were critical of standards of literacy, but their main concern was the proliferation of unnecessary detail and the inadequacy of analysis. Judges, too, cherish brevity and clarity (Bond and Sandhu, 2005) and reports which are poorly written or structured are likely to result in a negative opinion of the writer which is hard to reverse, however commendable their subsequent performance.

All of these areas can be addressed in the practice learning setting, by devising specific tasks, based on actual case records, which could include all, or some, of the following:

- compiling a genogram or chronology (neither of which should contain any opinion – a fact often overlooked);

- reducing large amounts of information without losing essential material or compromising fairness and balance;

- distinguishing between fact, analysis and opinion;

- expressing a rationale for opinions and decisions;

- presenting relevant theoretical and research material to support a rationale, including that which may not support the case being put forward;

- critical analysis of, and clarity in, use of language, including the identification and minimal use of jargon and acronyms.

Cross-examination

As the aim of cross-examination is to expose any flaws in the evidence, it follows that evidence which has been properly prepared and presented by people who are familiar with their material, confident in their role and clear about the rationale for any opinions expressed, has the best chance of standing up to scrutiny. An effective cross-examiner is one who succeeds in obtaining from another party's witness evidence which assists their client's case, which means obtaining answers which the witness accepts are accurate, or at least more accurate than their previous evidence (Seymour and Seymour, 2011, p153).

Although witnesses in the UK should never be coached on their actual evidence (unlike in the United States, where witness coaching is widely practised), preparation for the experience of being cross-examined can be facilitated by:

- compiling and maintaining records in such a way as to make them suitable to be shared with people who may have different interests in the case;

- anticipating the grounds on which evidence of fact might become subject to challenge (perception, memory, bias or prejudice, untruthfulness);

- anticipating the grounds on which evidence of opinion might be challenged (level or range of qualifications, experience or expertise, rationale);

- considering the influence of, and personal responses to, the cross-examiner's personal style;

- learning to recognise different types of question and their relationship to the sort of response sought;

- developing strategies to establish some control over the process, such as objectivity, controlling the pace, seeking clarification where necessary and keeping responses brief and focused.

The extensive transcripts of the Climbié Inquiry (**www.nationalarchives.gov.uk**) provide a fascinating insight into the reality of cross-examination and are an invaluable learning resource for students.

After the hearing

At one level the justice system can be understood as the major institutional way we deal with losses, largely around our expectations of how other people will behave towards us.

(Dawes, in Thompson, 2002, p176)

Any court experience is likely to involve loss for one or more of the people involved and this can provide a theoretical framework within which to plan responses in the aftermath of what could be distressing and damaging experiences. Potential losses range from those which are severe and permanent, such as the decision to place a child for adoption, to those from which recovery is possible and lessons can be learned, such as the restriction of liberty by means of a community sentence or having part, or all, of your evidence rejected by a court. For social workers, knowledge of models and theories of loss and of variations in the cultural needs of people experiencing loss can potentially make a significant difference to their own experiences and those of others who have been involved in the process. Supervision which actively encourages reflection and the application of relevant theories to practice will help students develop the confidence and independence of thought to question and critically analyse legal and court processes, which in turn will encourage them to see themselves as equal players in the court setting.

Conclusion

Social workers often describe their court experience as the most demanding of their career (Seymour and Seymour, 2011, p168). Sometimes the experience is viewed negatively, but with effective preparation and support, it offers opportunities and challenges which do not arise in other areas of work. This article has sought to encourage practice assessors to help students build the foundations for developing the necessary knowledge and skills during the course of practice learning opportunities in which court work is undertaken.

Where the law meets social work, there may be a new mix of skills that brings together the principles and values of both professions and applies them to the task of developing lawful, ethical social work practice.

(SCIE, 2005, p187)

Brammer, A (2015) *Social work law*, 4th edn. London: Pearson.

This is a comprehensive, practical and accessible guide to the legal framework related to social work.

OFSTED (2010) *Children on family justice: a report of children's views for the Family Justice Review Panel by the Children's Rights Director for England.* London: TSO. Available from: **www.lgcplus.com/Journals/3/Files/2011/2/15/Children%20on%20family%20justice.pdf**

As part of the Family Justice Review, this report asked 125 children and young people in care or living away from home to give their opinions on questions being investigated by the Review Panel.

Seymour, C and Seymour, R (2011) *Courtroom and report writing skills for social workers*, 2nd edn. Exeter: Learning Matters.

This guide is a very readable text on legal and courtroom processes and procedures.

Slapper, G (2013) *How the law works*, 3rd edn. London: Routledge.

This is a plain English guide to the legal system in the UK.

Smeeton, J and Boxall, K (2011) Birth parents' perceptions of professional practice in child care and adoption proceedings: implications for practice. *Child and Family Social Work*, 16(4): 444–53.

This insightful paper, based on a previous 2010 Cafcass research paper, explores non-relinquishing birth parents' experiences of contested child care and adoption proceedings.

Family Law Week

Register at **www.familylawweek.co.uk** to receive a free weekly summary of family court judgements, research and articles by lawyers.

Full text court judgements

www.bailii.org/

You will be able to search for full text court judgements with a neutral citation number from the above link.

Ministry of Justice

www.justice.gov.uk/

The above link provides information for users of courts and tribunals.

Social Work Evidence Template

http://coppguidance.rip.org.uk/social-work-evidence-template/

This link to the Research in Practice website provides written and video resources for the jointly developed (ADCS and Cafcass) template.

Appendix 4
Rights, justice and economic well-being

Chris Willetts

Social workers should recognise the fundamental principles of human rights and equality, and that these are protected in national and international law, conventions and policies. This should have been a core feature of your qualifying education.

Rights

Firstly, it is imperative that social workers know relevant law and work within it in order to work legitimately and non-oppressively so as to advance human rights and promote social justice and economic well-being for the benefit of service users and society as a whole. These are grand aspirations enshrined as key social work values by the Standards of Conduct, Performance and Ethics (HCPC, 2016), Knowledge, Skills and Professional Capabilities Frameworks (DH, 2015; DfE, 2014; BASW, 2015) and BASW's (2012) Code of Ethics.

Social work is a 'rights' based form of practice where, in the 1950s and 1960s and even since its beginnings, social work was at the forefront of campaigning to extend rights to some of the more marginalised groups, such as disabled people, people in mental institutions and those either homeless or in extreme poverty, needing the support of the welfare state.

The history of social work's more radical campaigning can be read in McLaughlin (2008) and Fergusson and Woodward (2009). Both sources ponder whether we need social work to return, in part, to its more campaigning roots.

The rights movement in social welfare and policy has a long history: significant was the UK's commitment to the UN Declaration of Human Rights (1948) following the widespread rights abuses and genocide up to and during the Second World War. At the same time, Britain signed up to the Council of Europe's Convention on Human Rights (1950).

Britain has no written constitution, unlike the USA whose citizens have a constitutional Bill of Rights. In the UK, much law is common law (laid down in legal precedent); common law gave some protection for UK citizens (along with Britain's signing of the UN Declaration and the European Convention). On admittance to the European Economic Community in 1973 (now the EU), Britain eventually came into line with many other EU states and the European Convention by passing the Human Rights Act 1998 into UK law, which legally enshrines these human rights. More latterly, the Equality Act 2010 became law. Two good resources on law for social workers are Brammer (2015) and Johns (2014).

As well as understanding the relationship between social work and the law, there are many ways in which social workers are expected to use law, such as the Children Act (2004), Children and Young Person Act (2008) or the Mental Health Act and Amendment (1983, 2007) and Mental Capacity Act 2005, to identify a few examples of important legislation.

Thompson (2011, 2012) suggests that, in promoting equality and upholding rights, you should have a good working knowledge of the provision of relevant legislation and to cite and use it in order to promote or protect rights. Certainly in my own professional practice over many years with disabled people, I was able to use my knowledge of disability discrimination legislation, the Human Rights Act and the Equality Act to ensure, using persuasion and eloquent challenging alongside service users, the provision of equal services and access for people with disabilities when not provided. Therefore, the social worker should study the provision and requirements of key legislation such as the Human Rights Act 1998 and Equality Act 2010.

However, the issue of rights and equality is complex. For example, how do we balance the right to free speech with the consequence that people have the right to say things that may offend others? The concept of equality is problematic: should policies promote equality of *opportunity* or equality of *outcome*? There are fundamentally differing approaches to promoting equality. There is a good discussion of 'rights' and 'equality' in Blakemore and Booth (2013), Bochel (2009) and Taylor-Gooby (2008). On promoting equality, see Thompson (2011) as well as Nzria and Williams (2009) on anti-oppressive practice.

See also the Equality and Human Rights Commission website: **www.equalityhuman rights.com/**.

FURTHER READING

Social justice and economic well-being

Levitas (2005), Pierson (2010) and Wilkinson and Pickett (2009) are influential texts on how poverty and social exclusion can have profound effects on individual and societal health, levels of crime and disorder and educational achievement, to name just a few areas of concern.

For Pierson (2010), exclusion is more than poverty and low income; it is also about lack of access to the jobs market, thin or non-existent social supports and networks, the impoverishment of the local area or neighbourhood and exclusion from services.

It is not just a matter of absolute poverty but, as Wilkinson and Pickett point out, it is relative poverty and inequalities that are harmful, when there are gross or increasing differences between the 'haves' and 'have nots', a society characterised by wide inequalities.

Although there have been many attempts to measure relative poverty and inequality, such as Townsend (1979), some useful indicators of relative poverty and exclusion are:

- The most recent annual Joseph Rowntree Foundation (JRF) Monitoring Poverty and Social Exclusion (PSE) Report is dated December 2015. The links to the reports for the last 10 years, for comparison of trends, can be found via the JRF website (**www.jrf.org.uk**).

- The Poverty and Social Exclusion site (**www.poverty.ac.uk/free-resources**) is a resource which is part of an Economic and Social Research Council project.

- The Equality Trust: data on national and international inequalities can be accessed at **www. equalitytrust.org.uk**.

For tackling social exclusion, poverty and social injustice read Levitas (2005), Pierson (2010, 2016) and Thompson (2011).

There is an excellent online resource on social exclusion by the Governance and Social Development Resource Centre (GSDRC) at the University of Birmingham: **www.gsdrc.org/go/topic-guides/social-exclusion**.

For discussion of social security and welfare for people in economic hardship, see Fitzpatrick (2012), McKay and Rowlingson (2014) and Alcock with May (2014).

This list of resources is not exhaustive, but will provide you with further understanding of how we can all uphold and extend the exercise of rights and promote greater equality and social justice.

Appendix 5
Diversity

Chris Willetts

PROFESSIONAL CAPABILITIES FRAMEWORK

This appendix will help you demonstrate the following ASYE-level capability:

3. Diversity: recognise diversity and apply anti-discriminatory and anti-oppressive principles in practice.

KNOWLEDGE AND SKILLS STATEMENTS

This appendix will help you demonstrate the following requirements:

Child and family:

2. Communication.

Adult:

2. The role of social workers working with adults.
6. Effective assessments and outcome based support planning.

Recognising individuality

Recognising the individuality of every service user and the uniqueness of their situation, and not allowing any personal prejudice about them to affect your service to them, is one of the core values of social work (e.g. see Standards of Conduct, Performance and Ethics (HCPC, 2016); Knowledge and Skills Frameworks (DH, 2015; DfE 2014); Professional Capabilities Framework (BASW, 2015); BASW (2012) Code of Ethics). Organisational policies and employment contracts also have to meet statutory obligations to respect diversity and promote equal treatment through the employer duties under the Human Rights Act 1998 and Equality Act 2010.

On the surface, working by this core value seems to be straightforward. However, what follows are some reflection points which highlight some of the complexities around the topic of diversity.

All social workers should easily recognise that societies like the UK have very diverse populations. Two good accounts of the changing demography of Britain can be found on the Office for National Statistics Population and Migration and Cultural Identity portals (see **www.ons.gov.uk/peoplepopulationandcommunity/population andmigration** and **www.ons.gov.uk/peoplepopulationandcommunity/cultural identity**). The latest 2011 census data is available at **www.ons.gov.uk/peoplepopula tionandcommunity/populationandmigration/populationestimates/bulletins/2011 census/2013-05-16**.

However, there are theoretical and practical problems with thinking of diversity just in terms of highly visible ethnic or racial differences. For instance, it ignores all the other many ways in which the UK population is diverse:

- there are significant social differences between the experiences of men and women (also people who are transgender);

- diversity in terms of age, social class, religion or belief, sexual orientation and identity;

- diversity in our health status, and whether we may be differently able (have a disability), and so on.

There are good chapters in core sociology texts such as Giddens and Sutton (2013) and Haralambos and Holborn (2013) as a starting point on different social identities such as race and ethnicity, gender, sexual identity, age diversity and social class.

Valuing diversity

Really valuing diversity is a complex challenge for any social worker. Valuing diversity means not just accepting but sometimes defending the social rights of those deemed 'other' (Thompson, 2016). We cannot demand having our own rights and freedom to express our identity as we want, without accepting that as a right or freedom for others.

Read good overviews of the potentially problematic and oppressive aspect of labels and social categorisations in Thompson (2011, 2016), Nzira and Williams (2009) and about 'othering' in Dominelli (2002). One possible conclusion about labels is well put by Central England People First (2000): 'jars should be labelled, not people!'

Despite problems with the accuracy of labels, people who share the characteristics of an excluded or marginalised group can be subject to oppression and discrimination as a result of other people's scapegoating, stereotyping and prejudice. Dominelli (2002) and Thompson (2011, 2016) recognise that multiple oppressions can occur when a person experiences discrimination, which may be amplified if they are deemed to belong to a second or additional stigmatised group.

As practitioners, we should reflect on how much knowledge we really have of the identity and experiences of people who may differ in their social identity from ourselves.

The equality duties (Equality Act, 2010) require us to make reasonable proactive adjustments to accommodate and offer equal, non-discriminatory services to people from diverse social backgrounds. It is also good practice to update ourselves about the possible experiences and needs of anyone who might use our service. The following suggestions are made by Nzira and Williams (2009) and Thompson (2016).

- Newly qualified (and experienced) social workers should routinely search literature and websites to find out about the lived experiences of different social groups. Examples include:

  o The Equality and Human Rights Commission website (**www.equalityhumanrights. com/en**);

  o Age UK (**www.ageuk.org.uk/**);

  o Friends, Families and Travellers, and Travellers' Times websites with resources about the travelling, Romani and Gypsy communities (**www.gypsy-traveller.org/**);

  o Stonewall – about the lived experiences and challenges still faced by the lesbian, gay, bisexual and transgender communities (**www.stonewall.org.uk/**);

  o The Beaumont Society (**www.beaumontsociety.org.uk/**) and the TransgenderZone (**www.transgenderzone.com/**) offer internet support groups for people who are transgender;

  o The Big Issue/Big Issue website (**www.bigissue.com/**), along with other homeless charities including Shelter, Crisis and Barnardo's;

  o Amnesty International (**www.amnesty.org.uk/** especially on their refugee and asylum page which covers experiences in the UK) and also the Refugee Council (**www. refugeecouncil.org.uk/**) and Refugee Welcome Trust (**http://togethernow.org.uk/**) websites;

  o Websites documenting faith-based oppression, such as Islamophobia Watch, or anti-Semitism, recorded in the Community Security Trust's (2012; see **https://cst.org.uk/**) Anti-Semitic Incidents Report.

Clearly this list is not exhaustive, but do carry out your own literature or web research to locate professional training resources to enable you to meet the valuing diversity capability and related knowledge and skills statements. Also think about:

- Holding regular team training events and workshops to explore how to meet the needs of diverse groups and what adjustments and resources could help you meet diverse needs. Invite guest facilitators from different social groupings to lead the discussion.

- Making respecting and valuing diversity a routine agenda item in regular supervision and appraisal meetings.

- Drawing up a personal action plan about how you can enhance your own capability to respect and value diversity. Discuss progress in regular supervision meetings.

- How the team and service can better address diversity and make reasonable adjustments could be a regular minuted agenda item on all team or departmental meetings.

- Reviewing and auditing current service/departmental policy and practice, using the expertise of people from different social groupings to help with your audit and review of what works and what needs improvement.

- Sharing your experience with other teams and local services by holding joint training or awareness-raising meetings, sharing resources and information.

These are just a few ideas but they show how much we can all do to enhance our skills and capability to value diversity and more fully and equally meet the needs of people who use our services.

FURTHER READING

BASW (2012) Code of Ethics: Available from: **www.basw.co.uk/codeofethics/**

Equality Act (2010) Available from: **www.legislation.gov.uk/ukpga/2010/15/contents**

HCPC (2016) Standards of Conduct, Performance and Ethics. Available from: **www.hpc-uk.org/ aboutregistration/standards/standardsofconductperformanceandethics/**

Human Rights Act (1998) Available from: **www.legislation.gov.uk/ukpga/1998/42/contents**

Thompson, N (2016) *Anti-discriminatory practice*, 6th edn. Basingstoke: Palgrave Macmillan.

Chapters 1 and 2 are a particularly good overview.

Appendix 6

Child protection for newly qualified social workers

Jill Davey and Richard Williams

PROFESSIONAL CAPABILITIES FRAMEWORK

This appendix will help you to demonstrate the following ASYE-level capability:

7. Intervention and skills: use judgement and authority to intervene with individuals, families and communities to promote independence, provide support and prevent harm, neglect and abuse.

KNOWLEDGE AND SKILLS STATEMENTS

This appendix will help you demonstrate the following requirements:

Child and family:

1. Relationships and effective direct work.
3. Child development.
5. Abuse and neglect of children.
6. Child and family assessment.
8. The law and the family and youth justice system.

Adult:

4. Safeguarding.
7. Direct work with individuals and families.

Introduction

Before we start this appendix in earnest it is important to point out that the Department for Education has issued a Knowledge and Skills Statement for social workers working with children and families (DfE, 2014). If you have not already, it is essential that you familiarise yourself with this document that can be accessed from their website:

www.gov.uk/government/uploads/system/uploads/attachment_data/file/379033/ Consultation_on_knowledge_and_skills_for_child_and_family_social_work_-_ government_response.pdf

The statement can be found on pages 14–18 of this document.

Child protection is a complex matter. To work alongside families with complex issues requires a considerable amount of skill and judgement. The impact of high profile cases, such as Victoria Climbié and Peter Connelly, make entry into the specialism of child protection a matter for serious consideration. In theory, the overwhelmingly negative media portrayal of social workers should deter the most enthusiastic social work student and steer them speedily away from working with children and families. Yet, there is something about working with children, young people and their respective families and carers that can provide the most challenging and rewarding of experiences. For what the media forgets, or fails to portray, is what a privilege it is to work with such families and the personal knowledge that by supporting them you can have a positive and significant impact in their lives. Also, crucially, for the overwhelming majority of cases, social workers make a positive difference in the lives of children and families.

To look at child protection in any detail would certainly take more than the space we are permitted within this book and therefore we can only hope to give you some signposts for those starting out in this worthwhile area of practice. Remember, you don't have to be a childcare practitioner to become involved in child protection matters; safeguarding is a priority for every social worker. At the end of this appendix we have highlighted key reading related to safeguarding children.

Know the policy and procedures
Whatever organisation you work within, you have to know your own organisation's child protection policies and procedures. Every one of us has a responsibility towards the protection of children. It is essential for you to know where and how to refer to such matters and to whom to refer them, at the very start of your employment.

Use supervision well
The unique opportunities we have as social workers to receive supervision should be received with enthusiasm and viewed as such – Chapter 5 should be especially helpful to you in this regard. Asking for advice, assistance or support should never be seen as a weakness, but as strength and a way of evidencing your desire to grow as a practitioner. It is essential you use this opportunity to explore both the professional and personal impact of child protection work. As Chapter 2 has reminded you, the need to critically reflect on your practice is not something just for the newly qualified social worker, but is an ongoing process throughout your career. Use supervision effectively by being open and honest about how you are managing.

Joint working: learning from the multidisciplinary team

Shadowing and joint working opportunities are essential for newly qualified social workers and allow you to observe experienced practitioners at work. This will allow you to become familiar with procedures and policies and to see the skilled prac-titioners communicating with families, empowering families and assessing risk. You do not just have to rely on your immediate colleagues to gain experience; col-leagues from other professions all contribute to the protection of children. Chapter 7 is a useful section of this practice guide as it is all about joining and contributing to a team.

The Child Protection Conference and Children Subject to a Child Protection Plan

Children Subject to a Child Protection Plan are those children and young people for whom a multidisciplinary child protection conference has decided there are signifi-cant child protection risks and on whose behalf a child protection plan has been devised; the implementation of this plan is co-ordinated by the social worker with case responsibility for the child/young person. All agencies must work together to support the child and their family and thereby address any issues of concern.

Legal duties

The legal duties and powers with regard to child protection are, as you know, exten-sive and complex. You will need to retain up-to-date knowledge of these and you may find the following publication a practical resource: Davis, L (2014) *The social worker's guide to children and families law,* 2nd edn. London: Jessica Kingsley.

Recognising and managing risk

The recognition and management of risk is a fundamental part of being a social worker, whatever specialism you choose. For child protection social workers it has to be at the forefront of your decision-making processes. The recognition of risk is often drawn out through the assessment process and the enquiring nature of the social worker. Making decisions regarding child protection issues is not the responsibil-ity of any one social worker, whether newly qualified or not. Child protection is a joint responsibility both within your organisation and on a multi-professional basis. It is therefore essential that you become familiar with the structure of your organi-sation, including with whom you discuss such issues and the availability of relevant staff. Discussing such matters anywhere other than within the professional arena is a serious breach of confidentiality.

The process of assessment has been developed to respond to needs early and thereby work proactively to prevent crises happening. The Common Assessment Framework (CAF) is the generic tool to assess the needs of children and young people using an ecological approach. Each local authority has developed its own version of the CAF and you will need to familiarise yourself with the relevant local policy.

Confidentiality

Issues of confidentiality are often seen as confusing. Professionals are aware of the tensions that may occur between sharing information that may breach the Data Protection Act 1998 and the need to uphold someone's human rights. However, when it comes to child protection, we must be clear – we must share information of which we become aware. We must share concerns via the appropriate procedures. Never 'hold back' information because it would be easier to do so, or because you have been asked to do so by a person who uses services. If you believe the information is relevant and of a serious nature, then it should be referred immediately to the appropriate person and always recorded in your records, including the outcome of your referral.

Record keeping

Finally, although Appendices 1 and 2 have already touched on writing skills, it is essential that you follow your employer's guidance on record keeping. Not only should you record contact with people who use services but also your decision-making processes. Anyone who has authorisation to access the file should be able to see how the case is progressing, the decision-making process and the relevant supervision notes. Remember that case recordings should accurately reflect your work and input into the case.

Summary of key points

- Familiarise yourself with your organisation's child protection policy and procedure.

- Use supervision well.

- Learn from the multidisciplinary team and recognise that child protection is a joint responsibility.

FURTHER READING

Children and Families Act 2014

Available from: **www.legislation.gov.uk/ukpga/2014/6/contents/enacted**

Department for Education

We recommend the following recent publications:

DfES (2015) *Working together to safeguard children: a guide for interagency working to safeguard and promote the welfare of children.* London: TSO. Available from:

www.gov.uk/government/publications/working-together-to-safeguard-children-2

DfES (2015) *What to do if you are worried a child is being abused.* London: DfES.

Available from: **www.gov.uk/government/publications/what-to-do-if-youre-worried-a-child-is-being-abused-2**

Calder, M with Archer, J (2016) *Risk in child protection*. London: Jessica Kingsley.

A useful, up-to-date publication for anyone involved in the safeguarding of children and young people.

Cocker, C and Allain, L (2011) *Advanced social work with children and families*. Exeter: Learning Matters.

A clear guide on legislation and practice for child and family social workers.

Appendix 7

Safeguarding adults

Di Galpin and Lucy Morrison

PROFESSIONAL CAPABILTIES FRAMEWORK

This appendix will help you to demonstrate the following ASYE-level capabilities:

5. Knowledge: apply knowledge of social sciences, law and social work practice theory.
7. Intervention and skills: use judgement and authority to intervene with individuals, families and communities to promote independence, provide support and prevent harm, neglect and abuse.

KNOWLEDGE AND SKILLS STATEMENTS

This appendix will help you demonstrate the following requirements:

Child and family:

4. Adult mental ill health, substance misuse, domestic abuse, physical ill health and disability.
6. Child and family assessment.
8. The law and the family and youth justice systems.
10. Organisational context.

Adult:

1. The role of social workers working with adults.
2. Person-centred practice.
4. Safeguarding.
5. Mental capacity.
9. Organisational context.

Introduction

Safeguarding Adults is increasingly a core activity for all those who work with adults across the health and social care sector. However, the Care Act 2014 has placed responsibility with local authorities, in partnership with public sector organisations such as the police and NHS, to ensure they lead a process to protect adults with care and support needs from abuse and neglect. This has professional implications for all qualified practitioners across adult and mental health services and that includes the newly qualified social worker. It's also a complex matter and why we have written this extended appendix.

Government and society expect professionals in practice to demonstrate a high level of skill, as they seek to protect those most vulnerable and at risk of harm in society, whilst also striving to protect individuals' right to live their lives as they choose. This will often involve striking a balance between non-intervention and intervention, and a professional approach to integrated practice by liaising with a wide range of partner agencies, people who use services and their families in a spirit of cooperation. Throughout this process all practitioners are required to demonstrate professional judgement and decision-making in complex situations, whilst managing high levels of risk.

Practice in Safeguarding Adults must be compliant with the law as outlined in Section 1 and 42–46 of the Care Act 2014 as it establishes a framework for practice focused on promoting well-being. The Care Act 2014 puts in place a new framework for adult safeguarding and includes measures to guard against provider failure to ensure this is managed without disruption to services.

The Care Act 2014; Sections 42–46

These sections replace the 'No Secrets' (2000) guidance. The Care Act 2014 states that safeguarding duties apply to an adult who:

- has needs for care and support (whether or not the local authority is meeting any of those needs) and;

- is experiencing, or at risk of, abuse or neglect; and

- as a result of those care and support needs is unable to protect themselves from either the risk of, or the experience of, abuse or neglect.

These safeguarding duties have a legal effect in relation to organisations other than the local authority, for example the NHS and the police.

Roles, responsibilities and training in local authorities, the NHS and other agencies

Where someone is 18 or over but is still receiving children's services and a safeguarding issue is raised, the matter should be dealt with through adult safeguarding arrangements. For example, this could occur when a young person with substantial and complex needs continues to be supported in a residential educational setting until the age of 25. Where appropriate, adult safeguarding services should involve the local authority's children's safeguarding colleagues as well as any relevant partners (e.g. the police or NHS) or other persons relevant to the case. However, the level of needs is not relevant, and the young adult does not need to have eligible needs for care and support under the Care Act, or be receiving any particular service from the local authority, in order for the safeguarding duties to apply.

Local authority statutory adult safeguarding duties apply equally to those adults with care and support needs regardless of whether those needs are being met, regardless of whether the adult lacks mental capacity or not, and regardless of setting, other than prisons and approved premises where prison governors and National Offender Management Service (NOMS) respectively have responsibility. However, senior representatives of those services may sit on the Safeguarding Adults Board and play an important role in the strategic development of adult safeguarding locally. Additionally, they may ask for advice from the local authority when faced with a safeguarding issue that they are finding particularly challenging.

Adult safeguarding: what it is and why it matters

Safeguarding means protecting an adult's right to live in safety, free from abuse and neglect. It is about people and organisations working together to prevent and stop both the risks and experience of abuse or neglect, while at the same time making sure that the adult's well-being is promoted including, where appropriate, having regard to their views, wishes, feelings and beliefs in deciding on any action. This must recognise that adults sometimes have complex interpersonal relationships and may be ambivalent, unclear or unrealistic about their personal circumstances.

Organisations should always promote the adult's well-being in their safeguarding arrangements. People have complex lives and being safe is only one of the things they want for themselves. Newly qualified social workers should work with the adult to establish what being safe means to them and how that can be best achieved. Professionals and other staff should not be advocating 'safety' measures that do not take account of individual well-being, as defined in Section 1 of the Care Act.

The Care Act requires that each local authority must:

- Make enquiries, or cause others to do so, if it believes an adult is experiencing, or is at risk of, abuse or neglect. An enquiry should establish whether any action needs to be taken to prevent or stop abuse or neglect, and if so, by whom;
- Set up a Safeguarding Adults Board (SAB);
- Arrange, where appropriate, for an independent advocate to represent and support an adult who is the subject of a safeguarding enquiry or Safeguarding Adult Review (SAR) where the adult has 'substantial difficulty' in being involved in the process and where there is no other suitable person to represent and support them;
- Co-operate with each of its relevant partners (as set out in Section 6 of the Care Act) in order to protect the adult. In their turn each relevant partner must also co-operate with the local authority.

The aims of adult safeguarding are to:

- stop abuse or neglect wherever possible; prevent harm and reduce the risk of abuse or neglect to adults with care and support needs;

- safeguard adults in a way that supports them in making choices and having control about how they want to live;

- promote an approach that concentrates on improving life for the adults concerned;

- raise public awareness so that communities as a whole, alongside professionals, play their part in preventing, identifying and responding to abuse and neglect;

- provide information and support in accessible ways to help people understand the different types of abuse, how to stay safe and what to do to raise a concern about the safety or well-being of an adult and address what has caused the abuse or neglect.

In order to achieve these aims, it is necessary to ensure that everyone, both individuals and organisations, is clear about their roles and responsibilities to:

- create strong multi-agency partnerships that provide timely and effective prevention of and responses to abuse or neglect;

- support the development of a positive learning environment across these partnerships and at all levels within them to help break down cultures that are risk-averse and seek to scapegoat or blame practitioners;

- enable access to mainstream community resources such as accessible leisure facilities, safe town centres and community groups that can reduce social and physical isolation.

The following six principles apply to safeguarding adults and all sectors and settings including care and support services, further education colleges, commissioning, regulation and provision of health and care services, social work, healthcare, welfare benefits, housing, wider local authority functions and the criminal justice system. The principles should inform the ways in which newly qualified social workers and other staff work with adults and underpin all safeguarding work.

Empowerment
People being supported and encouraged to make their own decisions and informed consent. 'I am asked what I want as the outcomes from the safeguarding process and these directly inform what happens.'

Prevention
It is better to take action before harm occurs. 'I receive clear and simple information about what abuse is, how to recognise the signs and what I can do to seek help.'

Proportionality
The least intrusive response appropriate to the risk presented. 'I am sure that the professionals will work in my interest, as I see them and they will only get involved as much as needed.'

Protection

Support and representation for those in greatest need. 'I get help and support to report abuse and neglect. I get help so that I am able to take part in the safeguarding process to the extent to which I want.'

Partnership

Local solutions through services working with their communities. Communities have a part to play in preventing, detecting and reporting neglect and abuse. 'I know that staff treat any personal and sensitive information in confidence, only sharing what is helpful and necessary. I am confident that professionals will work together and with me to get the best result for me.'

Accountability

Accountability and transparency in delivering safeguarding. 'I understand the role of everyone involved in my life and so do they.'

Making safeguarding personal

In addition to these principles, it is also important that all safeguarding partners take a broad community approach to establishing safeguarding arrangements. It is vital that all organisations recognise that adult safeguarding arrangements are there to protect individuals. We all have different preferences, histories, circumstances and lifestyles, so it is unhelpful to prescribe a process that must be followed whenever a concern is raised; the case study below helps illustrate this.

CASE STUDY A7.1

Two brothers with mild learning disabilities lived in their family home, where they had remained following the death of their parents some time previously. Large amounts of rubbish had accumulated both in the garden and inside the house, with cleanliness and self-neglect also an issue. They had been targeted by fraudsters, resulting in criminal investigation and conviction of those responsible, but the brothers had refused subsequent services from adult social care and their case had been closed.

They had, however, had a good relationship with their social worker, and as concerns about their health and well-being continued it was decided that the social worker would maintain contact, calling in every couple of weeks to see how they were, and offer any help needed, on their terms. After almost a year, through the gradual building of trust and understanding, the brothers asked to be considered for supported housing; with the social worker's help they improved the state of their house enough to sell it, and moved to a living environment in which practical support could be provided.

Making safeguarding personal means it should be person-led and outcome-focused. It engages the person in a conversation about how best to respond to their safeguarding

(Continued)

---

situation in a way that enhances involvement, choice and control as well as improving quality of life, well-being and safety. Nevertheless, there are key issues that local authorities and their partners should consider if they suspect or are made aware of abuse or neglect.

What are abuse and neglect?

This section considers the different types and patterns of abuse and neglect and the different circumstances in which they may take place. This is not intended to be an exhaustive list but an illustrative guide as to the sort of behaviour which could give rise to a safeguarding concern.

Local authorities should not limit their view of what constitutes abuse or neglect, as they can take many forms and the circumstances of the individual case should always be considered, although the criteria in section 42 will need to be met before the issue is considered as a safeguarding concern. Exploitation, in particular, is a common theme in the following list of the types of abuse and neglect.

- Physical abuse – including assault, hitting, slapping, pushing, misuse of medication, restraint or inappropriate physical sanctions.

- Domestic violence – including psychological, physical, sexual, financial, emotional abuse; so-called 'honour' based violence.

- Sexual abuse – including rape, indecent exposure, sexual harassment, inappropriate looking or touching, sexual teasing or innuendo, sexual photography, subjection to pornography or witnessing sexual acts, indecent exposure and sexual assault or sexual acts to which the adult has not consented or was pressured into consenting.

- Psychological abuse – including emotional abuse, threats of harm or abandonment, deprivation of contact, humiliation, blaming, controlling, intimidation, coercion, harassment, verbal abuse, cyber bullying, isolation or unreasonable and unjustified withdrawal of services or supportive networks.

- Financial or material abuse – including theft, fraud, internet scamming, coercion in relation to an adult's financial affairs or arrangements, including in connection with wills, property, inheritance or financial transactions, or the misuse or misappropriation of property, possessions or benefits.

- Modern slavery – encompasses slavery, human trafficking, forced labour and domestic servitude. Traffickers and slave masters use whatever means they have at their disposal to coerce, deceive and force individuals into a life of abuse, servitude and inhumane treatment.

- Discriminatory abuse – including forms of harassment, slurs or similar treatment, because of race, gender and gender identity, age, disability, sexual orientation or religion.

- Organisational abuse – including neglect and poor care practice within an institution or specific care setting such as a hospital or care home, for example, or in relation to care provided in one's own home. This may range from one-off incidents to ongoing ill-treatment. It can be through neglect or poor professional practice as a result of the structure, policies, processes and practices within an organisation.

- Neglect and acts of omission – including ignoring medical, emotional or physical care needs, failure to provide access to appropriate health, care and support or educational services, the withholding of the necessities of life, such as medication, adequate nutrition and heating.

- Self-neglect – this covers a wide range of behaviour neglecting to care for one's personal hygiene, health or surroundings and includes behaviour such as hoarding.

Incidents of abuse may be one-off or multiple, and affect one person or more. Newly qualified social workers and others should look beyond single incidents or individuals to identify patterns of harm, just as the Care Quality Commission, as the regulator of service quality, does when it looks at the quality of care in health and care services. Repeated instances of poor care may be an indication of more serious problems and of what we now describe as organisational abuse. In order to see these patterns it is important that information is recorded and appropriately shared.

Spotting signs of abuse and neglect

Workers across a wide range of organisations need to be vigilant about adult safeguarding concerns in all walks of life including, amongst others in health and social care, welfare, policing, banking, fire and rescue services, trading standards, leisure services, faith groups and housing. GPs, in particular, are often well-placed to notice changes in an adult that may indicate they are being abused or neglected. Findings from Serious Case Reviews (e.g. see **www.hampshiresab.org.uk/learning-from-experience-database/serious-case-reviews/**) have sometimes stated that if professionals or other staff had acted upon their concerns or sought more information, then death or serious harm might have been prevented.

The following case study illustrates that someone who might not typically be thought of, in this case the neighbour, does in fact have an important role to play in identifying when an adult is at risk.

Anyone can witness or become aware of information suggesting that abuse and neglect is occurring. The matter may, for example, be raised by a worried neighbour (see above case study), a concerned bank cashier, a GP, a welfare benefits officer, a housing support worker or a nurse on a ward. Primary care staff may be particularly well-placed to spot abuse and neglect, as in many cases they may be the only professionals with whom the adult has contact.

CASE STUDY A7.2

Mr A is in his 40s, and lives in a housing association flat with little family contact. His mental health is relatively stable, after a previous period of hospitalisation, and he has visits from a mental health support worker.

He rarely goes out, but he lets people into his accommodation because of his loneliness. The police were alerted by Mr A's neighbours to several domestic disturbances. His accommodation had been targeted by a number of local people and he had become subjected to verbal, financial and sometimes physical abuse.

Although Mr A initially insisted they were his friends, he did indicate he was frightened; he attended a case conference with representatives from adult social care, mental health services and the police, from which emerged a plan to strengthen his own self-protective ability as well as to deal with the present abuse. Mr A has made different arrangements for managing his money so that he does not accumulate large sums at home. A community-based visiting service has been engaged to keep him company through visits to his home, and with time his support worker aims to help get involved in social activities that will bring more positive contacts to allay the loneliness that Mr A sees as his main challenge.

The adult may say or do things that hint that all is not well. It may come in the form of a complaint, a call for a police response, an expression of concern, or come to light during a needs assessment. Regardless of how the safeguarding concern is identified, everyone should understand what to do, and where to go locally to get help and advice. It is vital that professionals, other staff and members of the public are vigilant on behalf of those unable to protect themselves. This will include:

- knowing about different types of abuse and neglect and their signs;

- supporting adults to keep safe;

- knowing who to tell about suspected abuse or neglect;

- supporting adults to think and weigh up the risks and benefits of different options when exercising choice and control; and

- awareness campaigns for the general public and multi-agency training for all staff to achieving these objectives.

Reporting and responding to abuse and neglect

It is important to understand the circumstances of abuse, including the wider context such as whether others may be at risk of abuse, whether there is any emerging pattern of abuse, whether others have witnessed abuse and the role of family members and paid staff or professionals.

The circumstances surrounding any actual or suspected case of abuse or neglect will inform the response. For example, it is important to recognise that abuse or neglect may be unintentional and may arise because a carer is struggling to care for another person. This makes the need to take action no less important, but in such circumstances, an appropriate response could be a support package for the carer and monitoring. However, the primary focus must still be how to safeguard the adult. In other circumstances where the safeguarding concerns arise from abuse or neglect deliberately intended to cause harm, then it would not only be necessary to immediately consider what steps are needed to protect the adult but also whether to refer the matter to the police to consider whether a criminal investigation would be required or appropriate.

The nature and timing of the intervention and who is best placed to lead will be in part, determined by the circumstances. For example, where there is poor, neglectful care or practice, resulting in pressure sores for example, then an employer-led disciplinary response may be more appropriate; but this situation will need additional responses such as clinical intervention to improve the care given immediately and a clinical audit of practice. Commissioning or regulatory enforcement action may also be appropriate.

Early sharing of information is the key to providing an effective response where there are emerging concerns. To ensure effective safeguarding arrangements all organisations must have arrangements in place which set out clearly the processes and the principles for sharing information between each other, with other professionals and the SAB; this could be via an Information Sharing Agreement to formalise the arrangements. And no professional should assume that someone else will pass on information which they think may be critical to the safety and well-being of the adult. If a professional has concerns about the adult's welfare and believes they are suffering or likely to suffer abuse or neglect, then they should share the information with the local authority and/or the police if they believe or suspect that a crime has been committed.

Carers and safeguarding

Circumstances in which a carer (for example, a family member or friend) could be involved in a situation that may require a safeguarding response include:

- a carer witnessing or speaking up about abuse or neglect;
- a carer experiencing intentional or unintentional harm from the adult they are trying to support or from professionals and organisations they are in contact with; or
- a carer unintentionally or intentionally harming or neglecting the adult they support on their own or with others.

Assessment of both the carer and the adult they care for must include consideration of the well-being of both of them. Section 1 of the Care Act includes protection from abuse and neglect as part of the definition of well-being. As such, a needs or carer's assessment is an important opportunity to explore the individual's circumstances and consider whether it would be possible to provide information or support that prevents abuse or neglect from occurring, for example, by providing training to the carer about the condition that the adult they care for has or to support them to care more safely.

Where that is necessary the local authority should make arrangements for providing it. If a carer speaks up about abuse or neglect, it is essential that they are listened to and that where appropriate a safeguarding enquiry is undertaken and other agencies are involved as appropriate.

If a carer experiences intentional or unintentional harm from the adult they are supporting, or if a carer unintentionally or intentionally harms or neglects the adult they support, consideration should be given to whether, as part of the assessment and support planning process for the carer and/or the adult they care for, support can be provided that removes or mitigates the risk of abuse.

For example, the provision of training or information or other support may minimise the stress experienced by the carer. In some circumstances the carer may need to have independent representation or advocacy; in others, a carer may benefit from having such support if they are under great stress or similar and whether other agencies should be involved; in some circumstances where a criminal offence is suspected this will include alerting the police, or in others the primary healthcare services may need to be involved in monitoring.

Other key considerations in relation to carers should include:

* involving carers in safeguarding enquiries relating to the adult they care for, as appropriate;

* whether or not joint assessment is appropriate in each individual circumstance;

* the risk factors that may increase the likelihood of abuse or neglect occurring, and whether a change in circumstance changes the risk of abuse or neglect occurring.

A change in circumstance should also trigger the review of the care and/or support plan.

Policies and procedures

In order to respond appropriately where abuse or neglect may be taking place, anyone in contact with the adult, whether in a volunteer or paid role, must understand their own role and responsibility and have access to practical and legal guidance, advice and support. For the newly qualified social worker, this will include understanding local inter-agency policies and procedures.

In any organisation, there should be adult safeguarding policies and procedures. These should reflect statutory guidance and be for use locally to support the reduction or removal of safeguarding risks as well as to secure any support to protect the adult and, where necessary, to help the adult recover and develop resilience.

Such policies and procedures should assist those working with adults how to develop swift safeguarding responses and how to involve adults in decision-making. This, in turn, should encourage proportionate responses and improve outcomes for the people concerned.

The SAB should keep policies and procedures under review and report on these in their annual report as necessary. Procedures should be updated to incorporate learning from published research, peer reviews, case law and lessons from recent cases and Safeguarding Adults Reviews. The procedures should also include the provisions of the law – criminal, civil and statutory – relevant to adult safeguarding. This should include local or agency specific information about obtaining legal advice and access to appropriate remedies.

The Care Act requires that each local authority must arrange for an independent advocate to represent and support an adult who is the subject of a safeguarding enquiry or Safeguarding Adult Review where the adult has 'substantial difficulty' in being involved in the process and where there is no other suitable person to represent and support them (see Chapter 7 of Care Act).

The Mental Capacity Act 2005

People must be assumed to have capacity to make their own decisions and be given all practicable help before anyone treats them as not being able to make their own decisions. Where an adult is found to lack capacity to make a decision then any action taken, or any decision made for them, or on their behalf, must be made in their best interests.

Newly qualified social workers and other staff need to understand and always work in line with the Mental Capacity Act 2005 (MCA). You should use your professional judgement and balance many competing views. You will need considerable guidance and support from your employer if you are to help adults manage risk and put them in control of decision-making if possible. Regular face-to-face supervision from skilled managers is essential to enable you to work confidently and competently in difficult and sensitive situations.

Mental capacity is frequently raised in relation to adult safeguarding. The requirement to apply the MCA in adult safeguarding enquiries challenges many newly qualified workers and requires utmost care, particularly where it appears an adult has capacity for making specific decisions that nevertheless places them at risk of being abused or neglected.

The MCA created the criminal offences of ill-treatment and neglect in respect of people who lack the ability to make decisions. The offences can be committed by anyone responsible for that adult's care and support – paid staff but also family carers as well as people who have the legal authority to act on that adult's behalf (i.e. persons with power of attorney or court-appointed deputies).

These offences are punishable by fines or imprisonment. Ill-treatment covers both deliberate acts of ill-treatment and also those acts which are reckless which result in ill-treatment. Wilful neglect requires a serious departure from the required stand-ards of treatment and usually means that a person has deliberately failed to carry out an act that they knew they were under a duty to perform. If someone has con-cerns about the actions of an attorney acting under a registered Enduring Power of Attorney (EPA) or Lasting Power of Attorney (LPA), or a Deputy appointed by the Court of Protection, they should contact the Office of the Public Guardian (OPG – see **www.gov.uk/government/organisations/office-of-the-public-guardian**).

The OPG can investigate the actions of a Deputy or Attorney and can also refer con-cerns to other relevant agencies. When it makes a referral, the OPG will make sure that the relevant agency keeps it informed of the action it takes. The OPG can also make an application to the Court of Protection if it needs to take possible action against the attorney or deputy. Whilst the OPG primarily investigates financial abuse, it is important to note that that it also has a duty to investigate concerns about the actions of an attorney acting under a health and welfare Lasting Power of Attorney or a personal welfare deputy. The OPG can investigate concerns about an attorney acting under a registered Enduring or Lasting Power of Attorney, regardless of the adult's capacity to make decisions.

Multi-agency safeguarding role

Local authorities must cooperate with each of their relevant partners, as described in section 6(7) of the Care Act 2014, and those partners must also cooperate with the local authority, in the exercise of their functions relevant to care and support includ-ing those to protect adults.

Relevant partners of a local authority include any other local authority with whom they agree it would be appropriate to co-operate (e.g. neighbouring authorities with whom they provide joint shared services). The following agencies or bodies who operate within the local authority's area include:

- NHS England;

- Clinical Commissioning Groups (CCGs);

- NHS trusts and NHS Foundation Trusts;

- Department for Work and Pensions;

- the police;

- prisons; and

- probation services.

Local authorities must also co-operate with other such agencies or bodies as it considers appropriate in the exercise of its adult safeguarding functions, including (but not limited to) those listed in section 6(3) of the Care Act 2014: general practitioners; dentists; pharmacists; NHS hospitals; and housing, health and care providers.

Agencies should stress the need for preventing abuse and neglect wherever possible. Observant professionals and other staff making early, positive interventions with individuals and families can make a huge difference to their lives, preventing the deterioration of a situation or breakdown of a support network. It is often when people become increasingly isolated and cut off from families and friends that they become extremely vulnerable to abuse and neglect. Agencies should implement robust risk management processes in order to prevent concerns escalating to a crisis point and requiring intervention under safeguarding adult procedures.

Partners should ensure that they have the mechanisms in place that enable early identification and assessment of risk through timely information sharing and targeted multi-agency intervention. Multi-agency safeguarding hubs may be one model to support this but are not the only one. Policies and strategies for safeguarding adults should include measures to understand the circumstances, including isolation, which make adults vulnerable to abuse.

CASE STUDY A7.3

Miss P's mental health social worker became concerned when she had received reports that two of Miss P's associates were visiting more regularly and sometimes staying over at her flat. Miss P was being coerced into prostitution and reportedly being physically assaulted by one of the men visiting her flat. There was also concern that she was being financially exploited. Miss P's vulnerability was exacerbated by her mental health needs and consequent inability to set safe boundaries with the people she was associating with.

The social worker realised that the most appropriate way to enable Miss P to manage the risk of harm was to involve Miss P's family, to which she agreed, and other professionals to develop and coordinate a plan which would enable her to continue living independently but provide a safety net for when the risk of harm became heightened. Guided initially by Miss P's wish for the two men to stay away from her, the social worker initiated a planning meeting between supportive family members and other professionals such as the police, domestic violence workers, support workers and housing officers. Although Miss P herself felt unable to attend the planning meeting, her social worker ensured that her views were included and helped guide the plan. The meeting allowed family and professionals to work in partnership, to openly share information about the risks and to plan what support Miss P needed to safely maintain her independence.

(Continued)

Tasks were divided between the police, family members and specialist support workers. The social worker had a role in ensuring that the plan was coordinated properly and that Miss P was fully aware of everyone's role. Miss P's family were crucial to the success of the plan as they had always supported her and were able to advocate for her needs.

They also had a trusting relationship with her and were able to notify the police and other professionals if they thought that the risk to Miss P was increasing. The police played an active role in monitoring and preventing criminal activity towards Miss P and ensured that they kept all of the other professionals and family up to date with what was happening. Miss P is working with a domestic violence specialist to help her develop personal strategies to keep safer and her support worker is helping her to build resilience through community support and activities.

Responding to abuse and neglect in a regulated care setting

It is important that all partners are clear where responsibility lies where abuse or neglect is carried out by employees or in a regulated setting, such as a care home, hospital or college. The first responsibility to act must be with the employing agency as the provider of the service. However, social workers and other professionals may need to be involved in order to support the adult to recover.

When an employer is aware of abuse or neglect, they are under a duty to correct this and protect the adult from harm as soon as possible and inform the local authority, CQC and CCG where the latter is the commissioner. Where a local authority has reasonable cause to suspect that an adult may be experiencing or at risk of abuse or neglect, then it is still under a duty to make (or cause to be made) whatever enquiries it thinks necessary to decide what if any action needs to be taken and by whom. The local authority may well be reassured by the employer's response so that no further action is required. However, a local authority would have to satisfy itself that an employer's response has been sufficient to deal with the safeguarding issue and, if not, to undertake any enquiry of its own and any appropriate follow-up action (e.g. referral to CQC, professional regulators).

The employer should investigate any concern (and provide any additional support that the adult may need) unless there is compelling reason why it is inappropriate or unsafe to do this. For example, this could be a serious conflict of interest on the part of the employer, concerns having been raised about non-effective past enquiries or serious, multiple concerns, or a matter that requires investigation by the police.

An example of a conflict of interest where it is better for an external person to be appointed to investigate may be the case of a family-run business where institutional abuse is alleged, or where the manager or owner of the service is implicated. The circumstances where an external person would be required should be set out in the local multi-agency procedures. All those carrying out such enquiries should have received appropriate training.

There should be a clear understanding between partners at a local level when other agencies such as the local authority, CQC or CCG need to be notified or involved and what role they have. ADASS, CQC, LGA, ACPO and NHS England have jointly produced a high-level guide on these roles and responsibilities – see our Further Reading section.

Commissioners should encourage an open culture around safeguarding, working in partnership with providers to ensure the best outcome for the adult. A disciplinary investigation, and potentially a hearing, may result in the employer taking informal or formal measures which may include dismissal and possibly referral to the Disclosure and Barring Service (see **https://www.gov.uk/government/publications/dbs-referrals-factsheets**).

Local authority's role in carrying out enquiries

Local authorities must make enquiries, or cause others to do so, if they reasonably suspect an adult who meets the criteria in section 42 is, or is at risk of, being abused or neglected. An enquiry is the action taken or instigated by the local authority in response to a concern that abuse or neglect may be taking place. An enquiry could range from a conversation with the adult, or if they lack capacity, or have substantial difficulty in understanding the enquiry their representative or advocate, prior to initiating a formal enquiry under section 42, right through to a much more formal multi-agency plan or course of action. Whatever the course of subsequent action, the professional concerned should record the concern, the adult's views and wishes, any immediate action taken and the reasons for those actions.

The purpose of the enquiry is to decide whether or not the local authority or another organisation should do something to help and protect the adult. If the local authority decides that another organisation should make the enquiry, for example a care provider, then the local authority should be clear about timescales, the need to know the outcomes of the enquiry and what action will follow if this is not done.

Professionals and other staff need to handle enquiries in a sensitive and skilled way to ensure distress to the adult is minimised. It is likely that many enquiries will require the input and supervision of a social worker, particularly the more complex situations and to support the adult to realise the outcomes they want and to reach a resolution or recovery. For example, where abuse or neglect is suspected within a family or informal relationship it is likely that a social worker will be the most appropriate lead. Personal and family relationships within community settings can prove both difficult and complex to assess and intervene in. The dynamics of personal relationships can be extremely difficult to judge and rebalance. For example, an adult may make a choice to be in a relationship that causes them emotional distress which outweighs, for them, the unhappiness of not maintaining the relationship.

Whilst work with the adult may frequently require the input of a social worker, other aspects of enquiries may be best undertaken by others with more appropriate skills and knowledge. For example, health professionals should undertake enquiries and treatment plans relating to medicines management or pressure sores.

Well-being and the Care Act 2014

Local authorities must promote well-being when carrying out any of their care and support functions in respect of a person. This may sometimes be referred to as 'the well-being principle' because it is a guiding principle that puts well-being at the heart of care and support. The well-being principle applies in all cases where a local authority is carrying out a care and support function, or making a decision, in relation to a person. For this reason it is referred to throughout this guidance. It applies equally to adults with care and support needs and their carers. In some specific circumstances, it also applies to children, their carers and to young carers when they are subject to transition assessments.

'Well-being' is a broad concept, and it is described as relating to the following areas in particular:

- personal dignity (including treatment of the individual with respect);
- physical and mental health and emotional well-being;
- protection from abuse and neglect;
- control by the individual over day-to-day life (including over care and support provided and the way it is provided);
- participation in work, education, training or recreation;
- social and economic well-being;
- domestic, family and personal;
- suitability of living accommodation;
- the individual's contribution to society.

The individual aspects of well-being or outcomes above are those which are set out in the Care Act, and are most relevant to people with care and support needs and carers. There is no hierarchy, and all should be considered of equal importance when considering 'well-being' in the round.

Promoting well-being
Promoting well-being involves actively seeking improvements in the aspects of well-being set out above when carrying out a care and support function in relation to an individual at any stage of the process from the provision of information and advice to reviewing a care and support plan. Well-being covers an intentionally broad range of the aspects of a person's life and will encompass a wide variety of specific considerations depending on the individual.

The principle of promoting well-being should be embedded through the local authority care and support system, but how the local authority promotes well-being in practice will depend on the particular function being performed. During the assessment process, for instance, the local authority should explicitly consider the most relevant aspects of well-being to the individual concerned, and assess how their needs impact on them. Taking this approach will allow for the assessment to identify how care and support, or other services or resources in the local community, could help the person to achieve their outcomes.

During care and support planning, when agreeing how needs are to be met, promoting the person's well-being may mean making decisions about particular types or locations of care (for instance, to be closer to family).

The well-being principle applies equally to those who do not have eligible needs but come into contact with the system in some other way (for example, via an assessment that does not lead to ongoing care and support) as it does to those who go on to receive care and support, and have an ongoing relationship with the local authority. It should inform the delivery of universal services which are provided to all people in the local population, as well as being considered when meeting eligible needs. Although the well-being principle applies specifically when the local authority performs an activity or task, or makes a decision, in relation to a person, the principle should also be considered by the local authority when it undertakes broader, strategic functions, such as planning, which are not in relation to one individual. As such, 'well-being' should be seen as the common theme around which care and support is built at local and national level.

In addition to the general principle of promoting well-being, there are a number of other key principles and standards which local authorities must have regard to when carrying out the same activities or functions. These are listed as follows:

- The importance of beginning with the assumption that the individual is best-placed to judge the individual's well-being. Building on the principles of the Mental Capacity Act, the local authority should assume that the person themselves best knows their own outcomes, goals and well-being. Local authorities should not make assumptions as to what matters most to the person.

- Considering the person's views and wishes is critical to a person-centred system. Local authorities should not ignore or downplay the importance of a person's own opinions in relation to their life and their care.

- The importance of preventing or delaying the development of needs for care and support and the importance of reducing needs that already exist. At every interaction with a person, a local authority should consider whether or how the person's needs could be reduced or other needs could be delayed from arising.

- The need to ensure that decisions are made having regard to all the individual's circumstances (and are not based only on their age or appearance, any condition they have, or any aspect of their behaviour which might lead others to make unjustified assumptions about their well-being). Local authorities should not make judgements based on preconceptions about the person's circumstances, but should in every case work to understand their individual needs and goals.

- The importance of the individual participating as fully as possible in decisions about them and being provided with the information and support necessary to enable the individual to participate. Care and support should be personal, and local authorities should not make decisions from which the person is excluded.

- The importance of achieving a balance between the individual's well-being and that of any friends or relatives who are involved in caring for the individual. People should be considered in the context of their families and support networks, not just as isolated individuals with needs. Local authorities should take into account the impact of an individual's need on those who support them, and take steps to help others access information or support.

- The need to protect people from abuse and neglect. In any activity which a local authority undertakes, it should consider how to ensure that the person is and remains protected from abuse or neglect. This is not confined only to safeguarding issues, but should be a general principle applied in every case.

- The need to ensure that any restriction on the individual's rights or freedom of action that is involved in the exercise of the function is kept to the minimum necessary for achieving the purpose for which the function is being exercised. Where the local authority has to take actions which restrict rights or freedoms, they should ensure that the course followed is the least restrictive necessary.

All of the matters listed above must be considered in relation to every individual, when a local authority carries out a function as described in this guidance. Considering these matters should lead to an approach that looks at a person's life holistically, considering their needs in the context of their skills, ambitions and priorities – as well as the other people in their life and how they can support the person in meeting the outcomes they want to achieve. The focus should be on supporting people to live as independently as possible for as long as possible.

Well-being throughout the Care Act

Well-being cannot be achieved simply through crisis management; it must include a focus on delaying and preventing care and support needs, and supporting people to live as independently as possible for as long as possible. Promoting well-being does not mean simply looking at a need that corresponds to a particular service. At the heart of the reformed system will be an assessment and planning process that is a genuine conversation about people's needs for care and support and how meeting these can help them achieve the outcomes most important to them. Where someone is unable to fully participate in these conversations and has no one to help them, local authorities will arrange for an independent advocate.

In order to ensure these conversations look at people holistically, local authorities and their partners must focus on joining up around an individual, making the person the starting point for planning, rather than what services are provided by what particular agency.

In particular, the Care Act is designed to work in partnership with the Children and Families Act 2014, which applies to 0–25-year-old children and young people with SEN and disabilities. In combination, the two Acts enable areas to prepare children and young people for adulthood from the earliest possible stage, including their transition to adult services.

Promoting well-being is not always about local authorities meeting needs directly. It will be just as important for them to put in place a system where people have the information they need to take control of their care and support and choose the options that are right for them. People will have an opportunity to request their local authority support in the form of a direct payment that they can then use to buy their own care and support using this information.

Control also means the ability to move from one area to another or from children's services to the adult system without fear of suddenly losing care and support. The Care Act ensures that people will be able to move to a different area without suddenly losing their care and support and provides clarity about who will be responsible for care and support in different situations. It also includes measures to help young people move to the adult care and support system, ensuring that no one finds themselves suddenly without care on turning 18. It is not possible to promote well-being without establishing a basic foundation where people are safe and their care and support is on a secure footing.

Summary of key points

- Know what safeguarding, abuse and neglect are and why they matter.

- Familiarise yourself with local policies and procedures to do with safeguarding adults.

- Develop understanding of the notion of 'well-being' and its application in practice.

- Develop skills and knowledge in application of law and policy which support good practice in safeguarding adults.

- Develop understanding of the inter-relationship between mental capacity, risk and safeguarding activity.

- Develop communication skills to facilitate a multi-agency approach to safeguarding adults.

FURTHER READING

Abuse of vulnerable adults in England report

www.hscic.gov.uk/catalogue/PUB13499/abus-vuln-adul-eng-12-13-fin-rep.pdf

The Care Act 2014

www.legislation.gov.uk/ukpga/2014/23/contents/enacted

Discrimination: your rights

www.gov.uk/discrimination-your-rights/types-of-discrimination

The Modern Slavery Act 2015

www.legislation.gov.uk/ukpga/2015/30/section/54/enacted

Safeguarding adults: roles and responsibilities guidance

www.local.gov.uk/documents/10180/11779/Safeguarding+adults+-+Roles+and+responsibilities+in+health+and+care+services/d7564e6f-53a4-4d0a-af2f-9c235f9b379b

Safeguarding policy: protecting vulnerable adults

www.justice.gov.uk/downloads/protecting-the-vulnerable/mca/safeguarding-policy.pdf

The following publications will further support your understanding of safeguarding adults.

Galpin, D (2012) The role of social defences and organisational structures in facilitating the abuse and maltreatment of older people. *Journal of Adult Protection,* 14(5): 229–36.

Galpin, D (2014) Reading between the lines: the role of discourse in shaping responses to safeguarding older people. *Journal of Adult Protection,* 16(6): 399–410.

Galpin, D (2016) *Safeguarding adults at risk of harm.* Birmingham: Learn to Care.

Galpin, D and Hughes, D (2011) A joined up approach to safeguarding and personalisation: a framework for practice in multi-agency decision-making. *Journal of Adult Protection,* 13(3): 150–9.

Parker, J and Galpin, D (2013) Safeguarding adults with a learning disability in England and Wales: money, markets and ethically sustainable care. *Journal of Care Service Management,* 6(4): 149–55.

References

Adair J (2010) *Decision-making and problem solving strategies*. London: Kogan Page.

Adams, J, Hayes, J and Hopson, B (1976) *Transition: understanding and managing personal change*. London: Martin Robertson.

Adams, R (2005) Working within and across boundaries: tensions and dilemmas, in Adams, R, Payne, M and Dominelli, L (eds) *Social work future*. London: Routledge, pp99–114.

Adams, R (2009) Encountering complexity and uncertainty, in Adams, R, Dominelli, L and Payne, M (eds) *Practising social work in a complex world*, 2nd edn. Basingstoke: Palgrave Macmillan, pp15–32.

Adams, R, Dominelli, L and Payne, M (2002) *Social work: themes, issues and critical debates*. Basingstoke: Palgrave.

Alcock, P (2008) *Social policy in Britain*, 3rd edn. Basingstoke: Palgrave.

Alcock, P with May, M (2014) *Social policy in Britain*, 4th edn. Basingstoke: Palgrave.

Argyris, C and Schön, D (1974) *Theory in practice: increasing professional effectiveness*. San Francisco, CA: Jossey-Bass.

Argyris, C and Schön, D (1978) *Organizational learning: a theory of action perspective*. Reading, MA: Addison Wesley.

Ashencaen Crabtree, S, Parker, J, Azman, A and Carlo, D P (2012) Epiphanies and learning in a postcolonial Malaysia context: a preliminary evaluation of international social work placements. *International Social Work*. Advance Access doi: 10.1177/0020872812448491.

Ashencaen Crabtree, S, Parker, J, Azman, A and Masu'd, F (2015) Typologies of learning in international student placements. *Asia Pacific Journal of Social Work and Development,* 25(1): 42–53.

Baginsky, M, Moriarty, J, Manthorpe, J, Stevens, M, MacInnes, T and Nagendran, T (2010) *Social workers workload survey: messages from the frontline*. London: Department for Children, Schools and Families.

Barr, H, Goosey, D and Webb, M (2008) Social work in collaboration with other professions, in Davies, M (ed) *The Blackwell companion to social work,* 3rd edn. Oxford: Blackwell, pp277–86.

BASW (British Association of Social Workers) (2012) *Code of ethics.* Available from: **www.basw.co.uk/codeofethics/**

BASW (2015) PCF – The Professional Capabilities Framework. Available from: **www.basw.co.uk/resource/?id=1137**

Bates, N, Immins, T, Parker, J, Keen, S, Rutter, L, Brown, K and Zsigo, S (2010) 'Baptism of fire': the first year in the life of a newly qualified social worker. *Social Work Education,* 29(2): 152–70.

Beckett, D and Hager, P (2002) *Life, work and learning: practice in postmodernity*. London: Routledge.

Beresford, P (2007) *The changing roles and tasks of social work from service users' perspectives: a literature informed discussion paper*. London: Shaping Our Lives.

Blair, S (2000) The centrality of occupation during life transitions. *British Journal of Occupational Therapy,* 63: 231–7.

Blakemore, K and Booth, L (2013) *Social policy: an introduction*, 4th edn. Maidenhead: Open University Press.

Blakemore, K and Griggs, E (2007) *Social policy: an introduction,* 3rd edn. Maidenhead: Open University Press.

Blewitt, J and Tunstall, J (2008) *Fit for purpose? The social work degree in 2008*. London: GSCC.

Bochel, H (2009) Ethical theory, Chapter 4 in Bochel, H, Bochel, C, Page, R and Sykes, R (eds) *Social policy: issues and developments,* 2nd edn. Harlow: Pearson/Prentice Hall.

Bond, T and Sandhu, A (2005) *Therapists in court: providing evidence and supporting witnesses*. London: Sage.

Borrill, C, West, M, Carter, M and Dawson, J (2003) The relationship between staff satisfaction and patient satisfaction, research paper. Aston: Aston Business School.

Bostock, L, Bairstow, S, Fish, S and Macleod, F (2005) *Managing risk and minimising mistakes in services to children and families*. London: SCIE. Available from: **www.scie.org.uk/publications/reports/report06.asp**

Bradley, G (2006) Using research findings to change agency culture and practice. *Research Policy and Planning,* 24(3): 135–48.

Brammer, A (2010) *Social work law,* 3rd edn. Harlow: Pearson Education.

Brammer, A (2015) *Social work law*, 4th edn. Harlow: Pearson.

Brandon, M, Belderson, P, Warren, C, Howe, D, Gardner, R, Dodsworth, J and Black, J (2008) *Analysing child deaths and serious injury through abuse and neglect: what can we learn? A biennial analysis of serious case reviews 2003–2005*. London: DCSF. Available from: **webarchive.nationalarchives. gov.uk/20130401151715/https://www.education.gov.uk/publications/eorderingdownload/ dcsf-rr023.pdf**

Brechin, A, Brown, H and Eby, M (eds) (2000) *Critical practice in health and social care*. London: Sage.

Brown, K, Immins, T, Bates, N, Gray, I, Rutter, L, Keen, S, Parker, J and members of the Project's Steering Group (2007) *Tracking the learning and development needs of newly qualified social workers project*. Bournemouth: Bournemouth University.

Brown, K, Rutter, L, Keen, S and Rosenorn-Lanng, E (2012) *Partnerships, CPD and APL*. Birmingham: Learn to Care.

Brown, L, Tucker, C and Domokos, T (2003) Evaluating the impact of integrated health and social care teams on older people living in the community. *Health and Social Care in the Community,* 11: 85–94.

Bruce, L (2013) *Reflective practice for social workers*. Maidenhead: OUP.

Brumfitt, S, Enderby, P M and Hoben, K (2005) The transition to work of newly qualified speech and language therapists: implications for the curriculum. *Learning in Health and Social Care,* 4: 142–55.

Bryman, A (2015) *Social research methods,* 5th edn. Oxford: OUP.

Cafcass (2008) CAFCASS case recording and retention policy. London: CAFCASS.

Cafcass (2015) CAFCASS case recording and retention policy. Available from: **www.cafcass.gov.uk/ media/268740/case_recording_and_retention_policy.pdf**

Cameron, C (2003) Care work and care workers, in *Social care workforce research: needs and priorities*. King's College London: Social Care Workforce Research Unit.

Carpenter, J, Patsios, D, Wood, M, Shardlow, S, Blewett, J, Platt, D, Scholar, H, Haines, C, Tunstill, J and Wong, C (2011) *Newly Qualified Social Worker Programme evaluation report on the second year (2009–2010).* Available from: **http://dera.ioe.ac.uk/12191/1/NQSW_Y2_final_report_with_front_cover.pdf**

Carpenter, J, Patsios, D, Wood, M, Platt, D, Shardlow, S, Scholar, H, Haines, C, Wong, C and Blewett, J (2012) *Newly Qualified Social Worker Programme: final evaluation report (2008–2011).* London: Department for Education. Available from: **http://www.kcl.ac.uk/sspp/policy-institute/scwru/pubs/2012/reports/carpenteretal2012nqswfinal.pdf**

Carpenter, J, Shardlow, S, Patsios, D and Wood, M (2015) Developing the confidence and competence of newly qualified child and family social workers in England: outcomes of a national programme. *British Journal of Social Work*, 45, 153–76.

Carpenter, J, Webb, C, Bostock, L and Coomber, C (2012) Effective supervision in social work and social care: SCIE research briefing 43. London: SCIE. Available from: **www.scie.org.uk/publications/briefings/briefing43/**

CEC (Commission of the European Communities) (2007) *Action plan on adult learning: it's always a good time to learn.* Brussels: Commission of the European Communities. Available from: **http://eur-lex.europa.eu/legal-content/EN/TXT/?uri=URISERV%3Ac11102**

Central England People First (2000) *About us.* Available from: **www.peoplefirst.org.uk/default.aspx?page=26482**

Centre for Human Services Technology (undated) *What is research mindedness.* Available from: **www.resmind.swap.ac.uk/content/02_what_is/what_is_02.htm**

Charles, M and Butler, S (2004) Management of organisational change, in Lymbery, M and Butler, S (eds) *Social work ideals and practice realities.* Basingstoke: Palgrave, pp40–50.

Children Act (2004) Available from: **www.legislation.gov.uk/ukpga/2004/31/contents**

Children and Young Person Act (2008) Available from: **www.legislation.gov.uk/ukpga/2008/23/contents**

Collins, S (2007) Resilience, positive emotion and optimism. *Practice,* 19(4): 255–70.

Collins, S (2008) Statutory social workers: stress, job satisfaction, coping, social support and individual differences. *British Journal of Social Work*, 39: 1173–93.

Community Security Trust (CST)'s *Antisemitic Incidents Report, 2011*, published on 2 February 2012. Available from: **www.brin.ac.uk/2012/anti-semitic-incidents-2011/**

Cooper, P (2006) *Reporting to the court under the Children Act,* 2nd edn. London: Stationery Office.

Cottrell, S (1999) *The study skills handbook.* Basingstoke: Macmillan.

Council of Europe (1950) *Convention on human rights.* Available from: **www.hri.org/docs/ECHR50.html**

Covey, S (1989) *The 7 habits of highly effective people.* New York: Simon Schuster.

Covey, S (2004 [reprinted]) *The 7 habits of highly effective people.* New York: Simon Schuster.

Cree, V E (2013) *Becoming a social worker: global narratives,* 2nd edn. London: Routledge.

Crisp, B, Anderson, M, Orme, J and Lister, P (2003) Knowledge Review 1. *Learning and teaching in social work education. Assessment.* London: Social Care Institute for Excellence (SCIE).

Croisdale-Appleby, D (2014) Re-visioning social work education: an independent review. London: DH. Available from: **www.gov.uk/government/publications/social-work-education-review**

Cull, L A and Roche, J (eds) (2001) *The law and social work.* Basingstoke: Palgrave.

Cunningham, J and Cunningham, S (2008) *Sociology and social work.* Exeter: Learning Matters.

CWDC (2008) *Newly qualified social worker pilot programme 2008–2011: outcome statements and guidance.* Leeds: CWDC.

CWDC (2008a) *CWDC social work projects: annexe B and C.* Leeds: CWDC.

Davis, L (2014) *The social worker's guide to children and families law*, 2nd edn. London: Jessica Kingsley.

Department for Education (DfE) (2014) *Knowledge and Skills Statement for Child and Family Social Work.* Available from: **https://www.gov.uk/government/uploads/system/uploads/attachment_data/file/379033/Consultation_on_knowledge_and_skills_for_child_and_family_social_work_-_government_response.pdf**

DfES/DH (2006) *Options for excellence: building the social care workforce of the future.* London: DfES/DH.

DH (1998) *Modernising social services.* London: TSO.

DH (2000) *The framework for the assessment of children in need and their families.* London: TSO. Available from: **http://webarchive.nationalarchives.gov.uk/20130107105354/http://www.dh.gov.uk/en/Publicationsandstatistics/Publications/PublicationsPolicyAndGuidance/DH_4008144**

DH (2000a) *No secrets: guidance on developing and implementing multi-agency policies and procedures to protect vulnerable adults from abuse.* London: HMSO.

DH (2002) *Requirements for social work training.* London: HMSO.

DH (2005) *Mental capacity act.* London: TSO.

DH (2006) *Reward and recognition.* London: DH. Available from: **http://webarchive.nationalarchives.gov.uk/20130107105354 www.dh.gov.uk/en/publicationsandstatistics/publications/publicationspolicyandguidance/dh_4138523**

DH (2007) *Putting people first: a shared vision and commitment to the transformation of adult social care.* Available from: **http://webarchive.nationalarchives.gov.uk/20130107105354/http://www.dh.gov.uk/en/Publicationsandstatistics/Publications/PublicationsPolicyAndGuidance/DH_081118**

DH (2012) *Caring for our future: reforming care and support.* Available from: **www.gov.uk/government/uploads/system/uploads/attachment_data/file/136422/White-Paper-Caring-for-our-future-reforming-care-and-support-PDF-1580K.pdf**

DH (2014) The Care Act. London: Department of Health. Available from: **http://goo.gl/uvShns**

DH (2015) *Knowledge and Skills Statement for Social Workers in Adult Services.* Available from: **www.gov.uk/government/uploads/system/uploads/attachment_data/file/411957/KSS.pdf**

Dickens, J (2004) Risks and responsibilities: the role of the local authority lawyer in childcare cases. *Child and Family Law Quarterly,* 16: 17.

Dickens, J (2005) The 'epitome of reason': the challenges for lawyers and social workers in care proceedings. *International Journal of Law, Policy and the Family,* 19: 73–101.

Dickens, J (2006) Care, control and change in childcare proceedings: dilemmas for social workers, managers and lawyers. *Child and Family Social Work,* 11(1): 23–32.

Doel, M and Kelly, T (2014) A–Z of groups and groupwork. Basingstoke: Palgrave Macmillan.

Dominelli, L (2002) *Anti-oppressive social work theory and practice.* Basingstoke: Palgrave Macmillan.

Dominelli, L (2005) Social work research: contested knowledge for practice, in Adams, R, Dominelli, L and Payne, M (eds) *Social work futures: crossing boundaries, transforming practice.* Basingstoke: Palgrave, pp223–36.

Dyrbye, L N, West, C P, Satele, D, Boone, S, Tan, L, Sloan, J and Shanafelt, T D (2014) Burnout among US medical students, residents, and early career physicians relative to the general US population. *Academic Medicine*, 89(3): 443–51.

Edwards, D, Hawker, C, Carrier, J and Rees, C (2015) A systematic review of the effectiveness of strategies and interventions to improve the transition from student to newly qualified nurse. *International Journal of Nursing Studies*, 52(7): 1254–68.

Equality Act (2010) Available from: **www.legislation.gov.uk/ukpga/2010/15/contents**

ESWDQET (Evaluation of Social Work Degree Qualification in England Team) (2008) *Evaluation of the new social work degree qualification in England. Volume 1: Findings.* London: King's College Social Care Workforce Research Unit.

Everitt, A and Hardiker, P (1996) *Evaluating for good practice.* Basingstoke: BASW/Macmillan.

Fergusson, I and Woodward, R (2009) *Radical social work in practice: making a difference.* Bristol: Policy Press.

Fish, S, Munro, E and Bairstow, S (2008) *SCIE guide 24: leading together to safeguard children: developing a multi-agency systems approach to case reviews.* London: SCIE. Available from: **www.scie.org.uk/publications/guides/guide24/index.asp**

Fitzpatrick, T (2012) Cash transfers, Chapter 10 in Baldock, J, Mitton, J, Manning, N and Vickerstaff, S (eds) *Social policy,* 4th edn. Oxford University Press.

Fook, J and Askeland, G A (2007) Challenges of critical reflection: nothing ventured, nothing gained. *Social Work Education,* 26(5): 520–33.

Fouad, N A and Bynner, J (2008) Work transitions. *American Psychologist,* May–June: 241–51.

Fowler, A (1996) *Employee induction: a good start.* London: IPD.

Gabbay, J and le May, A (2004) Evidence based guidelines or collectively conducted 'mindlines'? Ethnographic study of knowledge management in primary care. *British Medical Journal,* 329: 1013–16.

Galpin, D (2009) Who really drives the development of post-qualifying social work education and what are the implications of this? *Social Work Education,* 26: 65–80.

Gardner, A (2011) *Personalisation in social work.* Exeter: Learning Matters.

Gibbs, G (1988) *Learning by doing: a guide to teaching and learning methods.* Oxford: Further Education Unit, Oxford Polytechnic.

Gibson, F, McGrath, A and Reid, N (1989) Occupational stress in social work. *British Journal of Social Work,* 19: 1–16.

Giddens, A and Sutton, P (2013) *Sociology,* 7th edn. Cambridge: Polity Press.

Gilligan, P (2007) Well motivated reformists or nascent radicals: how do applicants to the degree in social work see social problems, their origins and solutions. *British Journal of Social Work,* 37: 735–60.

Gilzean, T (2011) Communicating chaos, regaining control: the implications for social work of writing about self-injury. *Journal of Social Work Practice*, 25(1): 35–46.

Goldsmith, L (1999) *Recording with care: inspection of case recording in social services department.* London: DH. Available from: **http://webarchive.nationalarchives.gov.uk/+/www.dh.gov.uk/en/ Publicationsandstatistics/Publications/PublicationsPolicyAndGuidance/DH_4010129**

Goleman, D (1996) *Emotional intelligence.* London: Bloomsbury.

Goleman, D, Boyatzis, R and McKee, A (2013) *Primal leadership: unleashing the power of emotional intelligence.* Harvard: Harvard Business Review Press.

Gould, N and Baldwin, M (eds) (2004) *Social work, critical refection and the learning organization.* Aldershot: Ashgate.

Grant, L and Kinman, G (2014) (eds) *Developing resilience for social work practice.* London: Palgrave.

Grant, S, Sharidan, L and Webb, S (2014) *Readiness for practice of newly qualified social workers.* Glasgow: Glasgow Caledonian University.

Gray, I, Field, R and Brown, K (2010) *Effective leadership, management and supervision in health and social care.* Exeter: Learning Matters.

Gray, I, Parker, J, Rutter, L and Williams, S (2013) Developing communities of practice: a strategy for effective leadership, management and supervision in social work, in Lawler, J and Hafford-Letchfield, T (eds) *Perspectives on management and leadership in social work.* London: Whiting and Birch, pp118–39.

Hamm, RM (1988) Clinical intuition and clinical analysis: expertise and the cognitive continuum, in Dowie, J A and Elstein, A S (eds) *Professional judgement: a reader in clinical decision-making.* Cambridge: Cambridge University Press, pp78–105.

Handy, C (1993) *Understanding organisations,* 4th edn. London: Penguin.

Hansard (2007) *House of Lord Debates.* 8 October, column 88–94.

Haralambos, M and Holborn, M (2013) *Sociology: themes and perspectives,* 8th edn. London: Harper Collins Educational.

Harrison, K and Ruch, G (2007) Social work and the use of self: on becoming a social worker, in Lymbery, Mand Postle, K (eds) *Social work: a companion to learning.* London: Sage, pp40–50.

Hart, E and Bond, M (1995) *Action research for health and social care.* Buckingham: Open University Press (OUP).

Hawkins, P and Shohet, R (2007) *Supervising in the helping professions,* 3rd edn. Bucks: OUP.

HCPC (Health and Care Professions Council) (2016) *Standards of conduct, performance and ethics.* Available from: **www.hcpc-uk.org/aboutregistration/standards/ standardsofconductperformanceandethics/**

Health and Safety Executive (2015) *Work related stress, anxiety and depression statistics in Great Britain 2015.* Available from: **www.hse.gov.uk/statistics/causdis/stress/stress.pdf**

Healy, K (2000) *Social work practices: contemporary perspectives on change.* London: Sage.

Henwood, S and Lister, J (2007) *NLP and coaching for health care professionals.* Chichester: Wiley.

Higham, P (2013) Understanding continuing professional development, in Parker, J and Doel, M (eds) *Professional social work,* London: Sage, pp132–51.

Holmes, T H and Rahe, R H (1967) The social re-adjustment rating scale. *Journal of Psychosomatic Research,* 11: 213–18.

Holroyd J (2012) *Improving personal and organisational performance in social work*. London: Sage/ Learning Matters.

Howe, D (2008) *The emotionally intelligent social worker*. Basingstoke: Palgrave.

Howe, K and Gray, I (2012) *Effective supervision in social work*. London: Sage/Learning Matters.

Huczynski, A and Buchanan, D (2007) *Organisational behaviour,* 6th edn. Harlow: Pearson.

Hudson, B (2002) Interprofessionality in health and social care: the Achilles heel of partnership. *Journal of Interprofessional Care,* 16(1): 7–17.

Hull, C, Redfern, L and Shuttleworth, A (2004) *Profiles and portfolios: a guide for health and social care,* 2nd edn. Basingstoke: Palgrave Macmillan.

Human Rights Act (1998) Available from: **www.legislation.gov.uk/ukpga/1998/42/contents**

Humphries, B (2008) *Social work research for social justice*. Basingstoke: Palgrave Macmillan.

Hussein, S, Moriarty, J, Stevens, M, Sharpe, E and Manthorpe, J (2014) Organisational factors, job satisfaction and intention to leave among newly qualified social workers in England. *Social Work Education,* 33(3): 381–96.

Huxley, P, Evans, S, Gately, C, Webber, M, Mears, A, Pajak, S, Kendall, T, Medina, J and Katona, C (2005) Stress and pressures in mental health social work: the worker speaks. *British Journal of Social Work,* 35: 1063–79.

Ingleby, E (2006) *Applied psychology for social work*. Exeter: Learning Matters.

Ingram, R. (2015) *Understanding emotions in social work: theory, practice and reflection.* Oxford: OUP.

International Federation of Social Workers (2014) *Global definition of the social work profession*. Available from: **http://ifsw.org/policies/definition-of-social-work/**

Jack, G and Donnellan, H (2010) Recognising the person within the developing professional: tracking the early careers of newly qualified child care social workers in three local authorities in England. *Social Work Education,* 29(3): 305–18.

Jelphs, K and Dickinson, H (2008) *Working in teams*. Bristol: Policy Press.

Johns, C (1998) Opening the doors of perception, in Johns, C and Freshwater, D (eds) *Transforming nursing through reflective practice*. Oxford: Blackwell Science, pp1–20.

Johns, R (2009) *Using the law in social work* (Transforming Social Work Practice), 4th edn. Exeter: Learning Matters.

Johns, R (2014) *Using the law in social work* (Transforming Social Work Practice), 6th edn. Exeter: Learning Matters.

Johnson, B (1996) *Polarity management: identifying and managing unsolvable problems,* 2nd edn. Amherst, MA: HRD Press.

Jones, C, Ferguson, I, Lavalette, M and Penketh, L (2004) *Social work and social justice: a manifesto for a new engaged practice*. Available from: **www.socmag.net/?p=177**

Jordan, B and Drakeford, M (2012) *Social policy and social work under austerity*. Bristol: Policy Press.

Jordan, B and Jordan, C (2006) *Social work and the third way: tough love as social policy,* 3rd edn. London: Sage.

Joseph Rowntree Foundation (2007) *Monitoring poverty and social exclusion 2007.* Available from: **www. jrf.org.uk/publications/monitoring-poverty-and-social-exclusion-2007**

Joseph Rowntree Foundation (2008) *Monitoring poverty and social exclusion 2008.* Available from: **www. jrf.org.uk/publications/monitoring-poverty-and-social-exclusion-2008**

Joseph Rowntree Foundation (2009) *Monitoring poverty and social exclusion 2009.* Available from: **www.jrf.org.uk/report/monitoring-poverty-and-social-exclusion-2009**

Joseph Rowntree Foundation (2010) *Monitoring poverty and social exclusion 2010.* Available from: **www. jrf.org.uk/report/monitoring-poverty-and-social-exclusion-2010**

Joseph Rowntree Foundation (2011) *Monitoring poverty and social exclusion 2011.* Available from: **www. jrf.org.uk/report/monitoring-poverty-and-social-exclusion-2011**

Kahneman, D (2011) *Thinking, fast and slow.* London: Penguin Books.

Kamya, H (2000) Hardiness and spiritual well being among social work students: implications for social work education. *Journal of Social Work Education,* 36: 231–40.

Keeping, C (2006) *Emotional aspects of the professional identity of social workers.* Bristol: University of the West of England/Avon and Wiltshire NHS.

Keeping, C (2014) The process required for effective interprofessional working, in Thomas K, Pollard K and Sellman D (eds) *Interprofessional working in health and social care,* 2nd edn. Basingstoke: Palgrave Macmillan.

Kemmis, S (1985) Action research and the politics of reflection, in *Reflection: turning experience into learning.* London: Kogan Page, 139–64.

Kennedy, S, Kenny, A and O'Meara, P (2015) Student paramedic experience of transition into the workforce: a scoping review. *Nurse Education Today.* Available from: **http://dx.doi.org/10.1016/ j.nedt.2015.04.015**

Klein, G (2004) *The power of intuition.* New York: Currency Books.

Kneale, P (2003) *Study skills for geography students.* London: Hodder.

Knott, C and Scragg, T (eds) (2007) *Reflective practice in social work.* Exeter: Learning Matters.

Kobasa (1979) in Kamya, H (2000) Hardiness and spiritual well being among social work students: implications for social work education. *Journal of Social Work Education,* 36: 231–40.

Koerin, B, Harrigan, M and Reeves, J (1990) Facilitating the transition from student to social worker: challenges of the younger student. *Journal of Social Work Education,* 26: 199–208.

Kondrat, M E (1992) Reclaiming the practical: formal and substantive rationality in social work practice. *Social Service Review,* 66(2): 237–55.

Laming, H (2003) *The Victoria Climbié Inquiry.* London: TSO. Available from: **www.victoria-climbie-inquiry.org.uk**

Laming, H (2009) *The protection of children in England: a progress report.* London: The Stationery Office.

The Law Commission (2011) *Adult social care.* London: The Stationery Office.

Lawson, H (2004) The logic of collaboration in education and the human services. *Journal of Interprofessional Care,* 18(3): 225–37.

Levitas, R (2005) *The inclusive society? Social exclusion and New Labour.* Basingstoke: Palgrave Macmillan.

LGA (Local Government Association) (2014) *Standards for employers of social workers in England*. London: LGA. Available from: **www.local.gov.uk/documents/10180/6188796/The+Standards+- +updated+July+01+2014/146988cc-d9c5-4311-97d4-20dfc19397bf** or **http://cdn.basw.co.uk/upload/ basw_33012-2.pdf**

LGA (2014a) *What you should expect as a social worker?* London: LGA. Available from: **www.local.gov. uk/documents/10180/6188796/What_should_you_expect_as_social_worker.pdf/8e7fed0c-32d9- 4b6a-a213-b06e7c7d1e0d**

Lowes, L and Hulatt, I (eds) (2005) *Service users' involvement in health and social care research*. London: Routledge.

Lymbery, M (2006) United we stand? Partnership working in health and social care and the role of social work in services for older people. *British Journal of Social Work,* 36: 1119–34.

Lyons, K and Manion, K (2004) Goodbye DipSW: trends in student satisfaction and employment outcomes. Some implications for the new social work award. *Social Work Education,* 23: 133–48.

McBride, P (1998) *The assertive social worker*. Aldershot: Ashgate.

McDonald, C (2007) This is who we are and this is what we do: social work education and self-efficacy. *Australian Social Work,* 60: 83–93.

McFadden, P (2015) *Measuring burnout among UK social workers: a community care study*. Available from: **www.qub.ac.uk/schools/media/Media,513723,en.pdf**

McKay, S and Rowlingson, K (2014) Pensions, income maintenance and taxation, Chapter 9 in Bochel, H and Daly, G (eds) *Social policy*, 3rd edn. London: Routledge.

McLaughlin, H (2012) *Understanding social work research,* 2nd edn. London: Sage.

McLaughlin, K (2008) *Social work, politics and society: from radicalism to orthodoxy*. Bristol: Policy Press.

Maddi, S, Kahn, S and Maddi, K (1998) The effectiveness of hardiness training. *Consulting Psychology Journal, Practice and Research,* 50: 78–86.

Maher, B, Appleton, C, Benge, D and Perham, T (2003) *The criticality of induction training to professional social work care and protection practice*. Paper presented to the ninth Australasian Conference on Child Abuse and Neglect: Sydney.

Management Standards Centre (2015) Standards. Available from: **www.management-standards.org/ standards/standards**

Manthorpe, J, Moriarty, J, Hussein, S, Stevens, M and Sharpe, E (2015) Content and purpose of supervision in social work practice in England: views of newly qualified social workers, managers and directors. *British Journal of Social Work*, 45: 52–68.

Marsh, P and Triseliotis, J (1996) *Ready to practice? Social workers and probation officers: their training and their first year in work*. Avebury: Aldershot.

Mehra, A, Smith, B R, Dixon, A L and Robertson, B (2006) Distributed leadership in teams: the network of leadership perceptions and team performance. *The Leadership Quarterly,* 17: 232–45.

Mental Health Act (1983) Available from: **www.legislation.gov.uk/ukpga/1983/20/contents**

Mental Health Act (2007) Available from: **www.legislation.gov.uk/ukpga/2007/12/contents**

Miller, E and Cook, A (2007) *Users and carers define effective partnerships in health and social care: modernising adult social care initiative*. Birmingham: University of Birmingham.

Moon, J (2005) *We seek it here ... a new perspective on the elusive activity of critical thinking: a theoretical and practical approach.* Bristol: ESCalate.

Mor Barak, M, Travis, D, Pyun, H and Xie, B (2009) The impact of supervision on worker outcomes: a meta-analysis. *Social Service Review,* 83(1): 3–32.

Morhman, S A, Cohen, S G and Morhman, A M (1995) *Designing team based organisations.* San Francisco, CA: Jossey-Bass.

Moriarty, J and Murray, J (2007) Who wants to be a social worker? *British Journal of Social Work,* 37: 715–33.

Moriarty, J, Manthorpe, J, Steven, M and Hussein, S (2011) Making the transition: comparing research on newly qualified social workers with other professions. *British Journal of Social Work,* 41: 1340–56.

Morrison, T (2007) Emotional intelligence, emotions and social work: context, characteristics, complications and contribution. *British Journal of Social Work,* 37: 245–63.

Moscrip, S and Brown, A (2002) Child and youth care: the transition from student to practitioner. *The International Child and Youth Care Network,* 41. Available from: **www.cyc-net.org/cyc-online/cycol-0602-transitions.html**

MSH (Management Sciences for Health) and UNICEF (1998) *Welcome to managing for quality.* Available from: **http://erc.msh.org/quality/**

Munro, E (2009) Managing societal and institutional risk in child protection. *Risk Analysis,* 29(7): 1015–23.

Munro, E (2011) *The Munro review of child protection: final report – a child-centred system.* Available from: **www.gov.uk/government/collections/munro-review**

Musson, P (2011) *Effective writing skills for social work students.* Exeter: Learning Matters.

Narey, M (2014) Making the education of social workers consistently effective. London: DfE. Available from: **www.gov.uk/government/publications/making-the-education-of-social-workers-consistently-effective**

Nelson, P and Weatherald, C (2014) Cracking the code: an approach to developing professional writing skills. *Social Work Education,* 33(1): 105–20.

Nkateng, U and Wharton, S (2015) Genre exploration: a frame for understanding and teaching social work writing in Botswana. *Social Work Education,* 34(2): 182–98.

Novell, R (2014) *Starting social work: reflections of a newly qualified social worker.* Northwich: Critical Publishing.

NSWQB (2004) *Induction study: a study of the induction needs of newly qualified and non-nationally qualified social workers in health boards.* Dublin: NSWQB.

Nzira, V and Williams, P (2009) *Anti-oppressive practice in health and social care.* London: Sage.

O'Connor, J (2001) *NLP workbook.* London: Thorsons.

O'Connor, L and Leonard, K (2014). Decision-making in children and families social work: the practitioner's voice. *British Journal of Social Work,* 44(7): 1805–22.

OECD (Organisation for Economic Co-operation and Development) (2007) *Qualifications and lifelong learning. Policy brief.* April 2007. Paris: OECD. Available from: **www.ciaonet.org/attachments/11332/uploads**

Orme, J, MacIntyre, G, Green Lister, P, Cavanagh, K, Crisp, B, Hussein, S, Manthorpe, J, Moriarty, J, Sharpe, E and Stevens, M (2009) What a difference a degree makes: the evaluation of the new social work degree in England. *British Journal of Social Work,* 39(1): 161–78.

Ovretveit, J (2014) *Evaluating improvement and implementation for health.* Maidenhead: OUP.

Pare, A and Le Maistre, C (2006) Active learning in the workplace: transforming individuals and institutions. *Journal of Education and Work,* 19: 363–81.

Parker, J (2004) *Effective practice learning in social work.* Exeter: Learning Matters.

Parker, J (2007) Developing effective practice learning for tomorrow's social workers. *Social Work Education,* 26: 763–79.

Parker, J and Bradley, G (2014) *Social work practice,* 4th edn. London: Sage.

Parker, J and Doel, M (eds) (2013) *Professional social work.* London: Sage.

Parker, J, Whitfield, J and Doel, M (2006) *Effective practice learning in local authorities (2). Workforce development, recruitment and retention.* Leeds: Practice Learning Taskforce.

Parker, J, Ashencaen Crabtree, S, Baba, I, Carlo, D P and Azman, A (2012) Liminality and learning: international placements as a rite of passage. *Asia Pacific Journal of Social Work and Development,* 22(3): 146–58.

Parker, J, Ashencaen Crabtree, S, Azman, A, Carlo, DP and Cutler, C (2014) Problematising international placements as a site of intercultural learning. *European Journal of Social Work,* 18(3): 383–96.

Parkes, C M (1971) Psychosocial transitions: a field study. *Social Science and Medicine,* 5: 101–15.

Paterson, C (2002) in Trevithick, P (2005) *Social work skills: a practice handbook,* 2nd edn. Bucks: OUP.

Pawson, R, Boaz, A, Grayson, L, Long, A and Barnes, C (2003) *Types and quality of knowledge in social care, SCIE Knowledge Review 3.* Bristol: Policy Press. Available from: **www.scie.org.uk/publications/ knowledgereviews/kr03.pdf**

Penhale, B (2007) Ethics and charging for care, in Maclaren, S and Leathard, A (eds) *Ethics and contemporary challenges.* Bristol: Policy Press, pp185–97.

Peters, T (1989) *The customer revolution* (video). BBC training videos. London: BBC.

Phillipson, J (2002) Supervision and being supervised, in Adams, R, Dominelli, L and Payne, M (eds) *Critical practice in social work.* Basingstoke: Palgrave Macmillan, pp244–51.

Pierson, J (2010) *Tackling social exclusion,* 2nd edn. London: Routledge.

Pierson, J (2016) *Tackling poverty and social exclusion: promoting social justice in social work,* 3rd edn. London: Routledge.

Pietroni, P C (1991) Stereotypes or archetypes? A study of perceptions amongst health care students. *Journal of Social Work Practice,* 5: 61–9.

Preston-Shoot, M (2000) Making connections in the curriculum: law and professional practice, in Pierce, R and Weinstein, J (eds) *Innovative education and training for care professionals: a provider's guide.* London: Jessica Kingsley.

Preston-Shoot, M (2000a) Stumbling towards oblivion or discovering new horizons? Observations on the relationship between social work education and practice. *Journal of Social Work Practice,* 14(2): 87–98.

Preston-Shoot, M (2007) *Effective groupwork,* 2nd edn. Basingstoke: Palgrave Macmillan.

Preston-Shoot, M, Roberts, G and Vernon, S (1998) Social work law: from interaction to integration. *Journal of Social Welfare and Family Law,* 20(1): 65–80.

Quality Assurance Agency for Higher Education (QAA) (2000) *Social policy and administration and social work subject benchmark statements.* London: QAA.

Quality Assurance Agency (2008) *Benchmarks for social work.* Gloucester: Quality Assurance Agency.

Quinney, A (2012) *Collaborative social work practice,* 3rd edn. London: Sage/Learning Matters.

Quinney, A and Hafford-Letchfield, T (2012) *Interprofessional social work: effective collaborative approaches,* 2nd edn. London: Sage.

Quinney, A, Thomas, J and Whittington, C (2009) *Working together to assess needs, strengths and risks.* London: SCIE. Available from: **www.scie.org.uk/assets/elearning/ipiac/ipiac04/resource/ flash/index.html**

Rai, L (2006) Owning (up to) reflective writing in social work education. *Social Work Education*, 25(8): 785–97.

Rai, L and Lillis, T (2013) 'Getting it write' in social work: exploring the value of writing in academia to writing for professional practice, *Teaching in Higher Education*, 18(4): 352–64.

Revans, L (2008) Keeping a head above water: NQSW. *Community Care*, 81: 14–15.

Roets, G, Rutten, K, Roose, R, Vanderkinderen, C and Soetaert, R (2015) Constructing the 'child at risk' in social work reports: a way of seeing is a way of not seeing. *Children and Society*, 29(3): 198–208.

Rolfe, G, Freshwater, D and Jasper, M (2001) *Critical thinking for nursing and the helping professions.* Hants: Palgrave.

Rolfe, G, Freshwater, D and Jasper, M (2011) *Critical reflection in practice: generating knowledge for care,* 2nd edn. Hants: Palgrave.

Ronka, A, Oravala, S and Pulkkinen, L (2003) Time points in adults' lives: the effect of gender and amount of choice. *Journal of Adult Development,* 10(3): 203–15.

Roose, R, Mottart, A, Dejonckheere, N, van Nijnatten, C and De Bie, M (2009) Participatory social work and report writing. *Child and Family Social Work,* 14(3): 322–330.

Roscoe, K D and Marlow, M (2013) Case work in social work: exploring the use of reflective letters in the intensive Family Support Services. *Journal of Social Work Practice*, 27(4): 423–40.

Rosenberg, M (2003) *Life-enriching education.* Encinitas, CA: PuddleDancer Press.

Rossi, P H, Lispey, M W and Freeman, H E (2004) *Evaluation: a systematic approach,* 7th edn. Thousand Oaks, CA: Sage.

Rowlingson, K and McKay, S (2009) Income maintenance and taxation, Chapter 9 in Bochel, H, Bochel, C, Page, R and Sykes, R (eds) *Social policy: issues and developments,* 2nd edn. Oxford: Longman.

Rubin, A, Johnson, P J and De Weaver, K L (1986) Direct practice interests of MSW students: changes from entry to graduation. *Journal of Social Work Education,* 22: 98–108.

Ruch, G (2005) Relationship-based practice: holistic approaches to contemporary childcare social work. *Child and Family Social Work,* 10: 111–23.

Rutter, L (2012) *Continuing professional development in social work.* London: Sage/Learning Matters.

Rutter, L and Brown, K (2015) *Critical thinking and professional judgement in social work,* 4th edn. London: Sage/Learning Matters.

Sarason, S B and Lorentz, E M (1998) Crossing boundaries: collaboration, co-ordination and the redefinition of resources. San Francisco, CA: Jossey-Bass.

Schrader, A (2008) Hitchhiking across cultures from the classroom to the workplace. *Feliciter*, 2: 43–4.

Schraer, R (2016) Patchy implementation of the ASYE leaves newly qualified social workers facing unprotected caseloads. *Community Care*. 27 January. Available from: **www.communitycare. co.uk/2016/01/27/patchy-implementation-asye-leaves-newly-qualified-social-workers-facing-unprotected-caseloads/**

SCIE (2004) *Learning organisations: a self-assessment resource pack.* Available from: **www.scie.org.uk/ publications/learningorgs/index.asp**

SCIE (2005) *Teaching, learning and assessment of law in social work education.* Bristol: Policy Press.

SCIE (2006) *Knowledge about learning organisations.* Available from: **www.scie.org.uk/publications/ learningorgs/know/index.asp**

SCIE (2006a) *Learning organisation audit.* Available from: **www.scie.org.uk/publications/learningorgs/ files/key_characteristics_2.pdf**

SCIE (2012) *At a glance 01: learning together to safeguard children: a systems model for case reviews.* Available from: **www.scie.org.uk/publications/ataglance/ataglance01.asp**

SCIE (2013) *Effective supervision in a variety of settings.* London: SCIE. Available from: **www.scie.org.uk/ publications/guides/guide50/index.asp**

SCIE (2015) *Study resource: organisational change in social care.* Available from: **www.scie.org.uk/ publications/elearning/organisational-change-in-social-care/**

Sellick, K (2008) Children's social workers give degree poor marks. *Community Care,* 29 May 2008: 5.

Sellman, D (2010) Values and ethics in interprofessional working, in Pollard, K, Thomas, J and Miers, M (eds) (2010) *Understanding interprofessional working in health and social care.* Basingstoke, Hampshire: Palgrave Macmillan. Available from: **http://eprints.uwe.ac.uk/5346**

Senge, P M (1990) *The fifth discipline: the art and practice of the learning organisation.* London: Random House.

Senge, P (2006) *The fifth discipline: the art and practice of the learning organization,* 2nd edn. London: Random House Business Books.

Seymour, C and Seymour, R (2011) *Courtroom and report writing skills for social workers,* 2nd edn. Exeter: Learning Matters.

Sinclair, I (2008) Inspection: a quality-control perspective, in Davies, M (ed) *The Blackwell companion to social work,* 3rd edn. Oxford: Blackwell, pp449–57.

Skills for Care (2006) *Continuing professional development strategy for the social care workforce.* Leeds: Skills for Care.

Skills for Care/Children's Workforce Development Council (2007) *Providing effective supervision.* Leeds: SfC/CWDC. Available from: **www.skillsforcare.org.uk/Document-library/Finding-and-keeping-workers/ Supervision/Providing-Effective-Supervision.pdf**

Skills for Care (2010) *Keeping up the good work: a practical guide to implementing continuing professional development in the adult social care workforce.* Leeds: Skills for Care.

Skills for Care (2011) *Getting a good start: evaluation of the first year of the newly qualified social worker framework for adult services 2009/10.* Leeds: Skills for Care.

Skills for Care (2011a) *NQSW framework in adult services.* Leeds: Skills for Care.

Skills for Care (2011b) *Newly qualified social worker (NQSW) resource pack.* Leeds: Skills for Care.

Skills for Care (2012) *Assessed and supported year in employment.* Available from: **www.skillsforcare. org.uk/asye/**

Skills for Care (2013) *Concept to reality: implementation of the ASYE with social workers in adult services.* Leeds: Skills for Care. Available from: **http://goo.gl/dZc8QV**

Skills for Care (2015) *Overview of revised ASYE framework.* Leeds: Skills for Care. Available from: **www. skillsforcare.org.uk/Document-library/Social-work/ASYE-framework-2015/Overview-of-revised-ASYE-framework.pdf**

Skills for Care (2015a) Completing the critical reflection log. Leeds: Skills for Care. Available from: **www. skillsforcare.org.uk/Document-library/Social-work/ASYE-framework-2015/Guidance-critical-reflection-log-%28online-version%29.pdf**

Skinner, K (2005) *Continuing professional development for the social services workforce in Scotland.* Developing learning organisations, discussion paper 1. Dundee: Scottish Institute for Excellence in Social Work Education.

Social Work Task Force (2009) *Building a safe and confident future.* Available from: **http://webarchive. nationalarchives.gov.uk/20130401151715/https://www.education.gov.uk/publications/standard/ publicationdetail/page1/dcsf-01114-2009**

Stapleton, S R (1998) Team building: making collaborative practice work. *Journal of Nurse-Midwifery,* 43: 12–18.

Storey, J and Billingham, J (2001) Occupational stress and social work. *Social Work Education,* 20: 659–70.

Swinton, L (2008) *Honey and Mumford: learning style questionnaire.* Available from: **www.mftrou.com/ honey-mumford.html**

SWRB (2010) *Building a safe and confident future: one year on.* London: Social Work Reform Board. Available from: **www.education.gov.uk/swrb**

SWRB (2012) *Reform board guidance: introduction to the ASYE May 2012.* Available from: **www. skillsforcare.org.uk/asye/**

SWRB (2012a) *Standards for employers of social workers in England and supervision framework.* London: SWRB. Available from: **www.education.gov.uk**

SWRB (2012b) *Building a safe and confident future: maintaining momentum.* London: Social Work Reform Board. Available from: **www.education.gov.uk/swrb**

Taylor, B (2013) *Professional decision making and risk in social work.* London: Sage/Learning Matters.

Taylor, S, Leigh-Phippard, H and Grant, A (2014) Writing for recovery: a practice development project for mental health service users, carers and survivors. *International Journal of Practice Development,* 4(1): 1–13.

Taylor-Gooby, P (2008) Equality rights and social justice, Chapter 5 in Alcock, P, May, M and Rowlingson, K (eds) *The student's companion to social policy,* 3rd edn. Oxford: Blackwell.

Taylor-Gooby, P (2012) Equality rights and social justice, Chapter 4 in Alcock, P, May, M and Wright, S (eds) *The student's companion to social policy,* 4th edn. Oxford: Blackwell.

TCSW (The College of Social Work) (2012) *Professional Capabilities Framework for Social Workers.* Available from: **www.collegeofsocialwork.org/pcf.aspx**

TCSW (2012a) *Professional Capabilities Framework: Assessed and Supported Year in Employment (ASYE) Level.* Available from: **www.collegeofsocialwork.org/pcf.aspx**

TCSW (2012b) *Understanding what is meant by holistic assessment.* London: TCSW.

TCSW (2015) *Review of the Professional Capabilities Framework.* London: TCSW.

Tham, P and Lynch, D (2014) Prepared for practice? Graduating social work students' reflections on their education, competence and skills. *Social Work Education*, 33(6): 704–17.

The Poverty Site (ed. Palmer, G) (2011) *Indicators of poverty in the UK based on Joseph Rowntree Foundation Annual Monitoring Poverty and Social Exclusion Reports.* Available from: **www.poverty.org.uk/index.htm**

The Poverty Site (ed. Palmer, G) (2011) *Poverty and social exclusion.* Available from: **www.poverty.org.uk/summary/social%20exclusion.shtml**

Thomas, J, Whittington, C and Quinney, A (2009) *Building relationships, establishing trust and negotiating with other workers.* London: SCIE. Available from: **www.scie.org.uk/assets/elearning/ipiac/ipiac03/resource/flash/index.html**

Thomas, J, Whittington, C and Quinney, A (2009a) *Working collaboratively in different types of teams.* London: SCIE. Available from: **www.scie.org.uk/assets/elearning/ipiac/ipiac06/resource/flash/index.html**

Thompson, N (ed) (2002) *Loss and grief.* Basingstoke: Palgrave.

Thompson, N (2011) *Promoting equality: working with diversity and difference,* 3rd edn. Basingstoke: Palgrave Macmillan.

Thompson, N (2016) *Anti-discriminatory practice,* 6th edn. Basingstoke: Palgrave Macmillan.

Townsend's Deprivation Index, from Townsend, P (1979) Poverty in the United Kingdom, cited in Giddens, A (2009) *Sociology,* 6th edn. Cambridge: Polity Press.

Townsley, R, Abbott, D and Watson, D (2004) *Making a difference? Exploring the impact of multi-agency working on disabled children with complex health care needs, their families and the professionals who support them.* Bristol: Policy Press.

Trevithick, P (2005) *Social work skills: a practice handbook,* 2nd edn. Buckingham: OUP.

Trevithick, P (2012) *Social work skills and knowledge: a practice handbook,* 3rd edn. Buckingham: OUP.

Tuckman, B (1965) Developmental sequence in small groups. *Psychological Bulletin*, 63(6): 384–99.

Turner, M, Brough, P and Williams-Findlay, R B (2003) *Our voice in our future: service users debate the future of the welfare state.* London: Shaping Our Lives National User Network.

United Nations (UN) (1948) *Declaration of Universal Human Rights.* Available from: **www.un.org/en/universal-declaration-human-rights/index.html**

Unrau, Y A, Gabor, P A and Grinnell, R M (2007) *Evaluation in social work: the art and science of practice,* 4th edn. New York: Oxford University Press.

Vatcher, A and Jones, K (2014) Social work, in Thomas, K, Pollard, K and Sellman, D (eds) *Interprofessional working in health and social care*, 2nd edn. Basingstoke: Palgrave Macmillan.

Walker, H (2011) *Studying for your social work degree,* 2nd edn. Exeter: Learning Matters.

Walker, J, Crawford, K and Parker, J (2008) *Practice education in social work: a handbook for practice teachers, assessors and educators.* Exeter: Learning Matters.

Walker, S, Shemmings, D and Cleaver, H (2005) *Write enough: interactive training materials to support quality recording in children's social services.* Available from: **www.writeenough.org.uk**

Walter, I, Nutley, S, Percy-Smith, J, McNeish, D and Frost, S (2004) *Improving the use of research in social care practice (Knowledge review 7).* London: SCIE and The Policy Press.

Wangensteen, S, Johansson, I S and Nordstrom, G (2008) The first year as a graduate nurse: an experience of growth and development. *Journal of Clinical Nursing,* 17: 1877–85.

Warren, J (2007) *Service user and carer participation in social work.* Exeter: Learning Matters.

Watson, T J (2002) *Organising and managing work: organisational, managerial and strategic behaviour in theory and practice.* Harlow: Pearson Education.

Weick, K (1995) *Sensemaking in organizations.* Thousand Oaks, CA: Sage Publications.

Weiss-Gal, I, Levin, L and Krumer-Nevo, M (2014) Applying critical social work in direct practice with families. *Child and Family Social Work,* 19(1): 55–64.

Wenger, E (1998) *Communities of practice: learning, meaning and identity.* Cambridge: Cambridge University Press.

Wenger, E (2015) *Introduction to communities of practice.* Available from: **http://wenger-trayner.com/introduction-to-communities-of-practice/**

West, M, Eckert, R, Steward, K and Pasmore, B (2014) *Developing collective leadership for health care.* London: King's Fund. Available from: **www.kingsfund.org.uk/publications/developing-collective-leadership-health-care**

Whittington, C (2003) A model of collaboration, in Weinstein, J, Whittington, C and Leiba, T (eds) *Collaboration in social work practice.* London: Jessica Kingsley, pp39–62.

Whittington, C, Thomas, J and Quinney, A (2009) *An introduction to interprofessional and interagency collaboration.* London: SCIE. Available from: **www.scie.org.uk/assets/elearning/ipiac/ipiac01/resource/flash/index.html**

Whittington, C, Thomas, J and Quinney, A (2009a) *Professional identity and collaboration.* London: SCIE. Available from: **www.scie.org.uk/assets/elearning/ipiac/ipiac02/resource/flash/index.html**

Wilkinson, R and Pickett, K (2009) *The spirit level: why equality is better for everyone.* London: Penguin.

Williams, M and Penman, D (2011) *Mindfulness: a practical guide to finding peace in a frantic world.* London: Piatkus.

Williams, S, Rutter, L and Gray, I (2012) *Promoting individual and organisational learning in social work.* London: Sage/Learning Matters.

Woodward, C and Potanin, F (2004) *Winning: the story of England's rise to World Cup glory.* London: Hodder and Stoughton.

Index

Printed in Great Britain
by Amazon

84732835R00142